WITHDRAWN

RECONCILABLE DIFFERENCES

RECONCILABLE DIFFERENCES

Turning Points in Ethnopolitical Conflict

Sean Byrne and Cynthia L. Irvin
editors

Paul Dixon, Brian D. Polkinghorn, and Jessica Senehi
associate editors

KUMARIAN PRESS

Reconcilable Differences: Turning Points in Ethnopolitical Conflict

Published 2000 in the United States of America by Kumarian Press, Inc.,
14 Oakwood Avenue, West Hartford, Connecticut 06119-2127 USA.

Production and design by The Sarov Press, Stratford, Connecticut.
The text of this book is set in New Baskerville 10/13.5.
Index by Cynthia L. Irvin.

Printed in Canada on acid-free paper by
Transcontinental Printing and Graphics, Inc.
Text printed with vegetable oil-based ink.

∞ The paper used in this publication meets the minimum requirements
of the American National Standard for Information Sciences—Permanence of
Paper for Printed Library Materials, ANSI Z39.48–1984.

Library of Congress Cataloging-in-Publication Data
Reconcilable differences : turning points in ethnopolitical conflict / Sean Byrne
and Cynthia L. Irvin, editors.
    p.   cm.
Includes bibliographical references and index.
ISBN 1–56549–109–2 (cloth : alk. paper). — ISBN 1–56549–108–4
(pbk. : alk. paper)
    1. Ethnic relations—Political aspects. 2. Culture conflict. 3. Political violence.
4. Conflict management. I. Byrne, Sean, 1962– II. Irvin, Cynthia L.
GN496 .R44   2000
305.8—dc21   99–088100

09 08 07 06 05 04 03 02 01 00   10 9 8 7 6 5 4 3 2 1

First Printing 2000

Contents

Contents

Part 3: Strategies and Techniques in Conflict Resolution and Reduction

The editors Byrne and Irvin

would like to dedicate this book, respectively, to

Patricia and Michael Byrne and the late Frank Wright

Lorraine and Clarence Irvin.

Acknowledgments

THIS VOLUME IS THE RESULT of a series of ongoing conversations between the editors, Paul Dixon, Brian Polkinghorn, and Jessica Senehi, over the past five years about the role of transformational conflict resolution and peacebuilding in protracted ethnic conflicts. We are indebted to the rich discussions we have had together and with the other chapter contributors at various professional conferences where we have had the rare chance to meet and discuss our ideas. Our students have also provided us with a rich forum for thinking about those ideas and have given us valuable feedback. They have also demonstrated to us their interest in and commitment to constructive conflict resolution and social transformation. We also thank Simona Sharoni of American University whose many invaluable comments helped bring this project to fruition.

We wish to express our gratitude to the United States Institute of Peace for its support of our work. Cynthia Irvin also thanks the Harry Frank Guggenheim Foundation for its generous financial support which facilitated her field research and the final revisions of the book manuscript. Cynthia's thanks also go to the many people in Northern Ireland and the Basque country who gave of their time and shared their many insights with her.

In addition, we thank Linda Beyus, our editor at Kumarian Press, for her faith in this project and her assistance throughout the production process.

Finally, we are grateful to the comments offered by anonymous reviewers.

Introduction

AS HOROWITZ (1985, 12) HAS illustrated, ethnic conflict is at the center of politics in divided societies. Ethnic divisions at times pose challenges to both the cohesion of states and to peaceful relations among states. Indeed, as Gurr (1993) has noted, among twenty-four ongoing major armed conflicts since mid-1994, at least seventeen are a direct result of ethnic and religious rivalries, resurgent nationalism, or a struggle for self-determination or state control. Pundits now compete to paint a gloomy future of "The Coming Anarchy," "The Wrath of Nations," and "The Clash of Civilizations." The conflicts in the former Yugoslavia, Rwanda, Indonesia, not to mention the former Soviet Union, dominate the headlines and lend credence to these pessimistic diagnoses. However, as Horowitz (1985, 684) has demonstrated, while there are recurrent tendencies to ethnic cleavage and identifiable patterns of conflict, the outcomes of conflicts are more varied than uniform and "even in the most severely divided societies, ties of blood do not lead ineluctably to rivers of blood."

Failures by academics and policy analysts alike to recognize and to address both the pervasive and ubiquitous means by which ethnicity influences the political, social, economic, and territorial dimensions of multiethnic states have, undoubtedly, contributed to the exile, flight, homelessness, and deaths of those caught up in the violence that ethnic conflict so frequently produces. The objective of this book, then, is not simply to present descriptive accounts of ethnic conflict. Nor is our objective to render judgments of which side(s) may be in the "right." The purpose of the book is to identify and illuminate the causes, responses, and consequences of ethnic conflict, and its resolution. In doing so, we hope to refine, contribute, and improve the theoretical and practical understanding of ethnic conflict.

The book's conceptual and analytical reasoning is also policy relevant because it examines selected contemporary intercommunal conflicts that have institutional avenues for addressing grievances and preventing or limiting conflict, as well as those in countries without established constitutional means for protecting minority rights. Indeed, many of today's most serious conflicts occur precisely in those settings that lack institutional channels to limit their escalation. Given the perception among government officials and policymakers that intercommunal conflicts are becoming increasingly prominent in public debate, this volume serves as a broad foundation for those debates as well as furthering our understanding of conflict resolution techniques and contributing to theory building.

The contributors to this volume offer a rich mix of chapters that illustrate the value of synthesizing different disciplinary approaches to furnish a comprehensive study of intercommunal conflict. As our approach is explicitly interdisciplinary, the volume includes theories and research from the fields of international relations, geography, political science, political psychology, ethnic studies, conflict resolution, peace studies, and sociology. Most importantly, this volume will be useful to practitioners, students, and faculty interested in a more holistic picture of the field of ethnic conflict and conflict resolution than is typically offered in ethnic conflict edited volumes. The book is also designed to assist in integrating a field of study often subject to fragmentation as a result of the emergence of area-specific journals, issue- specific conflict resolution techniques, and professional societies.

It is our belief that this volume offers useful insights to those pursuing applied work as well as those interested in conflict theory. We seek to engage a wide range of readers: policymakers, general readers interested in intergroup conflict, and scholars in the fields of international relations, sociology, political science, geography, conflict resolution and peace studies, political psychology, and social science. Chapters combine critiques of existing theory with innovative strategies for conflict resolution and transformation, and an in-depth understanding of the causes of, and strategies and methods through which ethnic conflict is perpetuated. Hence, the book, although ideally suited for use in graduate seminars, is also a useful text for advanced undergraduate courses in the above mentioned disciplines.

Organization of the Book

This volume is divided into three substantive sections that reflect, respectively, the contributors' work on conflict analysis, peace studies, and conflict resolution. The first section of the book, *Ethnopolitical Conflicts: Causes and Theoretical Approaches,* discusses aspects of the underlying theoretical basis of understanding ethnic conflict and their links to different issues and responses to conflict. These theoretical chapters set the stage for the second section, *Conflict Resolution, Group Identity, and Human Needs,* that analyzes selected topics in conflict resolution such as needs manifestation and conflict, institutional responses to ethnopolitical and environmental conflicts, and grassroots beliefs about conflict and conflict resolution. The third part of the book. *Strategies and Techniques in Conflict Resolution and Reduction*, examines in-depth several cases of protracted conflicts in different geopolitical contexts to illustrate possible approaches to conflict prevention, de-escalation and settlement. Taken collectively, the chapters demonstrate a significant contribution to the study of ethnopolitical conflict at the regional, the national, and the international level.

Part 1: Ethnopolitical Conflicts: Causes and Theoretical Approaches

The first section of this book highlights the work of three researchers who analyze the underlying historical, socioeconomic, geopolitical, and psychocultural factors that tend to escalate ethnopolitical conflicts. The chapters demonstrate that these factors solidify competing communal identities and escalate tensions between groups.

Chapter One is written by John Agnew (University of California, Los Angeles). Agnew's research emphasizes recent political fragmentation and the emergence of "Divided Societies" in the context of the collapse of the Cold War geopolitical order. While the Cold War provided an international order for the development of late modernity, the collapse of Communism and the Cold War geopolitical order, Agnew notes, has contributed to the growing disempowerment of ideologies based on modern rationalism; the formation of a new transnational order with an integrated financial system, standards of production and consumption, and the decline of the centralized nation-state and modern territorial sovereignty. These trends, Agnew argues, have worked to reinforce local particularisms and allegiances in response to the economic identity constructed by the global market's transnational hegemonic order. Agnew's contribution sets the stage for understanding how the causes of ethnic conflict influence and are influenced by conflict situations in and between groups in divided societies.

Chapter Two is contributed by John Nagle (Syracuse University), Fred Pearson (Wayne State University), and Mark Suprun (Columbia University). They contend that American liberal internationalism has tended to see its own norms as universal and progressive, and therefore, transferable to other cultures. This intellectual tradition is so embedded within the field of conflict resolution, that it ignores that other cultures have developed their own norms, and indigenous mechanisms for conflict resolution. Nagle, Pearson, and Suprun's chapter suggests that the rampant economic and political uncertainty that engulfed Eastern Europe during the latter part of the 1980s encouraged a number of former communist leaders to play the "nationalist" card. Responding with repression to irredentism, the Zhivkov regime in Bulgaria, and the Ceausescu regime in Romania, for example, stepped up their campaign of "Regeneration" and the creation of nationally pure states. In Bulgaria, the "Regeneration Process" aimed to force assimilation under a national civil code and coerced Bulgarian Turks and Slavic Muslims (*pomaks*) to adopt Bulgarian names (Velev 1996). Regeneration was also responsible for closing mosques, forbidding the use of the Turkish language in public places, and discouraging cultural and religious practices, and the Islamic consultation creed (*sher'a*). The assimilatory policies adopted by the Romanian government to erase the Hungarian ethnic identity of the population in Transylvania were remarkably similar. In 1989, Zhivkov's nationalist campaign led to a mass exodus of Bulgarian Turks and *pomaks* to Turkey and had devastating repercussions for the Bulgarian economy that caused a chain of additional repressive measures by the regime. In the same year the massacre in Timisvar, Transylvania, triggered the Romanian anti-communist revolution and the fall of Ceausescu's totalitarian regime. Instead of a straightforward manifestation of laissez-faire capitalism, enshrined in the rule of law and prosperity under the constructivism of international liberalism or the postmodern "condition," the "new order," according to the authors, holds a surprising resemblance to pre-modern disorder fueled by instability and turmoil, counter mobilization, and ethnic cleansing for the pursuit of cultural homogeneity and ethnic purity.

Closing this section, *Chapter Three* features the work of Neal Carter (St. Bonaventure University) and Sean Byrne (Nova Southeastern University). In their examination of the parallels between the conflicts in Northern Ireland and in Quebec, the authors skillfully adapt the cube structure as a framework to examine six interrelated social forces at work in both cases. Comparing these prime examples of seemingly intractable ethnoterritorial conflict illuminates the interaction of significant psychological mechanisms and social identity issues with cultural, historic, religious, demographic, political, and economic forces. The comparison reveals some of the similarities and differences in these cases, with important implications for conflict resolution. Carter and Byrne argue that a culture of violence in Northern Ireland is reinforced by symbolism, stereotyping, competing national identities, and feelings of insecurity that interact in a complex social cube with economic inequality and political differences. In contrast, Canada has maintained relatively peaceful institutional conflict in part because federalism provides an institutional framework in which political identities need not be cast in mutually exclusive terms and political differences can be more readily accommodated.

Part 2: Conflict Resolution, Group Identity, and Human Needs

The second section of the volume, Chapters Four through Seven, involves four diverse case studies to outline some of the forces that drive conflicting parties to the peace table. This section also addresses the question: why are some conflicts more successfully resolved than others? In this way, this section helps to illuminate the resolution processes of ethnopolitical conflicts.

In contrast to Nagle, Pearson, and Suprun's view that the eruption of ethnonationalism in the "developed West" casts doubt on the prospects for integration and the future of multiethnic states, both Kathleen Cavanaugh and Paul Dixon remind us that the western liberal democratic state has tried to make ethnicity irrelevant by urging the integration of members of ethnic groups into the "mainstream," and as the peace accords in South Africa suggest, such attempts are not inevitably doomed to failure.

Chapter Four is written by Kathleen Cavanaugh (University College Dublin) who, through the applications of basic needs theory, demonstrates that failure to satisfy basic needs criteria precipitated a crisis of legitimacy and contributed to the sociopolitical instability in Northern Ireland since 1968. Consistent with the first stage of an analytical framework developed by Edward Azar, the historical antecedents (a colonial "divide and rule" legacy) together with communal composition (bicommunalism) established preconditions for protracted social conflict in Northern Ireland. Further application of Azar's model substantiates an interdependency of needs criteria, such that derivation of one need impacts other areas. However, a close analysis also reveals a hierarchy of needs with identity-related needs emerging as dominant. Cavanaugh argues that while basic needs such as equitable access to economic, social and decision-making institutions impact conflict, it is the manner in which these dynamics interact with identity that contributes to its protractedness.

Chapter Five highlights Brian Polkinghorn's (Nova Southeastern University) analysis of environmental and intercommunal disputes. Polkinghorn traces the evolution of intercommunal tensions and natural resource conflict using a human basic needs approach. Ongoing field research by the author in conjunction with others in Bosnia, Croatia, Israel, Northern Ireland, and South Africa on environmental resources conflict is providing evidence that a strong relationship exists between the physical and biological environments and the social environment. Although there are many types of group affiliation which come into play, the emphasis in this chapter is on the group identity that allows or hinders one from fully participating in government and citizen decision-making or from receiving or being denied the benefits of the system. For example, in South Africa, identity continues to center around race while in Bosnia ethnicity is based on religious identity and regional heritage. Polkinghorn demonstrates that groups throughout these research settings primarily focus on social issues and not the environment. However, when the environment becomes a central component of the data collection, he notes that almost everyone claims it for their group and blames others for its general demise. Some of the issues raised in this chapter relate to the question of how we can balance the social construction of environmental conflict into an ethical framework based on a systems approach that views environmental resource conflict from a social, physical, and biological systems approach. Although this approach is needs based, it focuses on all three systems needs which must be considered in any solution.

Chapter Six by Jessica Senehi (Syracuse University) focuses on the role of the storytelling process as an important component of transformational ethnic conflict resolution. As many conflict resolution practitioners have noted, historical biases, oppression and hatreds, strong group loyalties and core ethnic identities, collective memories of past glories, traumas and grievances have caused physical and emotional injury that have brutalized peoples. Bloody Sunday, Enniskillen, Hebron, Netzarim, Soweto, and the Boipatang Massacres, for example, have all left indelible marks in the memories, culture, and folklore of people in Northern Ireland, Israel, and South Africa.

Senehi demonstrates how storytelling can serve as a means by which participants in grassroots psychosocial recovery programs can effectively participate in personal and group reconciliation and recovery. Storytelling, Senehi argues, creates a space for people locked in protracted ethnopolitical disputes to think about the other group and about the nature of conflict. She considers storytelling as a low-tech means that is accessible to all people to help them address common needs, a shared identity, and the intangible bases of longstanding ethnic conflict.

Chapter Seven features the work of Ho-Won Jeong (George Mason University). This chapter addresses the issue of ethnicity that has to be seen as the point of identification. More specifically, it examines why ethnicity is a source of violent preferences. The social practice embedded in the modern condition is the main focus in conceptual strategies for explaining the emergence of violent conflict in the post Cold War period. Conflict resolution cannot be understood without looking at the nature of agency and modern practices. The paper concludes with a brief analysis of the political space of conflict resolution.

Part 3: Strategies and Techniques in Conflict Resolution and Reduction

Chapters Eight through Eleven examine variations in the prosecution of ethnopolitical conflicts in some of the most turbulent and conflictual regional trouble spots—the former Yugoslavia, Northern Ireland, Canada, and South Africa. The "local" regional trends and patterns of conflict resolution are presented in comparative fashion and illustrated by rich empirical source materials.

The primary purpose of this final section is to explore the context of a number of case studies and how they both limit and provide opportunities for the successful resolution of protracted ethnopolitical disputes. In these four chapters, the authors provide rich material for the "pracademic" to consider when designing intervention processes to de-escalate protracted intercommunal conflicts. The student of ethnopolitical conflicts is also provided insightful observations from the authors' personal experiences in the field to understand more fully the dynamics of successes and failures of conflict intervention in ethnically divided societies.

In *Chapter Eight,* Mitja Zagar (Institute for Ethnic Studies, University of Ljubljana) argues that Yugoslavia was, ironically, one of the few countries in the world that was constitutionally declared a multinational state. Its constitution provided for ethnic equality and the protection of ethnic minorities and was often cited as a successful example of how ethnic relations should have been constitutionally and legally regulated and what kind of ethnic policy should have been practiced by the state to assure ethnic coexistence. He contends that the role of ideology in the constitutional design uncovered two parallel systems that actually existed in this country. In combination with several other factors and circumstances, Zagar posits that the lack of constitutional mechanisms and procedures for management and peaceful resolution of conflicts was a crucial factor in this context.

Chapter Nine features the work of George McCall and Miranda Duncan (University of Missouri-St. Louis) who argue that even in socially diverse communities, who fights about what, and how different sorts of disputes get handled, are culturally patterned features of social living. Viewing South Africa's National Peace Accord as an innovative national approach to resolving widespread community conflicts, McCall and Duncan examine closely its emergence, design, and performance as a key element in that divided society's negotiated transition to democracy. Indeed, they show how the Accord allowed South Africa—perhaps uniquely in the world—to achieve that dramatic take-off in community conflict intervention which James H. Laue had envisioned as the best-case scenario ("the developmental track") for that field.

Chapter Ten is based on Paul Dixon's (University of Ulster-Jordanstown) speculation regarding the possible roles European integration might play in resolving the historic antagonism between unionists and nationalists in Northern Ireland. Dixon's study focuses on the tendency of closer European integration to increase the cultural and political importance of regions such as North-ern Ireland and the Basque region in Spain, rather than the creation of new and larger states. Against this background over the role of Europe in the resolu-tion of conflict in Northern Ireland, he suggests that the prospects of current proposals for European involvement can be more realistically assessed.

Chapter Eleven is provided by Cynthia Irvin (University of Kentucky) and is based on the analysis of recent peace negotiations in Northern Ireland and the changing political context in the Basque peoples' struggle for self-determina-tion and a redefinition of their relationship to both the French and Spanish states which divide their nation. Drawing on interviews with members of the Irish nationalist party, Sinn Fein, and the Basque nationalist party, Herri Batasuna, this chapter first examines the internal negotiation process that led to the declaration of the IRA cease-fire and its impact on the activities of the Basque militant nationalist organization, Euzkadi ta Askatasuna (ETA-Basque Homeland and Freedom). It then traces the development of the negotiations between Sinn Fein and the Irish and British governments, and ETA and the Spanish government. Finally, Irvin examines the interplay between internal Sinn Fein and Herri Batasuna politics and their strategies of negotiation with other relevant actors and illustrates the relationship between internal and external political dynamics.

References

Gurr, Ted Robert. 1993. *Global Minorities at Risk: A Global View of Ethnopolitical Conflicts.* Washington, D.C.: United States Institute of Peace Press.

Horowitz, Donald. 1985. *Ethnic Groups in Conflict.* Berkeley, Calif.: University of Califor-nia Press.

Part 1

Ethnopolitical Conflicts:
Causes and Theoretical Approaches

1

The Geopolitical Context of Contemporary Ethnopolitical Conflict

John A. Agnew

Introduction

THE DIVISION OF THE WORLD into territorial entities we call "states" produces actors that operate on a territorial definition of space—that is, a world divided into discrete and mutually exclusive blocks of space. Rather than a natural and universal process, however, this type of geographical division has a clear, if largely unexamined, historicity. It originated in seventeenth-century Europe both as a normative ideal (and representational space) about how politics *should be* organized geographically and as an alternative mode of socioeconomic organization to imperial or "node and network" (trading system) ideals. It was a central feature of the uniquely European development of an expansive capitalism that slowly emerged between the fifteenth and eighteenth centuries (Palen 1992). The development was fastest where city-states were least well established on the seaward and continental margins of Europe (Rokkan and Urwin 1983). There was not a movement from one to the other, as argued by Mumford (1970), among others. To the contrary, territorial states became established most strongly where city-state development was least entrenched. Only in the nineteenth century were the last of the city-state territories converted into the territorial states of Germany and Italy.

The system of territorial states developed important legal and economic underpinnings as a wide range of spatial practices became more and more bounded by state-territorial limits. Through a social process of recognizing other spaces as potentially "developed" and "modern" insofar as they acquired the trappings of territorial statehood (armies, judiciaries, etc.), the state-territorial form of spatial organization came to encompass in some degree most of the world's population. Since the early nineteenth century and, more especially since the Second World War, international organizations, especially the United Nations, have played a fundamental role in formalizing this process (Luke 1993; Murphy 1993). From one point of view, a territorial state can be said to exist because its flag flies outside the U.N. headquarters in New York, irrespective of its effectiveness as a political-economic entity.

The actual spatial organization of the world, however, has always been more complex than the simple assimilation of all social cleavages into a superordinate state-territorial spatial form assumed by most varieties of thinking about international political economy. In particular, the spatial practices of everyday life have maintained a place-specificity that defies the intellectual assumption of growing state-territorial homogeneity. The recent explosion of regional-ethnic politics around the world bears witness to this. More generally, social groups are often defined by their spatial configurations: their relative spatial isolation and claims to territory are the root and symbol of their existence. The persisting segregation of American ethnic and racial groups is one example of this. Furthermore, the globalization of the world economy in recent years has challenged the state territory as the basic building block of the world economy. The financial and informational flows at the heart of the new economy are not readily contained by territorial-state boundaries. They favor or disadvantage particular regions and localities within states rather than national territories in their entirety (Agnew 1987).

How can we best begin to make sense out of the historical evolution of the geographical basis to the international political economy? At the risk of dramatically oversimplifying a much more complex reality, in this chapter, I identify three geopolitical orders over the period 1815–1990 in which different forms of global spatial organization have been predominant. The third of these geopolitical orders has recently collapsed with the end of the Cold War and it is in this context that the cases discussed in this book best make sense.

The Three Geopolitical Orders

In using the concept of geopolitical order it is important to establish the time-limits and identify the criteria used to define each order. The first period (1815–75) is one of a European territorial balance of power in which Britain came to command and define the nature of the growing world economy outside of Europe (the Concert of Europe – British Geopolitical Order). Britain held the balance of power in Europe, enjoyed a significant edge in sea-power that allowed it a coercive role in imposing its policies around the world, and sponsored a set of economic doctrines—comparative advantage, free trade, and the gold standard—

that, while appearing universal, benefitted key interests in Britain.

This combination of European Concert and British domination outside of Europe gave way in a second period (1875–1945) to a destabilization of the European balance of power as certain other states (especially Germany) challenged British policies. National economies became increasingly autarkic and protectionist and the world economy lost its focus on free trade and the gold standard and divided into economic blocs. The two World Wars were an intrinsic part of this drift towards a state-territorial international political economy (the Geopolitical Order of Inter-Imperial Rivalry).

In the third period (1945–90), a Cold War Geopolitical Order arose out of the ashes of the Second World War. The two major victors in that war, the United States and the Soviet Union, divided the world into two spheres of influence with different political economic models of development (the First World of capitalist organization and the Second World of state-planned organization) and competed for influence in a third (the Third World of new states emerging from colonialism). American hegemony involved a structure similar to that sponsored by Britain in the nineteenth century but with much greater commitment to opening up the world to direct investment and trade and with a security apparatus that was much more extensive and intrusive than that exercised by Britain in its day. This neo-liberalism was also much more institutionalized in a set of security alliances (especially NATO) and global trade, investment, and monetary arrangements (the GATT, the IMF, the World Bank, etc.) than had been the British variety.

The net effect of the American-based hegemony, however, has been to create a "transnational liberal order" that is no longer uniquely associated with the United States. As this occurred, and with the disintegration of the Soviet Union and its sphere of influence in 1989–90, it signified the collapse of the Cold War Geopolitical Order. Only the outlines of a new geopolitical order can be glimpsed as yet, though it is clear that a new form of transnational liberalism will be central to it. (It also goes without saying that the beginnings and ends of each of the geopolitical orders embraces a period of "morbid disorder," as in the 1940s and 1990s. Each geopolitical order emerged from the unraveling of the previous one without the sudden transition that the use of precise dates might be taken to imply.)

The Concert of Europe – British Geopolitical Order (1815–75)

This British geopolitical order of 1815–75 provides strong evidence for the view that there are alternatives to rules of governance manifesting either total anarchy or strict hierarchy. The international political economy between 1815 and 1875 was characterized by a European Concert in which no one state "laid down the law" for the continent as a whole and an emerging British economic hegemony in much of the rest of the world. Putting it another way: "Great Britain's role as a world power did not translate into continental hegemony. The governance system in nineteenth-century Europe was a polyarchy, not a hegemony" (Holsti 1992, 56). These twin features are what set this period apart from later ones. After 1875 both the Concert and certain key features of British economic hegemony decayed rapidly as the fundamental supports of the order collapsed.

The main problem the Concert was designed to handle was revolution. Initially there was agreement that this meant preventing a French war of revenge or the restoration of the regime of Napoleon Bonaparte. Thereafter there was disagreement over the extent to which this justified unilateral interventions in small states to suppress rebellion. But a consensus evolved among the dominant political elites in Europe that 1) no one state in Europe could predominate within the continent and 2) Europe-wide wars were best avoided because of their potential for unleashing revolutionary forces. Even though the system of regular congresses largely collapsed, certain rules of behavior became widely accepted. Unilateral responses were decried. The great powers were co-managers who merited consultation on all of the major threats to international peace. As a result, wars to foment revolution or to acquire territory were seen as threats to a system based on a conception of a collective interest that transcended particular national interests. In practice many conflicts which would have found their way easily to the battlefield in the eighteenth century were prevented by concerted diplomacy.

Britain not only experienced an Industrial Revolution before the rest of Europe, it also traded with and invested in other continents on a much larger scale than other European countries (save possibly for the Netherlands). These were connected. The technical innovation and organizational efficiency of early nineteenth-century British industry produced goods for export and capital for investment overseas and a demand for certain raw materials (especially cotton). In addition, however, Britain acquired a competitive advantage over other European states in the growing world economy.

The British orientation towards external expansion contrasted throughout this period with the Euro-centeredness of the other European great powers. They were much too caught up with national economy-making, a process largely completed by Britain, to challenge British preeminence in the making of the world economy outside of Europe. By progressively opening up their domestic market from 1823 to 1840 through the sponsorship and unilateral practice of freer trade, British leaders created a worldwide network of trade and financial flows that presented their centrality as a by-product of the workings of a "world market" that operated to the benefit of all. British governments could claim with credibility that the growth of the British economy served not only a national interest but a "global" interest as well. This argument appealed particularly strongly to those upwardly mobile social elements in settler (and former settler) colonies and social groups elsewhere involved in trading and financial activities.

Under British auspices market exchange was effectively globalized as production for the market replaced the mere trading of goods. The British national economy became the locomotive of the world economy. As industrialization proceeded in Europe and markets there became more competitive, British capitalists were pushed into widening their markets elsewhere. The British Empire was an important part of this "internationalization." But the United States, China, and Latin America, regions outside formal British control, were also important. The internationalization of the British economy in the nineteenth century was a crucial element in the quickening pace and increasing spatial scope of the world economy.

In the 1870s Britain began to lose its central position within the Concert of Europe and also to sacrifice its industrial strength on the altar of free trade. In both respects, the political-economic rise of Germany and the explosive economic growth of the United States were the most significant developments. British concentration on the "old" industrial technologies of the steam era and its increased commitment to such geographically extensive activities as commerce and finance put it at a disadvantage relative to the two massive territorial economies with which it now had to compete. Neither country had Britain's fervent commitment to free trade. The newly unified Germany, in particular, was not willing to accept political subsidiarity to Britain, either in Europe or outside.

Fatefully, by 1875 Britain had also turned away from Europe and the United States towards its empire and those world regions where its hegemony was apparently more secure. This provided the impetus for the collapse of the Concert in Europe and the beginning of a British retreat from its constitutive role in the international political economy. Britain certainly maintained its absolute centrality to world commerce and finance for many years but it was without the almost unquestioned position of supremacy it had established during the period from 1815 to 1875.

One of the most important aspects of the Concert constructed in 1814–15 was its territorial equilibrium of power (Holsti 1992, 53). The main measure of state power was maintenance of national territory. Differences in terms of military might did not excite much concern and did not threaten the balance of power. Throughout the period Russia had by far the largest army and Britain had a substantial naval supremacy. These constants imposed a stability that until the 1860s made the Concert a territorial rather than a military balance of power. Thereafter changes in military technology evened out military potential and led to an emphasis on mobility, mobilization, and preparation for preemptive attack. Relative military strength "became the measure of the balance of power, and any increment was perceived as threatening to the equilibrium. Arms racing gave the appearance of rapid changes in relative power and generated fears of lagging behind. . . . Industrial dynamics replaced territory as the main metric of power analysis." (Holsti 1992, 53)

Perhaps of greatest importance, however, the Concert of Europe, though based initially on a set of states that had been active in European international relations for many years, eventually saw the addition of many new states that had originated in ethnic revolts against established states and empires. As the century wore on the Concert had to come to terms with the creation of new states from the fission and the fusion of its original members. Beginning with the emergence of Greece from within the Ottoman Empire in the 1820s, through the unification of Italy (at the expense of Austria) and Germany (at the expense of Austria and France), to the explosion of the Balkans (against the Ottoman and Austrian Empires) at the century's end, the creation of the new states effectively called into question the "principles" upon which the Concert had been based. The new states had no commitment to the old order. In their wars of independence and frequent attempts at territorial expansion they effectively undermined it.

The order had been designed to tame and repress the nationalism that spread throughout Europe after the French Revolution. Its founding states were territorial states. But they were organized around aristocratic and bourgeois elites rather than mobilized national groups. Throughout the nineteenth century a new conception of statehood based on the creation of nation-states came increasingly to the fore. These were states built upon ethnic/religious/language divisions and particularities. In the identity of state with nation, territorial sovereignty became fused with the fate of the nation. The "interests" of peoples were rigidly territorialized as the number of states in Europe tripled. This new system of states had no place for the rules that had governed the previous one.

The Geopolitical Order of Inter-Imperial Rivalry (1875–1945)

The German and American national economies worked very differently from the British national economy and from one another. What they shared was a competitive advantage in the size and dynamism of their domestic markets. The British economy was much more dependent on international transactions and increasingly lagged behind them in the new "cutting edge" electrical and chemical industries. But they differed in that the American economy had become the main beneficiary of British free-trade imperialism, joining together its now continental dimensions and vast resource base with access to British mediated capital flows and credit. Germany's economic development was based upon a state-sponsored industrialization that gave priority to military goods. Its external financial links remained heavily orientated to Britain.

This was an inherently unstable situation. Germany's military-industrial capability could not be translated into an enhanced global political role without upsetting both the Concert and the global flows of trade and capital centered around Britain. At the same time the increased industrial production of the United States and the European states undermined British industrial preeminence and led British business and governments into the use of political dominance and non-tariff barriers within its empire to restrict price competition and monopolize trade. The net result was an erosion of the system of interactional accumulation based around a set of national states and one international state (Britain) that had predominated previously and the emergence of a set of competitive imperial states dividing the world into zones based on territorial accumulation.

The inter-state system quickly polarized into two antagonistic groups. One, headed by Britain and France (with tacit American support), was orientated towards maintaining free-trade imperialism. The other, headed by Germany, was concerned with expanding its territorial possessions and challenging British financial hegemony. This division was apparent by the 1890s and gained its most famous early expression in the arms race between Britain and Germany known quaintly as "the Anglo-German naval rivalry." This polarization became the central feature of the geopolitical order as the ground for conflict shifted towards the territorial definition introduced by the Germans. It is no coincidence, therefore, that 1875–1945 produced the major peaks in, and the largest average annual number of, territorial changes, excluding those involving national independence, for the entire period 1815–1980 (Goertz and Diehl 1992, 41–44).

It is often contended that Britain fell from its zenith because when challenged by the Germans (and other potential enemies) it could no longer finance the military obligations that its empire and naval protection of free trade entailed. Available statistical evidence suggests that this was not the case. In terms of both percentage of national income and per capita spending for the years 1870–1910, and except for the years of the South African War, Britain had consistently lower figures than France and ones not much higher than Germany's. In addition, the "burden" imposed by the empire was one Britain managed successfully to impose upon its colonies. The various parts of the far-flung empire paid for more than their own local defense. India in particular paid a substantial amount of Home Charges for the defense of the "homeland." As Offer (1993, 232) concludes in his thorough survey of the evidence: "overseas investment paid for its [India's] defense and left a substantial margin of profit."

More to the point than the simplistic (and incorrect) "imperial overstretch thesis" (Kennedy 1987) is the fact that the increasing economic importance of the British Empire to the British economy provided a powerful incentive to defend it against erosion from foreign competition. In return, the empire offered a reservoir of resources and labor for the prosecution of war that increased the capacity of the "small island nation" to wage war against its challengers. The path to the two World Wars ran through London and Calcutta/Delhi as well as through Berlin.

Inter-state rivalry was powerfully fueled by the growing nationalism of the period. National-economy making through the extension of railways and the reorganization of economic space into national blocs brought a collective sense of national economies as "communities of fate." The spread of literacy in standardized vernacular languages through universal elementary education enabled the more effective dissemination to mass publics of nationalized histories and myths of national origins (and superiority). State boundaries were seen to define natural units whose limits were the product of differences in national "vitality" and "capability." Small ethnic groups could expect little if any positive reaction from the existing large states except when, as in the immediate aftermath of the First World War, successful belligerents dismembered the territories of their adversaries (as with the Austro-Hungarian and Turkish Empires) or faced violent revolts for which they had little fight (as with the British in Ireland).

The imperial vision of the period was initially challenged by growing socialist movements in Europe. Class rather than nation was their basic conceptual category. However, they also succumbed to a pervasive nationalism by organizing nationally and having to adjust to the distinctive institutional arrangements governing industrial relations and political parties in different countries. Both ideologies (e.g., revolutionary versus evolutionary) and strategies (e.g., parliamentary versus industrial) became increasingly different in different countries. Perhaps most disabling was the lack of a "global" vision. Appealing largely to the immediate material interests of industrial workers in the industrialized world, they were unable to articulate how subjugation and exploitation were now global in form rather than just factory-level or specifically national phenomena (though see Lenin, 1971).

The late nineteenth century saw a vast enlargement and deepening of the world economy largely through the "new imperialism" of the period. Whole regions inside and outside of Europe became specialized in the production of specific manufactured goods, raw materials, and food products. The new spatial division of labor saw regional industrial specialization within the national economies of Europe and the United States paralleled by regional specialization in raw material production elsewhere. The downturn in the world economy in the period 1883–96, due among other things to decreased profitability in manufacturing, ushered in a major spurt in the expansion of investment in raw material production. By 1900 not only was most of the world formally bound into the colonial empires which expanded rapidly after 1880 but more and more of the world's resources and population were drawn into a geographically specialized world economy. Bananas in Central America, tea in Ceylon (Sri Lanka), and rubber in Malaya are just three of the host of examples involved in this process of regional commodity specialization (Wolf 1982).

But what was most novel was that the "club" of Great Powers was no longer entirely European. It was the entry of the U.S. in the First World War that proved decisive militarily. Japan had become a major power in Asia. On the eastern flank of Europe the revolutionary regime that established itself after the Russian Revolution of 1917 created a new kind of political economy that was claimed to represent the future for workers all over the world. None of these states could be effectively integrated into the decaying cross-over trading system with Britain as its linchpin or was able to help bring about a new one. In the 1930s Japan embarked on a territorial strategy of empire building in East Asia. The United States after sponsoring the collective security system called the League of Nations withdrew from its active implementation. The Soviet Union saw itself as threatening to and threatened by the capitalist world economy. The "system" was the enemy to overthrow and not something to be reformed or revitalized. The climax came after the remilitarization of the German economy under Nazi rule. The fact that the Second World War involved the active alliance of Germany, Italy, and Japan, the three great powers with the most autarkic economies and the ones whose elites were most dissatisfied with the global status quo, indicates the extent to which inter-imperial rivalry or competition for control over territory had replaced the previous combination of geographical modes of economic accumulation and political regulation as well as restricted the possibility for much success by movements devoted to realizing the political ambitions of ethnic groups "trapped" within existing nation-states.

The Cold War Geopolitical Order (1945–90)

The completeness of the American-Anglo-Soviet victory over Nazi Germany and Imperial Japan had two immediate consequences. First, Soviet influence extended over Eastern Europe and into Germany. When the war ended Soviet armies were as far west as the River Elbe. This encouraged both a continuing American military presence in Europe and a direct confrontation with the Soviet Union as a military competitor and sponsor of an alternative image of world order. This was quickly to find its clearest expression in the geopolitical doctrine of "containment," whereby through alliances and military presence the United States government committed itself to maintaining the political status quo established in 1945. The American development of nuclear weapons and a demonstrated willingness to use them meant that the security of the United States itself was beyond doubt (Art 1991). Indeed, the relative geographical isolation of the United States from most of its historic adversaries has always been an American advantage; if one discounts threats from nuclear armed terrorists or states that reject the "norms" of inter-state behavior. What was in doubt in 1945–47 was the allegiance of other countries to the United States and its political-economic model.

Second, in economic and political terms the United States was without any serious competition in imposing its vision of world order on both its vanquished foes and most of its recent allies. Unlike after the First World War, when the United States turned its back on hegemony, this time there seemed to be no alternative. Europe and Japan were devastated. The reading of the origins of the Great Depression and the Second World War that predominated in the Roosevelt and Truman administrations suggested that the continued health of the American economy and the stability of its internal politics depended upon increasing rather than decreasing international trade and investment (Wachtel, 1988). Europe and Japan had to be restored economically, both to deny them to the Soviet Union and to further American prosperity. Morgenthau's early 1940s plan for the "ruralization" of Germany was quickly scrapped in 1945.

This is not to say that there was no opposition to the "internationalist" po-sition. Indeed, the Republican majorities in the U.S. Congress in the immedi-ate postwar years were generally as skeptical of the projection of the U.S. New Deal experience of government economic intervention overseas as they were of its application at home. U.S. forces demobilized rapidly after 1945. Only after 1947, with the growing fear of the Soviet Union as both foreign enemy and domestic subversive, did an internationalist consensus begin to emerge.

The period from 1945 to 1990 was one in which this consensus played itself out. The United States government set out in 1945–47 to sponsor a liberal in-ternational order in which its military expenditures would provide a protective apparatus for increased trade (and, less so, investment) across international boundaries. These would, in turn, redound to domestic American advantage. The logic behind this lay in the presumed transcendental identity between the American and world economies. The expansion of one was seen as good for the other. Achieving this involved projecting at a global scale those institutions and practices that had already developed in the United States, such as: mass pro-duction/consumption industrial organization; electoral democracy; limited state welfare policies; and government economic policies directed towards stimulat-ing private economic activities (Maier 1978; Rupert 1990). Ruggie (1983) calls the normative content of these policies taken together "embedded liberalism" because they were institutionalized in such entities as the IMF, the World Bank, the GATT, and the Bretton Woods Agreement.

Three features of the American economy were particularly important in underpinning the internationalism of American policy. The first was economic concentration. Continuing an intermittent trend from the 1880s, in almost every American industry control over the market came to be exercised by ever fewer firms. Expanding concentration was accompanied and encouraged by the growth of government, especially at the federal level. Much of this was related to military expenditures designed to meet the long-term threat from the Soviet Union. These trends were reinforced by what became the main challenge to the perpetuation of the model within the United States: the direct investment of U.S. corporations overseas. Much of this was in other industrialized countries. The axis of capital accumulation now ran through the core rather than between core and periphery. In the short run the repatriated profits benefitted the American economy. But by the late 1960s, as domestic technology and management followed capital abroad, traditional exports were replaced by foreign production of U.S. affiliates to the detriment of employment in the United States. American mass consumption was no longer fully supported by the relatively high wages of its workers in mass production. This has come to define the crisis or impasse facing the American model in the United States (Agnew 1987). What Arrighi (1990, 403) calls a Free Enterprise System—"free, that is, from . . . vassalage to state power"—has come into existence to challenge the inter-state system as the singular locus of power in the international political economy.

The spread, acceptance, and institutionalization of the American model was by no means a preordained or easy process. The key institutions and practices spread rapidly in the late 1940s and early 1950s. They were eventually accepted in all of the major industrialized countries either through processes of "external inducement" (Marshall Aid would be the classic example) and coercion (the British loan of 1946), or through direct intervention and reconstruction as in West Germany and Japan. In all cases, however, there was considerable compromise with local elites over the relative balance of growth and welfare elements in public policy (Ikenberry and Kupchan 1990).

Most of the key elements persisted until 1990, although some faded by the 1960s. They have been: 1) stimulating economic growth indirectly through fiscal and monetary policies; 2) commitment to a unitary global market based on producing the greatest volume of goods most cheaply for sale in the widest possible market by means of a global division of labor; 3) accepting the United States as the home of the world's major reserve-currency and monetary overseer of the world economy (the Bretton Woods system, 1944–71; dollar-based floating exchange rate system, 1971–present); 4) unremitting hostility to "communism" or any political-economic ideology that could be associated with the Soviet Union; and 5) the assumption of the burden of intervening militarily whenever changes in government or insurgencies could be construed as threatening to the political status quo established in 1945 (the Truman doctrine).

Not only international relations, therefore, but also the domestic social order of other states was at issue in constituting the geopolitical order of the Cold War period. All states ideally were international ones open to the free flow of investment and trade (Wood 1986). However, the system had a built in flexibility that allowed both for national particularities and adjustments over time (Gilpin 1987). For example, and with respect to the former, the GATT (now the World Trade Organization) is a trade regime initially formed in 1947 to encourage multilateral free trade, but it allows for domestic costs of adjustment. "The GATT tries less to override . . . domestic political calculations than to moderate their impact on the larger network of liberal trade" (Lipson 1982, 425). The Most Favored Nation clause is a critical element in the GATT, as it was in mid-nineteenth-century trade agreements, "but unlike its predecessor it is built on multilateral commitments, organized around regular consultations and periodic negotiations" (Lipson 1982, 426). Countries can escape from previous agreements if they can show that this will help their economic development.

It is little exaggeration to claim that in the five decades after 1945 American dominion was at the center of a remarkable explosion in "interactional" capitalism. Based initially on the expansion of mass consumption within the most industrialized countries, it later involved the reorganization of the world economy around a massive increase in trade in manufactured goods and foreign direct investment. But this was not a recapitulation of the previous world economy. Abandoning territorial imperialism, "Western capitalism . . . resolved the old problem of overproduction, thus removing what Lenin believed was the major incentive for imperialism and war" (Calleo 1987, 147). The major driving force behind this was the growth of mass consumption in North America, Western Europe, and Japan. The products of such industries as real estate, household and electrical goods, automobiles, food processing, and mass entertainment were all consumed within (and, progressively, between) the producing countries. The "Keynesian" welfare state helped sustain demand through the redistribution of incomes and purchasing power. The old "cross-over" trading system was no longer needed. If before the Second World War the prosperity of industrial countries depended on favorable terms of trade with the underdeveloped world, now demand was stimulated at home. Moreover, until the 1970s the income terms of trade of most raw materials and foodstuffs tended to decline. This trend had negative effects on the economies of the Third World as a whole, but it stimulated some countries to engage in new models of industrialization which later paid off as they found lucrative export markets for their manufactured goods. The globalization of production through the growth of these Newly Industrializing Countries and the increased flow of trade and foreign direct investment between already industrialized countries finally undermined the geographical production/consumption nexus (often referred to as "central Fordism") that was the leitmotif of the early postwar decades.

A vital element in allowing the U.S. to have such a dominant presence within the world economy was the persisting yet historically episodic political-military conflict with the Soviet Union. This had two major peaks in intensity in the late 1940s and the early 1980s when each side perceived the other to be increasingly hostile and dangerous. The mid-1970s was generally the period of greatest cooperation.

However, even in periods of detente or coexistence the overarching Cold War conflict served both to tie Germany and Japan firmly into alliance with the U.S. and to define two geographical spheres of influence at a global scale. For a long time this imposed an overall stability on the world political system, since the U.S. and the Soviet Union were the two major nuclear powers, even as it promoted numerous "limited wars" in the Third World of former colonies where each of the "superpowers" armed surrogates or intervened themselves to prevent the other from achieving a successful "conversion" (O'Loughlin 1989). For all their weakness, however, Third World and other small countries could not be treated as passive objects of imperialist competition. They had to be wooed and often they resisted. This limited the ability of the superpowers to extend their influence. Unlike in the previous period, the world map was no longer a "vacuum" waiting to be filled by a small number of Great Powers. But the boundaries and integrity of existing states were protected by the military impasse between the superpowers. Any disturbance of the status quo threatened the hegemony of each within its respective sphere of influence.

In the end, the Cold War geopolitical order came undone with the collapse of the Soviet Union and not the United States. In some quarters this ending has been greeted as a Hegelian "end of history" (Fukuyama 1989), with American hegemony in its widest senses—transnationalism, liberalism, democracy—now standing ready to fulfill its (non-) imperial missions abroad. Even parts of the Dark Continent—Africa—are said to be ready to embrace the light of reason and democratization (see Hawthorn 1993). But this conclusion is too self-serving and too simplistic. The Cold War Geopolitical Order came to a formal end in 1989–90 with the breakup of the Soviet Union, but the wider spatial and economic logics that it depended upon had been under attack since the mid-1970s. The Cold War Geopolitical Order was designed at Bretton Woods in 1944 as well as at Yalta the next year, and by 1980 very little remained of the

Bretton Woods system: international investment was growing faster than international trade, the EC and Japan were growing faster than the U.S., Keynesianism had been replaced by monetarism and supply-side economics, and exchange and interest rates were being set by so-called market forces. The breakup of the Soviet Union was not the only sign of an old order in demise; the Cold War geopolitical economy was also in disarray as mounting stagflation, indebtedness, and balance of payments disequilibria clearly and successively indicated.

A New World Order?

The Cold War era laid the groundwork for what we have seen around us in the late 1990s. In particular, existing territorial states have become less and less "full societies" (Williams 1983). At one and the same time they are both too large and too small. They are too large for full social identities and many real economic interests. But they are also too small for many economic purposes. They are increasingly "market sectors" within an intensely competitive, integrated yet unstable world economy. This is the paradox of fragmentation in the context of globalization that many commentators have noted about the world since the "slow end" of the Cold War in the 1980s. Though frequently seen as separate processes they are in fact related aspects of a geopolitical order that has been slowly emerging within an apparent period of disorder. It is in this context that an explosion of ethnopolitical conflict has occurred, in Europe and around the world.

Globalization

British hegemony in the nineteenth century made trade more free and independent. American hegemony during the Cold War went a step further in promoting the transnational movement of all of the mobile factors of production: capital, labor, and technology. Free trade could always be limited when production was organized entirely on a national basis. But today production as well as trade moves easily across national boundaries.

The evidence for this qualitative shift in the character of the world economy and the diminution in the economic importance of existing territorial states as the basic units of account is of various types. First of all, since the 1950s but at a rapidly expanding pace in the 1980s and 90s, world trade has expanded at a rate well in excess of that of earlier periods (e.g., Rogowski 1989, 88). Most of this growth in trade has occurred in the already industrialized regions of the world. It owes much to the declining importance of transportation costs and to institutional innovations such as the GATT (now the World Trade Organization) and the European Union. In a world of large-scale trade there is a premium placed upon maintaining openness and balance rather than territorial expansion and military superiority (Rosecrance 1986).

Second, transnational firms are major agents in stimulating a more open world economy. For example, even as the U.S. territorial economy's total share of world exports shrank by one quarter between 1966 and 1984, U.S.-based firms still accounted for the same proportion of world exports (Lipsey and Kravis 1987).

Third, even the relatively protectionist Japanese economy, the second largest in the world after the U.S., is increasingly internationalized and subject to stresses generated abroad (Higachi and Lauter 1987). For example, the "meltdown" of various Asian economies in 1997–98 had negative effects on Japan because of heavy Japanese involvement in that region through exports, investment, and production.

Fourth, the world financial system is increasingly globalized. The demands of institutional investors, such as pension funds and insurance companies, for more diversified portfolios, the deregulation of national stock markets and the floating of currency-exchange rates, have led to a transnationalization of finance. To serve their worldwide clienteles, many financial markets now operate around the clock and without the close government supervision that was once the case.

Fifth, and finally, various institutions and new social groups have emerged as agents of the globalization of production and exchange. The IMF and the World Bank, for example, have become both more powerful and more autonomous of their member states than was intended when they were founded in the 1940s. Private organizations such as the Trilateral Commission attempt to build an internationalist consensus among leading businessmen, journalists, and academics from the United States, Europe, and Japan (Gill 1990). Some commentators see the progressive growth of an international "bourgeoisie" or class of the managerial employees of transnational firms whose loyalties are to those firms more than to the states from which they come (Sklar 1976).

This new world economy is neither inherently stable nor irreversible. In particular, total levels of world trade and flows of foreign direct investment could be limited by the growth of world-regional trading blocs, such as the European Union and NAFTA (North American Free Trade Agreement), which divert trade and investment into more protected circuits and reduce the global flows that have expanded most in recent years.

Fragmentation

Paralleling economic globalization has been growth in within-state sectionalism, localism, regionalism, and ethnic separatism. This growing fragmentation seems to have two aspects to it. One is the redefinition of economic interest from national to regional, local, and ethnic-group scales. The other is the questioning of political identity as singularly a phenomenon of existing states.

The first of these is the direct result of the breakdown of the national economy as the basic building-block of the world economy. Economic restructuring has involved a collapse of regional-sectoral economic specializations in established industries (cars in Detroit, steel in Pittsburgh, etc.) and the decentralization of production to multiple locations, including many in other states. At the same time, markets are less and less organized on purely national grounds. One important political consequence has been a geographical redefinition of economic interests. Local areas are now tied directly into global markets where they must compete for investment with other localities and regions. Meanwhile, the stimulative and regulative activities of national governments have both weakened and become less effective. Geared towards a national economy that has fragmented into regional and sectoral parts, government policies can no longer shield local communities or ethnic groups from the impacts of competition or readily redistribute resources to declining or poorer areas.

The other aspect of fragmentation has been encouraged by the crumbling of national economies, but relates more to the emergence of new political identities often based on old but revitalized ethnic divisions. The past twenty years have seen the proliferation of political movements with secessionist or autonomist objectives. In Western Europe this trend can be related to the growing redundancy of national governments and increasing levels of relative deprivation between regions and ethnic groups. In Eastern Europe and the former Soviet Union the assertion of ethnic identities has more to do with the demise of strong national governments, the exhaustion of state socialism as an ideology that incorporated ethnic elites, and the settling of old political scores from the distant past. In Africa, and to a degree elsewhere, economic development and nation-building have been sacrificed, after the immediate euphoria of independence and the stasis imposed by the Cold War, to ethnic and regional interests seeking their own futures in a world in which state powers, weak as they were, are increasingly co-opted by international institutions such as the IMF and the World Bank, and can no longer guarantee a return on investment in state legitimacy.

Conclusion

A historicist perspective on geopolitical order suggests that the geography of political organization has gone through a series of significant mutations and associated periodizations over the past two hundred years. Three geopolitical epochs can be identified over the period 1815–1990 in which the relative position of territorial states and empires in general and the identity of dominant states in particular have undergone important shifts. Each of these epochs lasted for around sixty years. In the first the spread of national states was tempered by the existence of an "internationalizing" state (Britain) which facilitated trade and interaction between all states but which also allowed for the emergence of new states out of old ones. In the second period a set of rival imperialisms produced a world in which Great Powers and territorial empires ruled the roost. Only after major wars was there much potential for the creation of new states based on ethnic and national cleavages. In the third period a new internationalizing state (the United States) faced off against an autarkic state (the Soviet Union) in a conflict that inscribed existing state boundaries with deep significance in the ideological balance of power between the two competing sides.

The collapse of the third period of geopolitical order, that of the Cold War, has ushered in a period in which two propositions offer the best hope of understanding the emerging new world order. The first is that economic power is no longer a simple attribute of states that have more or less of it. The growth in world trade, the activities of transnational corporations, the globalized world financial system, global production, and regional trading blocs point towards an emerging global world order to which existing states must adjust with weakened powers. Second, state and society/economy are no longer mutually defining as they were previously. The economic restructuring associated with globalization ties local areas directly into global markets. Local areas and their populations are thus the communities of fate in a world in which there is less possibility of shielding from competition within larger territorial units. The net result of the impact of these propositions is that space is created for the flowering of new and revived political identities organized with reference to a wide range of social, ethnic, and geographical interests. Whether this will continue and deepen depends in large part on whether established territorial states can recover the powers they have lost to global markets and to other actors. Globalization and fragmentation are opposite sides of the same geopolitical coin that has produced the upwelling of ethnopolitical conflict of the past twenty years.

Suggested Study Questions

1. It is popular to think of ethnopolitical conflicts as involving "ancient hatreds." Why would this chapter suggest that this is not at all adequate as a way of thinking about them?

2. Ethnopolitical conflict has not been a historical constant of the past two hundred years. Rather it occurs in "spurts." What does this tell us about why it occurs?

3. The globalization and fragmentation going on in world affairs today might seem the opposite more than complementary. How can they be related to one another? Why is this useful to the student of ethnopolitical conflicts?

4. Take one ethnopolitical conflict with which you are familiar and relate it to the historical-geopolitical argument of this chapter.

References

Agnew, J. 1987. *The United States in the World Economy*. Cambridge: Cambridge University Press.

Art, R. J. 1991. "A Defensible Defense: America's Grand Strategy after the Cold War." *International Security* 15: 5–53.

Baker, C. 1981. "Economic Reorganization and the Slump in South and Southeast Asia." *Comparative Studies in Society and History* 23: 325–49

Bourdieu, P. 1977. *Outline of a Theory of Practice*. Cambridge: Cambridge University Press.

Bull, H. 1977. *The Anarchical Society: A Study of Order in World Politics*. New York: Columbia University Press.

Calleo, D. P. 1987. *Beyond American Hegemony: The Future of the Western Alliance*. New York: Basic Books.

Cox, R. W. 1981. "Social Forces, States and World Orders: Beyond International Relations Theory." *Millennium* 10: 126–55.

———. 1987. *Production, Power, and World Order*. New York: Columbia University Press.

Dehio, L. 1962. *The Precarious Balance: The Politics of Power in Europe, 1494–1945*. London: Chatto and Windus.

Dessler, D. 1989. "What's at Stake in the Agent-Structure Debate?" *International Organization* 43: 441–73.

Deudney, D. 1993. "Bringing Nature Back in: Problems and Trends in Physiopolitical Theory from the Greeks to the Greenhouse." Paper presented at the American Political Science Association annual meeting, Washington D.C.

Fukuyama, F. 1989. "The End of History." *The National Interest* 16: 3–16.

Giddens, A. 1984. *The Nation State and Violence*. London: Macmillan.

Gill, S. 1990. *American Hegemony and the Trilateral Commission*. Cambridge: Cambridge University Press.

Gilpin, R. 1987. *The Political Economy of International Relations*. Princeton, N.J.: Princeton University Press.

Goertz, G. and P. Diehl. 1992. *Territorial Changes and International Conflict*. London: Routledge.

Hawthorn, G. 1993. "Sub-Saharan Africa." *Prospects for Democracy*. D. Held, ed. Cambridge: Polity.

Higashi, C. and G. P. Lauter. 1987. *The Internationalization of the Japanese Economy*. Boston: Kluwer.

Hinsley, F. H. 1966. *Sovereignty*. New York: Basic Books.

Holsti, K. J. 1992. "Governance without Government: Polyarchy in Nineteenth-Century European Politics." In *Governance without Government: Order and Change in World Politics*. J. N. Rosenau and E. N. Czempiel, eds. Cambridge: Cambridge University Press.

Ikenberry, J. and C. Kupchan. 1990. "The Legitimation of Hegemonic Power." In *World*

Leadership and Hegemony. D. Rapkin, ed. Boulder, Colo.: Lynne Rienner.

Inayatullah, N. 1993. "Theories of Spontaneous Disorder: Generating Intentions in Waltz, Gilpin, and Adam Smith." Unpublished paper. Maxwell School, Syracuse University, Syracuse, N.Y.

Keal, P. 1984. *Unspoken Rules and Superpower Dominance.* New York: St. Martin's Press.

Kennedy, P. 1987. *The Rise and Fall of the Great Powers: Economic Change and Military Conflict from 1500 to 2000.* New York: Random House.

Keynes, J. M. 1972. *Essays in Persuasion.* London: Macmillan.

Kratochwil, F. 1989. *Rules, Norms and Decisions.* Cambridge: Cambridge University Press.

Krugman, P. R. 1991. "Is Bilateralism Bad?" *International Trade and Trade Policy.* E. Helpman and A. Razin, eds. Cambridge, Mass.: MIT Press.

Latham, A. J. H. 1978. *The International Economy and the Underdeveloped World.* London: Croom Helm.

Lenin, V. I. 1971. *Imperialism: the Highest Stage of Capitalism.* Peking: Foreign Languages Publishing House.

Lipsey, R. and I. Kravis. 1987. "The Competitiveness and Comparative Advantage of U.S. Multinationals, 1957–84." *Banca Nazionale del Lavoro Quarterly Review* 161: 147–65.

Lipson, C. 1982. "The Transformation of Trade." *International Organization* 36: 417–55.

———. 1989. "International Debt and International Security: Comparing Victorian Britain and Postwar America." In *The International Debt Crisis in Historical Perspective.* B. Eichengreen and P. Lindert, eds. Cambridge, Mass: MIT Press.

———. 1991. "Why Are Some International Agreements Informal?" *International Organization* 45: 495–538.

Luke, T. W. 1991. "The Discipline of Security Studies and the Codes of Containment: Learning from Kuwait." *Alternatives* 16: 315–44.

Maier, C. S. 1978. "The Politics of Productivity: Foundations of American International Economic Policy after World War II." In *Between Power and Plenty: Foreign Economic Policies of Advanced Industrial States.* P. Katzenstein, ed. Madison, Wisc.: University of Wisconsin Press.

Mumford, L. 1961. *The City in History.* New York: Harcourt Brace.

Murphy, C. N. 1993. *International Organization and Industrial Change: Global Governance since 1850.* Cambridge: Polity.

Nijman, J. 1992. "The Limits of Superpower: The United States and the Soviet Union since World War II." *Annals of the Association of American Geographers* 82: 681–95.

Offer, A. 1993. "The British Empire, 1870–1914: A Waste of Money?" *Economic History Review* 46: 215–38.

O'Loughlin, J. 1989. "World-power Competition and Local Conflicts in the Third World." In *A World in Crisis? Geographical Perspectives.* R. J. Johnston and P. J. Taylor, eds. Oxford: Blackwell.

Overbeek, H. and K. van der Pijl. 1993. "Restructuring Capital and Restructuring Hegemony: Neo-liberalism and the Making of the Postwar Order." In *Restructuring Hegemony in the Global Political Economy*. H. Overbeek, ed. London: Routledge.

Palen, R. 1992. "The European Miracle of Capital Accumulation." *Political Geography* 11: 401–406.

Rogowski, R. 1989. *Commerce and Coalitions*. Princeton, N.J.: Princeton University Press.

Rokkan, S. and D. Urwin. 1983. *Economy, Territory, Identity: Politics of West European Peripheries*. London: Sage Publications.

Rosencrance, R. 1986. *The Rise of the Trading State: Commerce and Conquest in the Modern World*. New York: Basic Books.

Ruggie, J. G. 1983. "International Regimes, Transactions and Change: Embedded Liberalism in the Postwar Economic Order." *International Regimes*. S. D. Krasner, ed. Ithaca, N.Y.: Cornell University Press.

Rupert, M. E. 1990. "Producing Hegemony: State-society Relations and the Politics of Productivity in the United States." *International Studies Quarterly* 34: 427–56.

Sklar, R. L. 1976. "Postimperialism: A Class Analysis of Multinational Corporate Expansion." *Comparative Politics* 9: 75–92.

Stein, A. 1984. "The Hegemon's Dilemma: Great Britain, the United States and International Economic Order." *International Organization* 38: 355–86.

Tomlinson, B. R. 1993. *The Economy of Modern India, 1860–1970*. Cambridge: Cambridge University Press.

Wachtel, H. M. 1986. *The Money Mandarins: The Making of a New Supranational Economic Order*. New York: Pantheon.

Wendt, A. 1992. "Anarchy Is What States Make of It: The Social Construction of Power Politics." *International Organization* 46: 391–425.

Williams, R. 1983. *The Year 2000: A Radical Look at the Future and What We Can Do to Change It*. New York: Pantheon.

Wolf, E. R. 1982. *Europe and the People without History*. Berkeley, Calif.: University of California Press.

Wood, R. 1986. *From Marshall Plan to Debt Crisis: Foreign Aid and Development Choices in the World Economy*. Berkeley, Calif.: University of California Press.

2

Overcoming Wilsonianism: American Conflict Resolution and Ethnic Nationalism in Eastern Europe and the Former Soviet Union

John D. Nagle
Frederic S. Pearson
Mark Suprun

Wilsonianism: An American Tradition of Liberal Internationalism in Conflict Resolution

AS LOUIS HARTZ HAS SAID, America is overwhelmingly dominated in its political history by the ideas and ideals of Liberalism. Even our conservatives are, in fact, mainly classical liberals at the core; while our liberals often have been attacked for deviating from classic nineteenth-century liberalism in the search for social equality or social justice, they in fact accept many of the classical liberal premises ranging from free trade to civil liberties (Hartz 1991).

This dominant liberal tradition is mirrored in American thinking about international relations and in conflict resolution among nations as well. America's successful liberalism has from the earliest years of the Republic put itself forward as a model for the Old World of Europe to emulate, even at a time when the United States was still a minor economic power, and was still divided into slave and free states. American self-confidence in its basic liberal principles has not been overly troubled by temporary economic setbacks or by significant failures to stand by these principles when dealing with either foreigners or native-born, but has rather seen the American experience as both exceptional and exportable. A clearly missionary sense has accompanied the advertisement of Americanism as the modern alternative for the continuing problems of the European Old World, as well as the newer Afro-Asian Third World.

Warren Kuehl (1969, 11), in his political history of American liberal idealism's mission to Europe, culminating in Woodrow Wilson's League of Nations proposals at the end of World War I, notes that Thomas Paine, in his 1791 essay on the *Rights of Man,* saw the formation of the American Confederation and later American Federalism as the model for the formation of a new combination of nations first into loose association and later into a more complete union. Kuehl remarks that the federation of the separate colonies itself was seen as a "great rehearsal" for the experiments in voluntary international cooperation to overcome war and national conflict consistent with the thinking of Immanuel Kant in his essay of 1795 on *Perpetual Peace.* In an era of continual European war-making and failed peacemaking from the outbreak of the French Revolution in 1789 through the final military victory over the Napoleonic armies in 1814, a core of American thinkers looked already to the American federal experience as a radically new and hopeful success formula.

American leaders saw the post-Napoleonic order, the Holy Alliance of European monarchs, as reactionary and insupportable, and in 1819 Secretary of State John Quincy Adams announced that the United States would refuse membership in the Concert of Europe, which was for most of the nineteenth century the international foundation for maintaining the European peace. In the American view, the concert rested upon a suppression of liberalism in Europe and expansion and restoration of colonies in the New World. The American Peace Society of 1828, growing out of local peace societies beginning in 1815, established in the course of the nineteenth century an American intellectual discourse on the abolition of war and armed conflict which involved many of the basic points of a "league of nations" as the ideal organizational form for overcoming national conflicts. This line of thought, which again rested on the peculiar American experience of federalism and federal expansion throughout the century, was already referred to by Europeans in the 1840s as the "American Plan" (Kuehl 1969, 14–15).

While the Peace Society's leaders' motivations were Christian and pacifist in great measure, it is clear also that they represented a new form of American liberal internationalism, which rejected or ignored the deep differences of ethnic national cultures and the historical weight of ethnic conflict in Europe in its views on the possibilities and methods for overcoming war and national conflict. Already with the Peace Society, vanguard American thinking on conflict resolution among nations represented a break with classic conservative European thinking, and began a new path of liberal internationalism based on an (idealized) understanding of the American experience. In this new path of discourse, the American understanding of "nation" and its conflation with the sovereign "nation-state," were core elements of the search for a voluntary "congress" or "league" of nations. This intellectual tradition would nurture, in another era of European wars, the ideas of Woodrow Wilson and other Americans concerned with international peace and conflict resolution among nations.

The First World War occasioned a new round of American plans, each with its own distinctive features and points of disagreement. These were grounded in a peculiarly American understanding of the basic concepts of "nation" and "state," which were to be the components in some new "United States of Europe" (the young historian Samuel Eliot Morison of Harvard) or a "new State, a new Power" (Darwin Kingsley of the League to Enforce Peace) which would use the Constitution of the United States as its model (Kuehl 1969, 250–59). Through direct contact by their proponents with the Anglophile, Colonel Edward House, Wilson's closest advisor, these ideas fed into the Fourteen Points and League of Nations proposals. When Wilson first proposed U.S. membership in a league of nations on May 27, 1916, he carried this American liberal internationalist tradition a step further into an era when American intervention in European wars carried much greater weight and American ideas would be judged in practice against European realities (Kuehl 1969, 225–26).

Wilson also set up a secret committee, the so-called Inquiry, in October 1917 to plan the new map of Europe after the war. This committee included the young journalist Walter Lippman, Sidney Mezez, President of City College of New York, David Hunter Miller, a New York law partner of Colonel House's son-in-law, James Shotwell, historian at Columbia University, and Isaiah Bowman, director of the American Geographical Society. This small group of liberal internationalists set out to redraw the borders of Eastern and Central Europe in accordance with the notion of "self-determination of nations," understood as ethnic nationalities; it was the first attempt to superimpose an American Plan for a peaceful Europe on the realities of the Old World (Pfaff 1992, 68).

When combined with French territorial manipulations to make up for the loss of ally Russia in the Bolshevik Revolution, this audacious Wilsonian experiment would produce the successor states in East and Central Europe after the defeat of Germany and the breakup of Austria-Hungary. However, it also immediately produced new minorities and antagonisms within each new state, and new border grievances against neighboring states. George Kennan judged that this exercise illustrated the "colossal conceit of thinking that you could suddenly make international life over into what you believed to be your own image, when you dismissed the past with contempt, rejected the relevance of the past to the future, and refused to occupy yourself with the real problems that a study of the past would suggest" (cited in Pfaff 1992, 68).

At the Versailles Conference in 1919, Wilsonianism was boldly proclaimed as a break with the European past; World War I had been "fought to do away with an old order and to establish a new one, and the center and characteristic of the old order was that unstable thing we used to call the 'balance of power'" (Mansbach and Vasquez 1981, 370). Immediately, the tremendous gap between the Wilsonian principles and the European victors' notions of how to apply them to the problems of post-war collective security and conflict prevention in Europe was revealed. This clash of interests and the set of misunderstandings between the European victors and the United States, culminating in the U.S. decision not to join the League and to retreat into "isolationism," led later "realists" to characterize Wilson as an "idealist" or a "utopian." Yet, even American "realists" carried much of the same Liberal intellectual baggage with them when discussing European conflicts and their possible resolution.

After World War II, and another round of European war-making and reluctant United States intervention, Liberal principles of the American plan for a postwar peace again rose to prominence, and this time could not simply be turned into mush by the chastened British and French allies (nor by the wartime Soviet ally). John Herz, the noted political scientist, saw the birth of the United Nations as the continuation of Wilson's objective: "A system of equal, free, and self-determining nationalities, each organized into its own state and living peacefully side by side" (1951, 67). In some ways, the Cold War system of a divided Europe allowed for a good part of Wilsonianism to triumph in the West, whether from a new conviction or from practical necessity on the part of British, French, German, and Italian leaders. Voluntary collective security based on equality of nations, liberal self-determination in a democratic framework, and abandonment of empire and old border claims was the apparent record in the Western alliance. The success of the alliance gave renewed life to American Liberal internationalism not only in Europe but also in the new "nations" of the non-Western world as well.

Inherent in the revived Wilsonian concept, revived after World War II, was the necessity and myth of self-determination by each nationality, which Robert Wendzel has described as both means and end. This presumed equality of nationalities, like the liberal notion of equality of citizens, was the prerequisite for demanding equal obligations and rights for states, and would remove the inequalities among nations which were such a major source of conflict. In this framework, collective "security rests upon cooperation, and "real" cooperation is possible only among states who are equal" (Wendzel 1981, 34.) Wendzel analyzes the ethical basis for this American Wilsonianism and the effects it has had on U.S. policy-making during the Cold War, as in Vietnam. In the eyes of U.S. policymakers, American intervention in Vietnam was ethically "superior," say to France's, in terms of stated commitment to liberal self-determination of nations, even if at the same time the U.S. was aiding a repressive Saigon regime in a power game against Russia and China. As Wendzel notes, this replicated in type Wilson's and the Inquiry's misunderstandings at Versailles, in that it did not take into account other, strongly felt and deeply rooted notions of rights, morality, and ethics in dealing with other nationalities. While American liberal internationalism has tended to see its own norms as universal and progressive, and therefore transferable with enough effort and enlightenment to any other society and any other culture, often over a longer period of time, these societies and cultures have developed their own norms which are also self-perceived as superior, and more importantly, as part of the very self-definition of their own people as a nation.

Understanding the New Post-Cold War
Birth of Nations and National Conflicts

With the end of the Cold War, as at the end of both world wars, there has been a breakup of empire (Soviet) and the struggle of ethnic nationalities to establish themselves as sovereign nation-states (Czech, Croat, Slovak, Macedonian, etc.). Initially, this new birth of nations was generally greeted by the West (the United States did have reservations about both Yugoslavia and Czechoslovakia) as part of the progressive agenda for dismantling communism and building in Eastern Europe and the former Soviet Union new, free, self-determined and capitalist nation-states. The early enthusiasm for the "parade of sovereignties" of 1990–91 was part of the initial euphoria over the victory of the United States in the Cold War: with the fall of communism in Europe, a new Liberal internationalism, backed by revitalized U.N. collective security on the Gulf War model, would fulfill in the East what it had presumably already achieved in the West. This is part of what George Bush, sounding very Wilsonian, termed a "New International Order."

One of the earliest voices warning against a simplistic replay of 1919 or 1945 was William Pfaff, longtime American expatriate writer in Paris and correspondent for the *New Yorker* magazine. Pfaff, a continental conservative most critical of American Cold War conservatism (which he might argue had been more akin to aggressive Liberal internationalism), feared that American intellectuals and leaders would view the end of the Cold War with a renewed missionary zeal to remake Eastern Europe and the successor states of the former Soviet Union in their own image, and ultimately to intervene in the myriad ethnic nationalist conflicts which he predicted were to erupt with the collapse of European communism. Writing in 1989, before the fall of the Berlin Wall and before the outbreak of ethnic warfare (except over Nagorno-Karabakh between Armenians and Azeris), Pfaff (1989, 23) warned that Europe (Eastern and Central, but even perhaps Western) had become dangerous again.[1] Pfaff, a determined critic of Wilsonianism, warned also that America might misunderstand once again the new conflicts of post-communism and the post-Cold War era in Europe, and in misunderstanding, would bring greater harm than good in its attempts at conflict solving. Pfaff argues that European thoughts are not American thoughts. European assumptions, imaginations, and ambitions are not American. European beliefs about elite education and responsibility; classes and races and their relations; the defects of democracy as well as its virtues; and the alternatives to democracy (unimaginable to Americans), the qualities of heroism, conquest, endurance—of pride, caste, sanctity: all these remain deeply un-American. That this is so, and has always been so, he suggests, lies at the source of the American uneasiness with Europe which has marked both societies from the seventeenth to the twentieth centuries (nearly to the twenty-first); but since 1945 this has resolutely been ignored on both sides (Pfaff 1989, 21).

For Pfaff, the Cold War, as an important interlude to be sure, changed some elements of national political cultures both West and East, but the longer historical traditions and understandings of nation, nationality, and identity were now reasserting themselves and nowhere more quickly and powerfully than in the ex-communist East where the empty intellectual space was being filled, mostly with distinctly un-American ideas, even by many opinion elites eager to profess their desire to "join the West."

Despite the emergence of some liberal elites in Eastern Europe, the Balkans, and the successor states of the former Soviet Union, Pfaff argued that the crucial notion of citizenship is still defined in ethnic terms, which challenges any strictly liberal Americanist approach to settlement of ethnic conflict, either for minorities within state borders or between neighboring states. In a follow-up article on the current absence of empire in Europe, Pfaff (1992, 68) saw once again the dangers of American misunderstandings over this key concept: Because citizenship in these Eastern European and Balkan states is ethnic and therefore exclusive (that is, it cannot be acquired in any way except by having been born to it) it is compromised if equal standing is accorded other nationalities within a country's borders. At the same time the frontiers between exclusive national groups within a country are usually indistinct or disputed, with different nationalities intermingled: hence today's ethnic wars. One might add that even Germany, which has undergone a thorough process of domestic liberal democratic transformation since 1945, and which has displayed the most consistent loyalty to liberal internationalist goals in the evolution of the European Community and now European Union, still adheres to a basically ethnic definition of German citizenship and who are "Germans." Ethnic Germans in Poland, Russia, Ukraine, or Yugoslavia are immediately entitled to German citizenship upon arrival in Germany, whereas ethnic Turks who have lived and worked in Germany for decades, or whose children were born and raised exclusively in Germany, are not. Chancellor Kohl, one of the most steady partners of the United States in Europe in the 1980s, only recently affirmed that "Germany is not a land of immigrants" (*"Deutschland ist kein Einwanderungsland"*), which seems strange to American ears, since in fact Western Germany after 1945 received over fourteen million German refugees and expellees as new immigrants from the East, and encouraged over four million Turks, Yugoslavs, Greeks, Italians, and Spaniards to come to Germany as "guest workers" (*Gastarbeiter*). What Kohl meant, of course, is that by German reckoning, ethnic Germans from the East were already Germans with the birthright to citizenship, whereas Turks and others might be welcomed as needed, but would (with some minor exceptions) never become "Germans." Only now in the 1990s are some parties, notably the Greens and parts of the Social Democrats, and some leading intellectuals (Jürgen Habermas), and media (the liberal *die Zeit*) calling for fundamental changes of citizenship laws.

One might even note that France, which along with Britain was the West European power most affected by classical liberalism, and which had long accepted a more open *"jus solis"* definition of who was "French," has recently retreated to an alternative tradition, in the direction of *"jus sanguinis"* under pressure from LePen's National Front and from strong traditional nationalists in the neo-Gaullist party. Indeed, on a worldwide scale—note the practices of ethnic citizenship in Japan and, with the exception of native Arabs, in Israel for example—it is the American understanding of this concept which is peculiar, although by no means unique among mainly settler societies (Canada, Australia, and New Zealand). This does not mean that the United States has in reality escaped the conflict between liberal individualism and notions of ethnic or group rights. Especially in its traumatic race relations it has exhibited severe ambiguity in according a black racial minority first citizenship and then some special group recognition in compensation for past oppression. But both latter day liberals, in their attack on segregation, discrimination, and racial exclusion, and conservatives, in their attack on compensatory affirmative action, are in the American context relying on classic Liberal individualism as the mainstream ideal which holds the highest legitimization, even when it is blatantly trounced in practice.

American politics has great difficulty in dealing with notions of group rights or recognition, even as temporary compensatory measures, be they racial, gender, or ethnic (for example, bilingual education). But debates on such issues have arisen because liberal principles of individual equality in the American context have so often been systematically ignored for whole groups.

The Legacy of Empires and the Challenge of Conflict Resolution

The United States was a post-imperial successor state, or in Lipset's terms "the first new nation," but it arose from the most liberally affected West European empire. Anglophiles such as Wilson could find ample justification for "open door" ideologies and leagues of nations in British thought if not practice. In administering its overseas empire, in fact, London practiced a form of divide and rule strategy which allowed for relative local princely autonomy within a Raj-like superstructure. Relatively few colonial administrators could thereby rule vast territories. At home, the effect of these policies over time was to dilute relative homogeneity with gradually emerging transplanted colonial resident populations (West Indian, South Asian, etc.). The French revolution had decidedly different effects on French colonial policy, with the rising myth of French nationality being spread to the colonies along with citizenship rights. Colonial administration was far more centralized than in the British case, but the results were similar in that French society in the metropole was forced to be somewhat open to ethnic identity. What one gathers from Colonial administration is at the very least a tacit acceptance of the colonized cultures. In this sense, a policy of "multiculturalism," although neither officially enunciated nor adopted, was visible in the French metropole.

In Eastern Europe and the successor states of the former Soviet Union, on the other hand, the trauma of multiple resident ethnic groups undergoing simultaneous transitions (geographic, political, economic) made citizenship an issue of immediate economic survival and future economic, educational, residential, cultural, and political opportunity. A clear popular expectation persisted that the dominant ethnic elite would purposefully disadvantage and perhaps even expel ("cleanse" or in the most extreme cases exterminate) ethnic minorities from long-standing places of work and residence.

What does this imply for attempts to apply conflict resolution techniques, which arise from American theory and practice, to the ethnic conflicts, latent and active in Eastern Europe and the former Soviet Union? Even if one does not agree with the entire range of criticisms leveled against American Liberal internationalism and its assumptions, and although many precepts are enshrined in international laws of human rights, it appears at least necessary for conflict resolution specialists from American backgrounds to take seriously the historical depth of ethnic nationalism which has, in the years of post-communism, shown tremendous resiliency and potential for disaster. But what does it mean to "take seriously" this very different history and concept of "nation?"

Pfaff foresees the possibility that a disillusioned America might recoil from its Cold War era of Liberal internationalism into its other tradition—semi-isolationism—which he does not entirely see as harmful. In any case, a serious re-thinking of the purposes and potentials of American ideas of conflict resolution in the current era of ethnic strife in Europe is a minimum first step. "But if Americans give up their older ideas, they must also give up the progressive, moralizing language connected to those ideas, which continues to be employed by conservatives quite as much as by liberals" (Pfaff 1989, 188). If one rejects isolationism as a desirable alternative, what kind of new synthesis might allow for American conflict resolution theory and practice to play a useful and constructive role in ethnic conflict situations in this new era?

Adapting Liberalism and Wilsonianism to Eastern Europe and the Successor States of the Former Soviet Union: Prospects for Success?

Arguably, Wilson's principle of self-determination was a mechanism designed to facilitate the germination of the central tenets of liberalism in the peoples of Eastern Europe immediately following World War I. Many liberal internationalists at that time believed that if the Eastern peoples were allowed the right to self-determination, they would opt for a representative form of government, thus reducing or altogether eliminating the prospects for war (hence ultimately the Kellogg-Briand Peace Pact).[2] One integral aspect, then, of conflict resolution between emergent states in Eastern Europe lies in the creation of suitable national structures (political, economic, and social) which are capable of resolving domestic tensions and which facilitate group cohesion and security within the new state apparatus. Another important aspect is "cultural opening" or changed attitudes about and awareness of other nearby cultures. However, representative democracy, in its Western style, is dependent upon the principle of one man, one vote. Only recently have democratic systems in the West (Canada and the United States) been forced to integrate group dynamics into representative democracy's calculus, and with limited success if one considers the plight of African-Americans and Native Americans. Thus, a normative dilemma occurs when one considers the role of the individual versus the role of the group in a representative democracy. Furthermore, in order to understand Wilsonianism and assess its appropriateness for Eastern Europe, one must first realize that it is an extension of the ideals expressed by Liberalism. To appreciate the dilemmas posed by Wilsonianism today, and the opportunities for its application in some form, Liberalism must be contrasted with the philosophical underpinnings of Eastern European society. This is extremely important for the twenty-first century, since one of the rationales for NATO's rushed expansion to the east has been to safeguard and nurture democracy there.

Classical liberalism regards the individual as the central point of social development in society and the state. Since the dawning of the Enlightenment, western European political thought has focused on reconciling the apparently conflicting aspirations of the state and the individual. Liberalism emerged from an educated elite, which sought a moral and philosophical justification for the ascendant status they enjoyed in the social and political organization of the eighteenth century. Thus, in the rarefied colonial atmosphere of North America, the individual and the protection of individual rights from government or state encroachment became the praxis of American Liberalism. As such, Liberalism is composed of three constituent parts, labeled by Macridis (1996, 22) as moral, political, and economic.

The moral core contains an affirmation of basic values and rights attributable to the "nature" of a human being—freedom, dignity, and life—subordinating everything else to their implementation. The political core includes primarily political rights—the right to vote, to participate, to decide what kind of government to elect, and what kind of policies to follow. It is associated with representative democracy. The economic core has to do with economic and property rights. It is still referred to as "economic individualism" and pertains to the rights and freedoms of individuals to produce and to consume, to enter into contractual relations, to buy and sell through a market economy, to satisfy their wants in their own way, and to dispose of their property and labor as they decide. Its cornerstones have been private property and a market economy that is free from state controls and regulations.

In terms of normative foundations for a society, many of these tenets are unfamiliar to east European thinking, and even more so in the former Soviet Union, although the economic core has recently received popular support from aspiring entrepreneurs. In western Europe, as Macridis suggests, "liberalism freed individuals from all attachments to groups and status that defined and structured their activities. The individual became the driving force within the social and political system" (1996, 191).

Obviously, there were variations in this among European countries (Sweden's greater acceptance of collectivism as compared to Britain, for example), and continental western Europe displays a generally greater collective norm than the United States. Liberalism's exclusion of group rights and responsibilities is one reason why it has not found fertile ground in eastern Europe. That is, if one examines the nature of the individual in east European society and the peoples of the former Soviet Union, it becomes clear that the individual is still very much attached to the group. Indeed, in many parts of eastern Europe and the former Soviet Union, the ethnic group defines the individual and structures his/her endeavors.

The politico-ideological development in east European societies and the populations of the former Soviet Union has evolved, since the eighteenth century (and arguably earlier) along a social-needs (that is, group) orientation. This is not to suggest that all the needs of the individual are completely subsumed by the needs of the community or state. However, an individual's immediate relationship as citizen to the state is not of ultimate importance when compared to the individual's relationship with the community, church, class, or ethnic group. For example, many east European philosophers speak about the concerns that beset the community, rather than the condition of individuals within the larger state, as western philosophers have done. Regarding the Russian Federation, George Fedotov[3] says: "From the parents man comes and to the parents he returns, into the womb of Mother Earth. During his earthly life, his whole existence is determined by the parents, by the will of the living, and by the traditions of the departed. For the freedom and will of the individual yet there is very little place. The consciousness of personality, its own ways, vocations and rights, developed tardily and slowly on the Russian soil both in pagan and in Christian times."

In East Europe and the former Soviet Union, the ethno-cultural communities (based on a multi-cultural map), along with traditional institutions such as the church, have, since the collapse of European continental communism, reasserted their historic role as a driving force within the emerging political and social systems.

Prior to his death, Lenin revealed his latent understandings of the Soviet system's inherent failure to overcome ethnicity by stating that: "We must be clearly aware that the attempt has failed and that it is impossible suddenly to change people's outlook and the habits they acquired over the ages. We can try to drive the population into the new system by force, but the question would still remain whether we would retain power in this all-Russian slaughter house."[4]

During the Gorbachev era, Lenin's earlier admonition was referred to as the "nationalities problem." In the Communist Party's 1986 program, Gorbachev declared that "the national question, which has remained from the past, has been solved in the Soviet Union."[5] In proclaiming the nationalities problem solved, Gorbachev, like his predecessors, tried to break with history in order to focus resources on the deepening economic crisis. Like his predecessors, Gorbachev underestimated the role the ethnic group has played in Soviet history, and at least implicitly relied upon "*Homo Sovieticus*" to play an active role in his reforms. However, the waning years of the Soviet system were plagued by an internecine war over Nargorno-Karabakh, riots in Alma-Ata over the removal of an ethnic Kazakh leader and his replacement by an ethnic Russian, and subsequent ethnic tensions and bloodshed (e.g., Georgia Abkhazia, and the Baltic republics). The Homo Sovieticus model never displaced the ethnic or group loyalties that have been the driving forces for social development through the centuries. Thus, in terms of conflict resolution in east Europe and the former Soviet Union, one is forced to reevaluate the practicality of many of those tenets of Liberalism which espouse elevating the individual above the group; instead it appears that solutions to ethnic conflict lie in creative approaches to channeling group loyalties and defusing fears, rather than the imposing or injecting of foreign ideas about state, institutions, and society. The sources of the tensions that lead to what has been called "identity" conflict and violence in places like eastern and central Europe do not necessarily originate solely in competing ethnicities themselves, vying for territory or other resources. Instead, the origins of ethnic conflict today are rooted in relationship-constructs that may be unique to the region and influenced by regional political history and competition. In part, such patterns result from a legacy of empire. Identity conflict is heightened and politically driven, as leaders exploit latent ethnic tensions to serve the power-and-property seeking purposes of elite cliques and both old and new *nomenklatura* networks.

During the final years of the nineteenth century when the Austro-Hungarian, Ottoman and Russian empires were faced with imminent collapse, the relationship between the ethnic group and the state emerged as a key contested issue. Under the administrative-bureaucratic structure of empire, various ethnic communities had relationships with the imperial apparatus and among themselves. What emerged was a set of triangular relationships, with structural defects along interactive lines. In more general terms, according to Robert K. Thomas (1996, 45), the colonial situation creates an environment where "[o]ne 'people' specifically administer the affairs of another, but in this case, by institutional relationships that are pulled up out of one economic level or one 'community' and placed in another one." Furthermore, in what Thomas (1996, 46) calls the hidden colonial model, "there is great differential power between the administrated and the administrators, and institutional decisions are made through the institutions of the administrators," and this subsequently results in the "decay of the subordinate people's own institutions." Thus, native or indigenous mechanisms for mediation and conflict resolution between and among ethnic groups are slowly eroded and replaced by an imperial apparatus or ideology that inherently ignores the cultural nuances and mores that have existed for centuries.

Indeed, many of the nation-states and nationalities that have emerged from the collapse of Soviet communism were once administered as subject colonies. The political structure within the former Soviet Union, some of it inherited from empire, and some of it strongly affected by large population movements of ethnic Russians, was a striking example of Machiavellianism. In offering his advice about methods to employ when administering new territories, Machiavelli (1995, 47–48) observed that:

When states newly acquired as I said have been accustomed to living freely under their own laws, there are three ways to hold them securely: first, by devastating them; next, by going and living there in person; thirdly, by letting them keep their own laws, exacting tribute, and setting up an oligarchy which will keep the state friendly to you. In the last case, the government will know that it cannot endure without the friendship and power of the prince who created it, and so it has to exert itself to maintain his authority.

Ukraine, for example, was administered as a colony of Imperial Russia. As is the case with conquered territories according to Machiavelli, the subject group is often coerced to abandon its cultural (political, social, economic, and ecological) traditions. As Subtelney (1989, 282) notes, "in July, 1863, Petr Valuev, the minister of internal affairs, secretly banned the publication in Ukrainian of all scholarly, religious, and especially pedagogical publications.[6] The minister declared that the Ukrainian language "never existed, does not exist and shall never exist" (Subtelney 1989, 282). The Ukrainian relationship with the imperial elite was thus, to say the least, strained and eventually led to feelings of estrangement. As time went on, these feelings of estrangement from the imperial administration were transmuted into feelings of animosity towards ethnic Russians, as they represented the dominant culture. The original source of tension between ethnic Russians and Ukrainians was not so much due to ethnic differences (indeed, these were relatively few when compared to Asian-Russian tensions) but in structural and political conflicts with the imperial administration. Soviet administration was not merely a continuation of Tsarist imperial administration. However, during the initial movements to consolidate political and economic power in the Soviet Union, the nationality policy imposed by Stalin continued to reflect the hues of Machiavellianism in Russian politics. Using a political language similar to Tsarist thinking, Stalin revealed the Soviet Union's drive toward the creation of a new Empire by stating that: "The essence of the national question in the Soviet [Union] is to liquidate the economic, political and cultural backwardness of the nationalities. We inherited this backwardness from the past. We do this in order to give the backward peoples the opportunity to catch up with central Russia both in governmental, cultural and economic respects."[7]

Although this policy recognizes competing differences among ethnic groups in the Soviet administrative super-structure, the purpose of this structure was to eliminate all vestiges of ethnic identification prevalent in the Soviet Union. It also facilitated a justification for the creation of a hegemonic bureaucratic-Union and, as Stalin put it, would "liquidate the economic, political and cultural backwardness of the nationalities." It was adopted with a sense of teleological fervor and brutal means were employed to ensure its success. The "hidden colonial model" invariably begins to treat other ethnic groups as objects, efficiently removing the human dimension from conciliation or other acts of mediation aimed at integration through cooperation or establishing principles for mutual coexistence.

Thus, when one considers the former Soviet Union as a modified extension of the Russian empire, the pervasive triangular relationship becomes clear. At one point of the triangle sat the imperial (or Soviet) bureaucracy (together with its associational institutions, such as the church), at another the dominant ethnic group, and at the third, the subject ethnic group. East and Central European imperial bureaucracies lacked the secular administration of liberal bureaucracies in western Europe and the United States, for example. As a result, many of the institutions that were integral to the social functions of the subject ethnic group were subordinated or completely dissolved. These institutions, once bureaucratized, can facilitate a feeling of collective intra-group security, thereby alleviating inter-ethnic tensions. If the local institutions are denied, or the subject ethnic group is forced into the dominant system, feelings of alienation and tensions are reinforced. The appearance of nationalism, according to Alastair Reid (1994, 51): "arises from situations in which a smaller country is taken over by a larger power, which imposes on it a new official identity, a culture, and often a new language, suppressing the native identity and driving it inward to become a secret private self. In conditions of such subjugation, a people is forced to become both bilingual and bicultural."

After 1940, Estonia, Latvia, and Lithuania again, after a brief independence of twenty years, fell under the administrative control of the Kremlin. These countries were politically, economically, socially, and culturally subject to the imposition of ethnic Russian practices. For example, the use of a patronymic (a practice unfamiliar to Estonians) is culturally unique to Russia. Notwithstanding the use of Russian language throughout the former Soviet Union and its psychological impact on subject colonies, the use of the patronymic was a constant reminder to ethnic Estonians of their status as subjects of Russian authority. Thus for many of the non-Russian nationalities, the communist experience under the Soviet Union became synonymous with Russian domination.

An argument can therefore be made that stability, security, and resolution of conflict in Eastern Europe and the former Soviet Union will only be achieved when subjugated ethnic groups create their own bureaucratic administration that at least nominally protects the rights and responsibilities of a formerly suppressed minority. The forms of such developments may not always look "democratic" to western eyes—for example, they might include set-aside schools, councils, or institutions. Additionally, lateral contacts (through education or an independent media) and negotiations between the two (or more) ethnic groups at the comers of the triangle must be promoted to ease what may be perceived as harsh political-administrative effects. The potential for conflict is exacerbated if the emerging bureaucratic-administrative elite, in conjunction with the state's political leadership, comes to violate other ethnic minorities. Therefore, when positing solutions to ethnic tensions in eastern Europe and the former Soviet Union, one must realize that the fundamental associational characteristic is the group. Political negotiations must be aimed at group accommodation, at least until the "new Europe" produces "homo-europa."

Conclusions

There exists a discrepancy between Wilsonian principles and the present reality of group loyalties and group politics in East and Central Europe. When treating ethnic conflict situations in the former Soviet Union or east Europe, one must separate short-term possibilities from long-term ideals. In the short term, conflict resolution initiatives must allow for the fact that group-based ethnic politics cannot change quickly, and therefore that group-based solutions are necessary. This means that individualized conflict resolution approaches, based on litigation or advanced dispute resolution (ADR), may not resolve essential social conflicts or promote democracy. It also means that liberal expectations of "one man, one vote" or even "equal protection under the law" may take a very long time to develop fully. This is not an apology for repression, but a factual statement calling for the development of appropriate measures to promote gradual and progressive inter-group acceptance. The Northern Irish agreements of 1998, with provision for various joint councils and cross-border guarantees might constitute a model, but as noted by conflict theorist Sean Byrne (1998), the proof will be in the degree of grass-roots social support it generates in the respective communities. Only a solidly popular settlement can resist attacks from extremists. The mind-sets of the older and perhaps the middle generations in east Europe and the former Soviet Union are not likely to change very rapidly, even as economic changes proceed. The pace of democratization can be retarded by income inequalities and economic distortion. It may be possible, however, to educate the younger generation about liberal principles, and gradually expand the civic cultural base. Generation theory, proposed by Inglehart (1990), tells us it is precisely among the young adults (17–25) that worldview formation takes place and is most open to change.

In order for Wilsonian principles to gain relevance for societies of east and central Europe, certain social structures require reconstruction. Liberal principles have relied upon an independent judiciary in the West. Indeed, one can argue that arbitration, mediation, and ADR in the West are almost impossible without a functional, independent, and open legal system. The legal systems of the former Soviet Union and much of east Europe, on the other hand, are in a similar state of disarray. In order for Wilsonianism and liberalism truly to take root in the worldviews of the younger generation, they must first have a referent legal system (as well as a political system) in which they can place their trust. Richard Rose (1994, 26) tells us that 60 percent of Russians distrust their court system. He also states that "distrust is a major obstacle to the emergence of a civil society in which representative institutions can link the interests of individuals and families with the actions of government (1994, 28). Yet, Zbigniew Kurchevsky found that even during the Communist era, Poles favored use of courts over ADR, even though they distrusted courts, because in the final analysis, court decisions were authoritative. Therefore, the potential would seem to exist for greater reliance on a reformed and efficient independent judiciary. There is hope for conflict management even though there exist numerous obstacles to the Wilsonian mode of intervention.

Finally, Western conflict resolution specialists also may be able to learn some important and positive lessons from the cases of group-based conflict resolution and negotiation—or traditional mediation—in east Europe and the former Soviet Union. Ultimately, apart from the earliest impact of inter-ethnic agreements reflected in the U.S. Constitution, noted by David Hackett Fisher (1989) in the penetrating analysis *Albion's Seed*, and Native-American treaty rights (usually breached in practice, unless economically useful—as in gambling casino authorization), the West has not done very well in devising group-rights solutions to ethnic conflict. Yet, as western society becomes more multicultural (Southern California, Southern Florida, Frankfurt, Leipzig, Marseilles, and Paris), there may a growing and dire need for group-based conflict resolution approaches there as well.

Suggested Study Questions

1. To what extent and in what way should ethnic conflict settlement be "democratic"?
2. How does a tradition of "American Exceptionalism" apply to American diplomatic initiatives?
3. How does ethnic conflict management in central and eastern Europe compare to that of other troubled regions?
4. What does a country's definition of citizenship indicate about its approach to ethnic conflict settlement?

5. In dealing with identity disputes, to what extent are we "prisoners of history" and to what extent can we successfully innovate?

Notes

1. Pfaff (1989, 65) further argues that the differences between Western Europe and the U.S. are also greater than we would like to believe, ". . . the West European nations have less in common with the United States than forty years of slogans about the free world and Atlantic civilization suggest. There are crucial values held in common, but the general and largely unanalyzed assumption made since the Second World War that all are societies going in the same direction, toward the same goal, led by the United States, must be challenged."

2. Recent findings show that democracies almost never fight each other. See, for example, *Debating the Democratic Peace*, ed. M. E. Brown, S. M. Lynn-Jones and S. E. Miller (Cambridge, Mass.: MIT Press, 1998).

3. George Fedotov, *The Russian Religious Mind* (Cambridge, Mass.: Harvard University Press, 1946), 6–11. Quoted in *Gnosis: A Journal of the Western Inner Tradition*, Spring 1994, (31): 16.

4. Lenin, cited in Uri Ra'anan and Igor Lukes, *Gorbachev's U.S.S.R.* (London: Macmillan, 1990), 82.

5. Gorbachev, cited in Yaroslav Bilinsky. "Nationality Policy in Gorbachev's First Year." *Orbis* (Summer 1986): 331–42.

6. Orest Subtelney. *Ukraine: A History,* Toronto: University of Toronto Press, 1989, 282. It should be noted that sometimes, as in Ataturk's reforms in Turkey, even modern nationalists can adopt Machiavellian tactics regarding their own people (i.e., repressing older cultural and language traditions).

7. Stalin, cited in Gregory Gleason, "Leninist Nationality Policy: Its Source and Style," in *Soviet Nationality Policies: Ruling Ethnic Groups in the USSR*, ed. Henry R. Huttenbach, (London: Mansell Publishing Limited, 1990), 14.

References

Bilinsky, Yaroslav. 1986. "Nationality Policy in Gorbachev's First Year." *Orbis* (Summer): 331–42.

Brown, M. E., S. M. Lynn-Jones and S. E. Miller, eds. 1998. *Debating the Democratic Peace.* Cambridge, Mass.: MIT Press.

Byrne, Sean. 1998. "Traditional Modes of Elite Bargaining and Common Ground Citizen Participation: Fifteen Years on and the Evolution of the Peace Process in Northern Ireland." Unpublished Manuscript.

Fedotov, George. 1946. *The Russian Religious Mind*. Cambridge, Mass.: Harvard University Press, 6–11. Quoted in *Gnosis: A Journal of the Western Inner Tradition*, Spring 1994,

(31): 16.

Fisher, David Hackett. 1989. *Albion's Seed:Four British Folkways in America.* New York: Oxford University Press.

Gleason, Gregory. 1990. "Leninist Nationality Policy: Its Source and Style." In *Soviet Nationality Policies: Ruling Ethnic Groups in the USSR.* Henry R. Huttenbach, ed. London: Mansell Publishing Limited.

Hartz, Louis. 1991. *The Liberal Tradition in America: An Interpretation of American Political Thought since the Revolution.* San Diego: Harcourt Brace Jovanovich.

Herz, John. 1951. *Political Realism and Political Idealism.* Chicago: University of Chicago Press.

Ingelhart, Ronald. 1990. *Culture Shift in Advanced Industrial Societies.* Princeton, N.J.: Princeton University Press.

Kuehl, Warren. 1969. *Seeking World Order.* Nashville: Vanderbilt University Press.

Machiavelli, Niccolo. 1995. *The Prince.* New York: Penguin Books.

Macridis, Roy C. 1996. *Contemporary Political Ideologies: Movements and Regimes.* New York: HarperCollins.

Mansbach, Richard and John Vasquez. 1981. *In Search of Theory: A New Paradigm for Global Politics.* New York: Columbia University Press.

Pfaff, William. 1989. *Barbarian Sentiments.* New York: Hill and Wang.

———. 1992. "The Absence of Empire." *New Yorker* (August 10): 68.

Ra'anan, Uri and Igor Lukes. 1990. *Gorbachev's U.S.S.R.* London: Macmillan.

Reid, Alastair. 1994. "The Scottish Condition." *Wilson Quarterly* (Winter): 51–70.

Rose, Richard. 1994. "Postcommunism and the Problem of Trust." *Journal of Democracy* 5(3): 18–30.

Subtelney, Orest. 1989. *Ukraine: A History.* Toronto: University of Toronto Press. Thomas, Robert. 1996. "Colonialism: Classic and Internal." *Journal of Ethno-Development* 3(2): 43–48.

Wendzel, Robert. 1981. *International Politics: Policymakers and Policymaking.* New York: Wiley.

3

The Dynamics of Social Cubism:
A View from Northern Ireland and Québec

Neal Carter
Sean Byrne

Introduction

STUDIES OF ETHNOTERRITORIAL politics typically either examine political and economic structures to emphasize the competing interests of groups or analyze psychological and cultural dimensions to emphasize the importance of interpersonal behavior. Researchers who do address both material and psychological factors often attempt to weigh their relative importance as causes of conflict (Reilly 1994). Ross (1993) emphasizes that subjective differences may be more important than structural inequalities. He advocates including interests and interpretations within attempts to regulate conflicts, but indicates that these are distinct aspects of conflicts. We, in contrast, propose that studies of ethnoterritorial conflict be modeled systematically from the perspective of social cubism, incorporating the complex interaction of material and psychological mechanisms in six facets of ethnoterritorial conflicts. With this more complex model, we can better examine the dynamic nature of ethnoterritorial conflicts (Byrne and Carter 1996). We combine this perspective with social identity theory to analyze the amelioration of the conflict in Northern Ireland and the fluctuating polarization of Québec politics.

The term "social cubism" evokes images useful to describe our perspective.[1] Much like Rubik's Cube, ethnoterritorial politics poses a multi-faced puzzle. People concentrating on only one aspect, or side of the puzzle, are unlikely to explain the situation fully. Progress toward more useful proposals of conflict regulation can be made only by considering the interrelations among the faces of the puzzle.

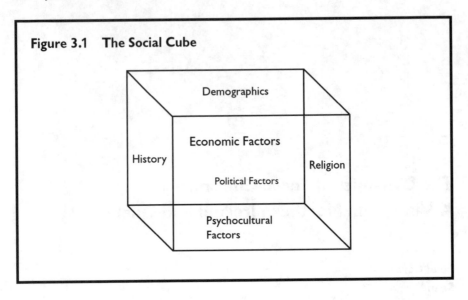

Figure 3.1   The Social Cube

In this paper, we examine politics in Northern Ireland and Québec from the standpoint of social cubism. The cases indicate the complexity of the relationship between psychological and material factors. These factors provide focal points for the mobilization of social groups. Specifically, we show the connections among history, religion, demographics, political activity, economics, and psychocultural symbolism in our two cases. As with Rubik's Cube, the faces are linked. For example, histories recounted by competing groups often evoke feelings about previous patterns of economic, political, or religious interaction. Interaction among factors produces patterns of intergroup behavior. Before proceeding to the analysis of the six facets of ethnoterritorial politics in explaining the apparent anomaly of the amelioration of the Northern Irish case and the fluctuation of the Québec case, we briefly examine the utility of social identity theory in linking these aspects to politics. Social identities should not be considered another face of the cube, as the identities frame the other aspects shaping perceptions of the conflict. Identities could be viewed as the internal structure of the social cube.

Social Identity and Ethnoterritorial Politics

Stories, history, and tradition promote in-group identity (Agnew 1989; Senehi 1996). Fundamental features of relationships among communities help people attach meaning to politics and group membership. Tajfel (1982) and Turner et al. (1987) show that individuals identify with several groups simultaneously, but exhibit behavior typical of the group whose importance is emphasized in a specific setting. Countervailing forces may weaken the influence of

Table 3.1 Interaction of the Six Forces

	NORTHERN IRELAND	QUÉBEC
Economic Factors	Used to support claims of discrimination based on religion. Could potentially mitigate ethnic cleavage with internal class divisions.	Primarily used to compare Québec and other provinces. Has been used to compare linguistic groups, especially during the Quiet Revolution.
Religious Factors	Used as a primary category label, replacing ethnicity and language. Decreases potential for compromise, as moral symbols are lent to conflicting parties.	Has lost salience with modernization, but helped shape a tradition of acceptance of hierarchy and compromise between two main linguistic groups, and divergent economic patterns. Its salience is now less than that of ethnicity and language.
Political Factors	Terrorism reinforces religious cleavage, reduces salience of economic factors, and contributes to historical backing for continued conflict. Reduction of violence may mitigate conflict. Constitutional status unacceptable to most citizens.	Terrorism was a minor issue, but killings for political ends deemed unacceptable. Political institutions, through their complexity, reduce the salience of cleavages. Political institutions have a mixed effect on histories, as nationalists and federalists selectively choose examples.
Psychocultural Factors	Generally these factors reinforce a bipolar conflict by emphasizing the threat of mutual destruction. May change with the cease-fire and confidence-building measures.	Some symbols promote overlapping loyalties with Québec and Canada, others indicate loyalty is mutually exclusive. English Canadian symbols are largely a reaction to Francophone nationalism, and slow to distance themselves from British symbols.
Historical Factors	Histories promote bicommunal view of the region through the recounting of past conflict. Commemoration of battles increases hostility.	Histories mixed between conflict and compromise. Figures of cooperation may also be seen as figures of co-optation.
Demographic Factors	Narrowing population gap increases Protestant fears of assimilation. Proximity increases need to maintain boundaries.	Decline in Québécois birthrates increases Francophone fears of assimilation and demand for increased control of cultural policies. Francophone dominance in Québec mitigates hostility.

particular groups, but we expect members of salient groups to exhibit similar patterns of behavior.

Elites often attempt to make various considerations salient to their constituents for political mobilization. Increased salience of specific issues provides group members with a frame of reference and set of norms from which to derive judgments about the political issues at hand. This is not to say that social identities are simply products of elite manipulation. Rather, elites are able to focus attention on specific characteristics that shape the way people think about political groups (Mosca 1939).

Brewer (1991) argues that people judge themselves in terms of similarity and difference. They need to view their groups as clearly distinct from others. Similarity helps establish necessary bonds among group members. The need to oppose an out-group often becomes encoded in the in-group's identity (Northrup 1989; Volkan 1988). If several political issues divide groups along the same fault lines, rather than forming cross-cutting cleavages, group members are likely to develop an "enemy image" of the out-group. Elites can exploit the tension between intragroup uniformity and intergroup difference to mobilize followers to pursue political action. In cases where groups are not monolithic and isolated, elites compete for the same constituents based on different group memberships by emphasizing the salience of different factors. For example, female Anglophone Québecers could be mobilized through appeals to their gender, their cultural heritage, territorial location, ideological views, or other such characteristics.

Political success often requires the mobilization of politically salient groups. Turner et al. (1987) list several important conditions that encourage the formation of a psychologically significant group (see also Brewer and Schneider 1990). Similarity among individuals within a category must be made salient; latent groups are unlikely to expend the energy to form a corporate entity unless something in the environment emphasizes their similarities. Second, group members must believe that they share a common fate (that is, they will share rewards or penalties from the social system due to their commonality with other group members). This notion is often supported by emphasis on group histories and traditions (Smith 1991). Third, the creation of a corporate entity is most likely when group members see themselves as interchangeable instances of the group category.

Political elites often attempt to instill a sense of common fate and group solidarity by emphasizing in-group similarities and out-group differences, depicting group members as interchangeable and personalizing inter-group conflict. This strategy of portraying issues in terms of social identities forms a nexus among the various facets of ethnoterritorial politics, to which we now turn. We attempt to show the relationship between these factors and social identity, and in turn, the relationship between social identities and the management of conflict.

Historical Factors

Histories are told to frame the context for current ethnic interaction. Stories of past events shape perceptions of political possibilities. When histories offer competing

interpretations of the nature of intergroup relations, conflicts may be increasingly characterized by misunderstandings and mistrust. This brief summary of Northern Irish and Québec history highlights only some of the historical events that are frequently evoked by the main parties involved. Rather than simply summarizing important dates, we attempt here to illustrate the conflicting interpretations of history.

Irish Catholics look to the Norman conquest of Gaelic Ireland in the twelfth century as the starting point of the present Troubles. Feudalism gripped the land but did not quite subjugate Gaelic customs and traditions. Indeed, subsequent attempts by the English monarchy to conquer the Gaelic inhabitants of Ireland failed (Byrne 1997). The English settlers intermarried with the indigenous people and "became more Irish than the Irish themselves."

The 1690 victory of William of Orange at the battle of the Boyne signaled a new era of Protestant economic and political dominance. However, the 1603 colonization of Ulster and the subsequent defeat of the Ulster Gaels ushered in an era of political, economic, and cultural change. The settlers or planters were to defend the political and economic interests of the English Crown against Catholicism (Bruce 1986). The present generation of extremist or ultra Protestants continues that tradition—protecting the Protestant religion and the Protestant community. Politics is viewed simply as a zero-sum situation (Whyte 1990).

The Home Rule movement of the late nineteenth century divided the island between unionists in the Northeast and nationalists in the agrarian South. The partition of Ireland in 1920, after a guerrilla war between the Irish Republican Army (IRA) and the British government, initiated a new series of hostile relations in the North that still lock the communities in sectarian strife. Since 1972 several attempts to formulate a devolved constitutional framework for governing Northern Ireland met with little success (O'Leary and McGarry 1993). Terrorism propagated by Republicans and Loyalists intensified polarization between communities. Negotiations concerning the status of Northern Ireland are usually followed by an escalation in terrorist activity. The recent Real IRA bombing in Omagh, County Tyrone has ensured that the present political climate is stalked by the potential escalation of violence by fringe paramilitary groups on both sides of the bicommunal divide.

President Clinton's visit to both parts of Ireland toward the end of November 1995 was an attempt to set the tone of the peace talks between the British and Irish governments, Unionists, Nationalists, and the paramilitaries. The "twin-track" approach to progress on the Northern Ireland problem, supported by the Mitchell Commission and President Clinton, reached an impasse; the PIRA refused the British government's ultimatum to decommission or surrender its arms to allow Sinn Fein to sit at the negotiating table (O'Brien 1995). The February 9, 1995, PIRA bombings in London effectively ended the Republican cease-fire, and the situation verged on complete breakdown of the Loyalist cease-fire and a resurgence of political violence (Crampton 1995). The Good Friday 1998 Agreement brokered by Senator Mitchell and elections to the Northern Ireland parliament may have brought all of the political actors to the same table in a new parliament but sectarian politics may yet prove difficult to transcend and transform.

Québecers recall a less violent past than the Northern Irish, but Francophones and Anglophones recount their histories differently (Bell 1992). Both groups celebrate heroes of their linguistic group and emphasize the importance of cultural survival. Francophones long considered themselves a distinct nation continually threatened with cultural extermination, while the more heterogeneous Anglophones struggled to maintain a Canadian identity distinct from the United States. Within the Francophone camp, two main interpretations of history—nationalist and federalist—compete (LaPierre 1992).

Québec's history can be divided into different phases of relations between French- and English-speakers. This history, and much of life in Québec, is heavily influenced by Québec's status as a province of Canada. After a period of colonial competition, France was forced to abandon New France in 1763. The decisive battle at the Plains of Abraham is cited as either a great victory or a terrible tragedy, and leaders commonly refer to it when discussing cultural policies or Québec-Canada relations. Political deadlock in British North America provided the incentive for a new set of institutions, so the colonies of New Brunswick, Nova Scotia, and Canada—divided into Québec and Ontario—formed the Dominion of Canada. This new arrangement produced a type of consociational federalism in which Anglophone and Francophone elites reached accommodation, typically within national parties. While Francophones tend to see the federation as a compact between two peoples, Anglophones generally consider it to have been an agreement between constituent territorial units. The rebellion of Francophone Métis leader Louis Riel exacerbated tensions, and continues to be evoked today to justify intergroup distrust. Federalism allowed different political cultures to develop in the provinces: Québec's predominantly Francophone society was long dominated by the Catholic Church and isolated from Anglophone culture.

During the "Quiet Revolution" of the 1960s and 1970s, a change in provincial leadership, educational reforms, and a decline in the Catholic Church's social influence reduced the province's parochial nature. A new group of nationalists advocated the creation of an economically competitive cadre of Francophones, birth rates plummeted, and Québec's legislature passed laws to promote the use of French in the workplace. The new Francophone outlook facilitated the 1976 election of the Parti Québécois, dedicated to seeking a new institutional arrangement of "Sovereignty-Association." Many Anglophones left the province following that election. The Quiet Revolution continues to be cited as a turning point in Québec history. Since then, the conflict over Québec's place in Canada has intensified. Recent history, especially regarding linguistic politics and the quest for constitutional recognition as a distinct society, will be addressed in other sections.

Histories focus attention on the struggles by which a group protects itself and promotes its interests. In Québec and Northern Ireland, these histories differ across groups and lead to widespread self-identification with the ethnocultural groups. Ethnoterritorial cleavages come to be expected, and develop into the basis on which constitutional change is evaluated.

Economic Factors

Leaders of ethnoterritorial movements exploit disparities in the distribution of economic resources to mobilize support for their demands. Awareness or suspicion of discrimination adds economic concerns to the overall categorization of the other. Categories used in economic analyses can greatly affect perceptions of intergroup differences.

In Northern Ireland, Protestants have greater access to political and economic resources than do Catholics (Agnew 1989; Cunningham 1994; Farrell 1980; MacLaughlin and Agnew 1986; O'Dowd et al. 1980). Catholic areas have higher unemployment rates than Protestant areas. Recruitment practices, lack of industrial development, emigration, and discrimination increase the economic gap between Protestants and Catholics, divide the working classes, and reinforce intergroup discrimination (Arthur and Jeffrey 1988; Cormack and Osborne 1983; Moxon-Browne 1983; Whyte 1990). Economic privileges in housing and employment enjoyed by Protestants reduced the salience of class conflict and may partly explain continued Protestant support for institutional links with Britain and devotion to British identity (Bew et al. 1995; Farrell 1980; McCann 1974). In rural Northern Ireland, however, farmers depend on each other's labor during the harvest season. The bicommunal divide is bridged for this specific purpose and controversial religious and political topics are avoided

(Harris 1972).

In Québec, the minority Anglophone population was generally advantaged. Protestantism correlated strongly with capitalism; Québec was dominated economically by the Protestant, Anglophone minority. After the Conquest, English Protestants tended to cluster in specific regions, especially Montreal and the Eastern Townships, and were relatively free to join the Canadian ethnic majority and business elite (Arnopoulos and Clift 1980; Robinson 1989). Francophone Catholics tended to shun capitalist ventures, although they often supplied the labor force. Eventually, however, a petty bourgeoisie emerged among Francophones, while workers faced great hardship. Class divisions formed an additional cross-cutting cleavage.

By the 1960s, studies of economic disparity showed vast differences in the economic welfare of Québec's two major linguistic communities (Mathieu and Lacoursière 1991; Porter 1965). Inequality helped change nationalist sentiment in Québec from church-dominated isolationism to secular cosmopolitanism as the Québécois began to seek political control of provincial resources. The federal and Québec governments initiated language laws to address new perceptions of economic discrimination against Francophones. In Québec, areas with larger proportions of Francophones still tend to have lower average incomes (Eagles et al. 1991).

Economic factors cannot be excluded from the analysis of ethnoterritorial conflict, but they are not, in and of themselves, enough to cause such conflict. Perceptions of intergroup inequalities rely on and reinforce social categories. The manner in which economic statistics are gathered and the statistical categories used, for example, can drastically influence the conclusions reached concerning the effects of public policies (Murphy 1988).

Political Factors

Several institutional and non-institutional political factors combine in ethnoterritorial conflicts. If credible institutional methods of settling disagreements exist, non-institutional, violent politics should be less prevalent (Duffy and Frensley 1991). Québec and Northern Ireland differ greatly in the extent to which they are incorporated into, and are significant within, the institutional frameworks of their states. Northern Ireland is marginalized, while Québec is a central player in the Canadian federation.

Institutional Politics

The 1921 creation of the state of Northern Ireland by the IRA-British government peace treaty ensured the dominance of the old Unionist party in the Stormont parliament (Bew et al. 1979, 1995). The Nationalist minority found its access to political institutions and power at the local and national levels stifled by a "Protestant parliament for a Protestant people" (Bew et al. 1979).

The 1972 introduction of direct rule from London did not alter the political structure much, nor did it increase institutional access for the Catholic community. Although Catholics could elect political representatives to local councils and the House of Commons, working-class Catholics felt the brunt of economic deprivation and social and political marginalization (McGarry and O'Leary 1995). Up until the 1995 Joint Framework for Peace Document and the recent Good Friday Agreement, the political structures and institutions continued to discriminate against Catholics in socioeconomic, cultural, and political terms (Cunningham 1994; Rowthorn and Wayne 1988).

In Canada, the tension between federalists and nationalists is strongly influenced by the federal government. Because Québec has about one-fourth of the seats in the Canadian House of Commons, it is virtually impossible for federal politicians to ignore Québec. Nevertheless, the struggle between nationalists and federalists contributes to a deep strategic ambiguity; it is commonly stated that "Québecers want a strong, independent Québec within a strong, united Canada."

The Canadian government, led by Québecer Pierre Elliott Trudeau, implemented the Constitution Act of 1982 over the protests of the Québec government. Québec demanded constitutional recognition of its status as a "Distinct Society." Two major rounds of national constitutional negotiations have failed to resolve this constitutional issue despite initial agreement by the First Ministers. The separatist but ideologically heterogeneous Bloc Québécois was founded following the 1990 failure of the Meech Lake Accord, and spent a term as the official opposition in the Canadian House of Commons.

The 1995 referendum on sovereignty showed the deep division in Québec, with only slightly more than one-half of Québecers voting to reject the sovereignty proposal. Aboriginal peoples, in separate referenda, voted overwhelmingly to reject a potential vote for sovereignty. It appears that most non-Francophones voted against the proposal, while about 60 percent of Francophones expressed approval. Premier Jacques Parizeau stated "don't forget that three-fifths of us voted Yes. It wasn't quite enough, but very soon it will be . . . and in the long run, finally, we will have our own revenge and we will have our own country" (Came 1995, 19). Parizeau later resigned and was replaced by former Bloc Québécois leader Lucien Bouchard. In 1998, the Supreme Court was asked to rule on the right of Québec to unilaterally declare independence. Québecers, be they Anglophone, Francophone, or speakers of other languages, continue to debate whether they form a nation with the right of self-determination, or are a segment of the Canadian nation.

Non-Institutional Politics

Terrorism has been used in both regions to draw attention to conflicts. Significantly, nationalist terrorism in Québec and initial Republican violence in Northern Ireland was aimed primarily at symbols of colonial or federal domination. Northern Irish Loyalists targeted Catholic civilians in retaliation, provoking sectarian retaliation from Republicans and producing a state of fear and powerlessness marked by a self-perpetuating pattern of deterrence and revenge (Feldman 1991; Wright 1988). Québec terrorism ended quickly after the October Crisis of 1970. Ideological acceptance of paramilitary violence as the only way of dealing with the other group in Northern Ireland fostered enduring conflict. A long history of violence, including the Enniskillen massacre of Protestants in 1987 and the 1991 sectarian murders of Catholic taxi drivers in Belfast, instills fear of genocide in both communities. Loyalist paramilitary violence escalates when British policy initiatives are perceived as a threat to abandon Ulster's loyal Protestants to Irish nationalism. These feelings, while mitigated, remain strong. While people continue to call for the disarming of the Provisional Irish Republican Army (PIRA), the Ulster Defense Association (UDA), and the Ulster Volunteer Force (UVF), such an event is unlikely until further confidence building measures increase support for institutional approaches of conflict management.

Violence polarizes Northern Ireland, thereby threatening moderate alternatives. Constitutional nationalists fear that if concessions are not forthcoming, then advocates of physical force such as the PIRA can claim to offer the only solution (McGarry and O'Leary 1995). The current cease-fire, in the wake of the Good Friday Agreement, has mitigated hostility to some extent; Sinn Fein (SF), the Social Democratic and Labor Party (SDLP), the Official Unionist Party (OUP), Alliance, and the Progressive Unionist Party (PUP) are working together to make the new powersharing parliament work. Nevertheless, the Loyalist Volunteer Force (LVF), the Real Irish Republican Army (RIRA), and the Continuity Irish Republican Army (CIRA) are conducting paramilitary attacks to sabotage the consociational, powersharing government. Also, punishment beatings by the rival paramilitary gangs continue unabated in working-class communities.

Québec has been less violent than Northern Ireland; federalists rejected terrorist retaliation and called instead on established institutions such as the police and the Army to maintain order. Québec has faced some violent challenges, but not to the degree experienced in Northern Ireland. The peak of terrorist activity in Québec was in the 1960s, involving groups like the Front de Libération du Québec (FLQ) who drew inspiration from anti-colonial and civil rights movements, as well as the PIRA (Vallières 1971). In the early 1960s, the

FLQ conducted a bombing campaign against symbols of colonial or federal domination. The FLQ appears to have had about thirty active members, most of whom were arrested in 1963. However, several apparently unconnected groups identified themselves as FLQ cells. Bombing activities intensified in 1968–69, and in 1970 British Trade Commissioner James Cross and Québec Labor Minister Pierre Laporte were abducted. These abductions appear to have been the acts of about ten people, but Canadian Prime Minister Trudeau used the War Measures Act, revoking protection of civil liberties, arresting some 450 suspects, destroying presses, and mobilizing ten thousand military and special police forces. Popular opinion, mildly in support of the FLQ, dropped dramatically when Laporte was executed by his abductors (Milner and Milner 1973; Robert 1975).

Terrorist activities often provoke a governmental backlash against the people (Gurr and Harff 1994). In Québec, this backlash failed to produce the reaction desired by the terrorists: instead of criticizing the federal government for invoking the War Measures Act, citizens blamed the agitators for disrupting a peaceful, if unequal, system. It should also be noted that Prime Minister Trudeau is from Québec, which may have increased the perceived legitimacy of using force against Québecers.

A difference between the two regions thus seems to be that the Québécois have access to institutions which they view to be legitimate, while some Northern Irish Catholics view political institutions as Protestant tools of repression (O'Leary and McGarry 1993). Institutional politics may reduce antagonistic views of the out-group, while violence will increase the mutual antagonism of groups. Furthermore, the importance of the Francophone minority in Canada mitigates the strict divisions between majority and minority. The danger still exists, however, that those who participate in cooperative institutions will be seen as co-opted sell-outs.

The legitimacy of institutional frameworks relies not only on the interests of the parties, but on their interpretations of the other group's motives. If groups view each other as inherently hostile, each will give little support to institutions that are supported by the other.

Religious Factors

Religion helps define the moral self-worth of a group, explains its highest goals, and establishes some clear delineations among groups. The communal nature of religion reinforces group identities and, if linked to other facets of ethnoterritorial conflicts, provides a solid basis of ethnocultural identity. Social and political institutions linked to religion polarize societies in Northern Ireland and Québec. In Northern Ireland, Protestants and Catholics attend separate schools and churches and live in separate neighborhoods for physical and psychological protection; religion preserves each group's way of life (Whyte 1986, 1990). In Québec, religious affiliation promoted distinct life-styles, as economic differences and parochial schools reinforced religious and linguistic polarization. The Catholic Church, however, has lost its traditional political power in Québec, and school boards have shifted from parochial to language-based differentiation.

Catholics in Northern Ireland are relatively homogeneous in their political beliefs and their identification with the Irish nation. Northern Ireland's Protestants are a heterogeneous group (Bruce 1986). Protestants, however, are generally loyal to the monarch in her role as head of the established church as well as head of the British state (Bruce 1986; Rose 1971; Whyte 1990). Parliament, however, lacks the religious legitimacy of the Queen; Northern Irish Protestants feel free to oppose the British Parliament since they are ultimately loyal not to political institutions but to their ethno-religious identity (Miller 1978). Protestants will remain loyal to Britain only as long as Britain guarantees a Protestant majority in Northern Ireland (Moxon-Browne 1983; Wallis et al. 1986).

Harris's (1972) study of the village of "Ballybeg" neatly outlines the importance of the religious dimension of the macro intercommunal conflict. Shunning or boycotting the "other" was used to ensure that Protestants and Catholics in the village lived intermixed but segregated and each group used "stereotypes in thinking and speaking of each other, for each remained basically a stranger to the other" (Harris 1972, 149).

These stereotypes produced drastically different perceptions of the conflict. Protestants claimed that Catholicism was authoritarian, undemocratic, and insensitive to their religious beliefs, and that Catholics represented a religious and politico-economic threat to the Protestant community. Discrimination was politically motivated. Catholics, on the other hand, claimed that society was dichotomized and they were targets of adverse discrimination. This view influenced how the Catholic community interpreted events at the local level, which in turn reinforced the original belief that society was indeed dichotomized (Harris 1972).

Religion has played a less divisive role in Québec. Religious loyalty prior to the 1960s helped Canada maintain relatively peaceful intergroup relations. Colonial patterns in New France failed to produce strong governmental institutions, leaving the Catholic Church as the most important communal organization. In 1659, Monseigneur de Laval, the bishop of Québec, established ultramontism, the doctrine that the Church is to be predominant in all social affairs and politically superior to the state (O'Sullivan See 1986). After the British Conquest of New France, the Québec Act of 1774 recognized and supported the Catholic Church's dominance of Québec, in exchange for acceptance of British rule. Protestants (primarily Anglophones) were allowed to establish separate facilities. Parochial schools reinforced the power of the Church and allowed each religious group to control the socialization of its members. In Québec, Irish Catholic immigrants often chose religion over language, and assimilated into the Francophone Catholic society. In a few areas they were concentrated enough to form Anglophone Catholic enclaves.

The history of ultramontism influenced the ethnonational identity of French-Canadians. As with Northern Irish Protestants, French-Canadian loyalty, especially in Québec, was to religion rather than to parliament or the crown. Religious identity promoted strong ties among members of a parish. The Church's decline as a social actor since the Quiet Revolution seems to have changed the focus of group loyalty. Most social functions historically performed by the Church, such as education, health, and welfare, now fall under provincial instead of federal jurisdiction. As the provider of these functions changes, so too does citizen identification with social institutions. This transfer of loyalty is illustrated by a change in self-identification: during the Quiet Revolution, French Canadians inhabiting Québec began to describe themselves as Québécois rather than Canadiens français (Dupont and Louder 1995). The transferral of loyalty from the Church to the province, increases the potential for rejecting the limited monarchy and the federation.

Demographic Factors

The major groups involved in each of our cases of ethnoterritorial conflict compare themselves to each other and seek to maintain distinct identities. Relative shifts in the welfare of the groups, their size, or their territorial distribution can alter the perceptions and interests of the groups. Here we examine the importance of boundaries and the notion of double minorities in helping to shape the multi-faceted conflicts.

Boundaries

Many community-based conflicts emphasize the territorial dimension of political institutions. In Québec, provincial boundaries allow the Québécois some control over a specific territory while remaining within the larger Canadian context, but a declaration of sovereignty could provoke boundary disputes. Northern Ireland, however, has a boundary that does not meet the demands of either main group.

Debate over the boundary in Northern Ireland increases group hostility as the salience of national identity becomes a tangible threat to the existence of Northern Ireland's position within the United Kingdom. The political partition of Northern Ireland from the Irish Free State in 1920 fostered sectarian politics (Arthur and Jeffrey 1988). While Nationalists continued to agitate for an independent Ireland, Unionists tried to maintain "peace through security," arguing that perceived threats and real terrorist attacks made special security arrangements necessary (Bew et al. 1979; 1995).

Both groups rigidly maintain their positions concerning the political status of Northern Ireland. Unionists are determined to safeguard the British link and their ethno-nationalist identity. Consequently, Unioists are resisting current proposals of a North-South institutional body to formulate policies. Nationalists, on the other hand, believe that the root of the conflict is the British presence in Northern Ireland, and politically support the creation of a future United Ireland. (Byrne 1995, 1997). Moderates from each community, however, will have to work together in the newly elected assembly if the peace process is to hold. Provincial boundaries in Canada enable the Québécois to control most of their cultural affairs. Leaders frequently debate the extent of power to be held at the provincial and federal levels of government, rather than questioning the existing boundaries. Because of their federal nature, these boundaries are less prone to conflict than the more institutionally divisive border in Northern Ireland. The ambiguous nature of federal boundaries increases the opportunity for shared identity among groups. The diverse effects of federalism on various groups complicates ethnoterritorial politics.

Debate over Québec's potential secession increases the significance of boundaries. The border between Québec and Newfoundland has never been formally delineated. Outstanding Aboriginal land claims and Anglophone enclaves challenge the legality of Québec's territorial claims. Some analysts have argued that Québec could leave with only its original (1867) boundaries and would be forced to cede all land granted to it, as a province, by the federal government (Koch 1990; Peritz 1991; Varty 1991). Federal Minister of Intergovernmental Affairs Stéphane Dion emphasized this possibility through the so-called "Plan B." While "Plan A" remains to convince Québecers of the value of continued membership in the federation, "Plan B" aims to convince Québecers that the costs would preclude secession. The potential partitioning of Québec is an emotionally significant part of this plan.

The intensity of ethnoterritorial identification produces greater hostility in Northern Ireland than Québec. Canada's federalist structure permits more peaceful conflict regulation. Northern Ireland's lack of a substantial strategic middle ground prevents cross-cutting cleavages, leading to institutional and constitutional impasse. Canada's political violence is mitigated by political institutions in which the communities are represented and by a tradition of mutual gestures of good will. Many Francophones belive they can achieve more by working within established institutions than they could achieve from armed conflict.

Double Minorities

Ross (1993, 111) states, "both because the resources of each side are almost never identical and because perceptions are selective, in many situations all parties see themselves as a vulnerable minority, and these conflicts are difficult to manage constructively." Group differences in Northern Ireland and Québec can be seen as demographic conflicts between "double minorities" (Jackson and McHardy 1984; Moxon-Browne 1983; Whyte 1978, 1990). Members of each group see themselves as minorities, but are simultaneously viewed by the other community as a threatening majority. Double minorities reinforce the need for security and recognition of each group's territorial claims.

In Northern Ireland, historical references to campaigns of genocide affect the perceptions and fears each group holds of the "other" (Byrne 1997; Farell 1980; Stewart 1977). In response, each group in Northern Ireland developed a pronounced "siege mentality." Protestants consider the Republic of Ireland as intent on destroying the Protestant "way of life" and thus oppose institutional links that could bring about a United Ireland.Catholics were marginalized by their treatment within Northern Ireland and look to the Republic of Ireland to protect their political interests. Each group, recalling a history of community conflict, seeks a majority within political institutions in order to prevent discrimination or suppression (Keogh and Haltzel 1994). The double minority in Northern Ireland thus decreases the potential for the formation of a solid political "middle ground" between the communities. The 1998 Good Friday Agreement, a newly elected parliament, and the recent cease-fire may have mitigated the severity of this mutual threat, providing room for some kind of political accommodation.

The idea of double minority could also describe the situation in Québec. The Francophone majority in Québec developed a mild "siege mentality," viewing itself as a minority population engulfed in a hostile Anglophone environment although it sustains a provincial majority. The Anglophone minority in Québec belongs to the majority Anglophone community in Canada and North America but still may feel threatened by Québec laws intended to promote the prominence of the French language. Some Anglophone Québecers think of themselves as a political minority in Québec, strongly oppose Québécois nationalist policies, and fear that the creation of an independent Québec would cut their ties with the rest of Canada. They stress the importance of maintaining the status and the freedom to use English in Québec.

The notion of double minorities improves our understanding of the combination of interpretations and interests in ethnoterritorial conflicts. Mutual perceptions of threat increase attention paid to a number of factors including birthrates, economic standing, and migration patterns that could affect the balance of power of the groups.

Psychocultural Symbolic Factors

Symbols create a sense of commonality among group members and help them categorize their political beliefs. Ethnoregional groups may promote prejudice and stereotyping by invoking group traditions to symbolize current problems (Byrne 1997; Coles 1986; O'Donnell 1978).

The Northern Irish conflict appears intractable because economic, religious, and national identity crises are embedded in everyday life, affecting such mundane issues as choice of a favorite sports team (McGarry and O'Leary 1995; Rose 1971). Northern Irish Protestants link their cultural symbols, flags, and holidays to the nature of the state (Wright 1988). Marches, conducted by both groups, include symbolic incursions into the enclaves of the opposing group. Orange marches are perceived as a "traditional expression of a legal right" to display Protestant values and symbols (Wallis et al. 1986). Likewise, Northern Irish Catholics wear Easter lilies to commemorate the Easter Rising of 1916. A strong link exists between Republican violence, Catholicism, and a pan-Celtic culture centered around the redemptive nature of a blood sacrifice (O'Brien 1986). Northern Irish Catholics often invoke the symbolic significance of "martyrs for the cause," such as IRA leaders Bobby Sands and Patrick Pearse (O'Brien 1986; Feehan 1986). These cultural and religious symbols reinforce in-group solidarity and out-group hostility.

In Northern Ireland, myths of siege, victory, massacre, and martyrdom permit two distinct cultural traditions to coexist (O'Leary and McGarry 1993; Stewart 1977). Symbolic issues exacerbate the bicommunal conflict by fostering sectarian stereotypes and prejudice. Children learn the images used to categorize people from the other community at an early age (Byrne 1997; Coles 1986; Greer 1985). Extremists depict the conflict as a struggle between good and evil (Todd 1987; Whyte 1990). Moderates, on the other hand, perceive the conflict in political and economic terms and not as religious issues (Whyte 1990). As debate turns from economic and political matters to symbolic questions of ethnoreligious identity, polarization weakens the middle ground (Agnew 1989).

Québec's split between nationalists and federalists generates competing symbolic representations of the nature of the Confederation (Taylor 1993; Watts and Brown 199). When politicians debate the constitution, symbolism dominates political communication (Russell 1992). Furthermore, federalists tend to combine some features of nationalist symbolism with the symbols of federal ties, as indicated in the combination of the Fleur-de-Lys and the Maple Leaf during the referendum campaign.

Lipset (1990) argues that Canada is a country of defeated nations, and therefore its symbolism reinforces notions of the challenge of survival for distinct societies in an inhospitable climate, faced with the ever-present threat of assimilation. Québec nationalists use symbolism effectively, emphasizing land, language, faith, and families. The feast of St. John the Baptist is held as Québec's national holiday. To intensify Québécois nationalism, activists used slogans such as "*Maîtres chez-nous*" (Masters in our own house) to represent a desire for self-determination and economic responsibility. With the increased Francophone attention to national symbolism, federalists responded with Canadian symbols: the Maple Leaf has been the insignia of Canada only since 1965; "O Canada" replaced "God Save the Queen" in 1967 (Lipset 1990).

Conclusions

In general, Northern Ireland experiences more problems with terrorism, geo-politics, and conflicting national identities than Québec because of the psychological and political insecurity of each ethnic group. Lack of control over policies, mutual suspicion of treachery, histories of inter-community violence, and symbolism that promotes a siege mentality all reduce the potential for Northern Ireland to create a sense of shared identity. The cease-fire and current peace process, however, have reduced the extent to which the security of one group is threatened by the other. While trust is not yet high, the extremes are beginning to lose credibility, and foreign investment is improving the economic situation as a reward for increased stability.

In contrast, Québec benefits from the existence of federalism, which reduces both groups to minority status and also promotes some mutual recognition. However, continued failure in the negotiation of constitutional matters is reducing good will on both sides of the debate. Despite the potential for accommodation presented by the positive aspects of double minorities, problems still threaten the equilibrium. The continuing struggle of Québec governments to establish a new status reduces the potential for accommodation.

We have identified a number of significant interrelated factors that are part of a multi-causal analysis of conflict in Northern Ireland and Québec. These components are interrelated and must be examined together if we are to understand ethnoterritorial politics and seek mechanisms of conflict resolution in these types of protracted intercommunal conflicts. As indicated in figure 3.1, the various factors produce different patterns of behavior and views of the conflict. In Québec, the complexity of the federal system partially explains the divisions between nationalist and federalist Francophones. The patterns in which the factors counteract each other mitigate the potential conflict between groups, since appeals to other factors may change the configuration. In Northern Ireland, however, the opposite appears to be the case. When approaching the conflict using many of the categories, it is possible to reinforce the divisions, and both sides seem to agree that the division is accurate. It may still be possible, however, to emphasize overarching factors. For example, emphasizing the economic difficulties which are aggravated by continued strife, or the personal losses suffered by both sides, may increase the perceived costs of conflict enough to reinforce peaceful movements. This process will be difficult and slow, as institutions and interpretation of the other group's motives are built gradually.

What stands out in our analysis is the way that practical and psychological dimensions interact to maintain or mitigate intergroup conflict. Entrenched sectarian attitudes result from political and economic institutions and cultural stereotypes that reinforce bigotry, suspicion, and polarization. A holistic, social cubism approach to intergroup conflict must account for structural and psychocultural dynamic interaction. Future research should address the interrelation of material and psychological mechanisms that shape ethnoterritorial politics.

Suggested Study Questions

1. How can history shape people's views of a political conflict? What other cases show the power of competing histories?
2. How do the psychocultural and structural factors interact? Why is this important?
3. How do each of the six sides of the social cube contribute to the construction of social identities?
4. Why isn't financial investment or foreign aid a simple solution to ethnoterritorial conflict?
5. How do conflicts change over time? Is de-escalation simply escalation in reverse, or are different mechanisms at play?
6. What is the relationship between leaders and the masses in ethnoterritorial conflicts?
7. How can third parties intervene to affect conflicts? How could they use a social cube perspective?

Notes

1. This image was suggested by Jessica Senehi during a conversation with the authors. For her views of conflict, see Senehi (1996).

References

Agnew, John. 1989. "Beyond Reason: Spatial and Temporal Sources of Ethnic Conflicts." In *Intractable Conflicts and Their Transformation*. L. Kriesberg, T. A. Northrup and S.J. Thorson, eds. Syracuse: Syracuse University Press.

Arnopoulos, Sheila M. and Dominique Clift. 1980. *The English Fact in Québec*. Montreal: McGill-Queen's University Press.

Arthur, Paul and Keith Jeffrey 1988. *Northern Ireland since 1968*. New York: Basil Blackwell.

Bell, David. 1992. *The Roots of Disunity: A Study of Canadian Political Culture*. Toronto: Oxford University Press.

Bew, Paul, Peter Gibbon and Henry Patterson. 1979. *The State in Northern Ireland, 1921–72: Political Forces and Social Classes*. Manchester: Manchester University Press.

———. 1995. *Northern Ireland, 1921–1994: Social Classes and Political Forces*. London: Serif.

Brewer, Marlin B. 1991. "The Social Self: On Being the Same and Different at the Same Time." *Personality and Social Psychology Bulletin* 17: 475–82.

Bruce, Steve. 1986. *God Save Ulster! The Religion and Politics of Paisleyism*. Oxford: Clarendon Press.

Byrne, Sean. 1995. "Conflict Regulation or Conflict Resolution: Third Party Intervention in the Northern Ireland Conflict—Prospects for Peace." *Terrorism and Political Violence,* 7(2): 1–25.

——— and Neal Carter. 1996. "Social Cubism: Six Social Forces of Ethnoterritorial Conflict in Northern Ireland and Québec." *Peace and Conflict Studies*, 3(2): 52–71.

———. 1997. *Growing Up in a Divided Society: The Impact of Conflict on Belfast Schoolchildren*. Cranbury, N.J.: Associated University Presses.

Came, B. 1995. "The Yes Side Vows to Continue the Fight." *Maclean's* 6 November: 18–19.

Coles, Robert. 1986. *The Political Life of Children*. Boston: Houghton Mifflin.

Cormack, Robert J. and Robert D. Osborne. 1983. *Religion, Education and Employment: Aspects of Equal Opportunity in Northern Ireland*. Belfast: Appletree Press.

Crampton, Robert. 1995. "The Dirty Peace." *Sunday Independent.* (December 2), 3–5.

Cunningham, Michael J. 1994. *The British Government and the Northern Ireland Question: Governing a Divided Community*. Sheffield: PAVIC.

Duffy, Gavin and Nathalie Frensley. 1991. "Community Conflict Processes: Mobilization and Demobilization in Northern Ireland." In *International Crisis and Domestic Politics: Major Political Conflicts in the 1980s.* J. Q. Lamare, ed. New York: Praeger.

Dupont, Louis and Dean Louder. 1995. "Quelles cultures reproduire?" Presented at the Association for Canadian Studies in the United States, Seattle, November 17.

Farrell, Michael. 1980. *Northern Ireland: The Orange State*. London: Pluto Press.

———. 1983. *Arming the Protestants: The Formation of the Ulster Special Constabulary and the Royal Ulster Constabulary 1920–27*. London: Pluto Press.

Feehan, John M. 1986. *Bobby Sands and the Tragedy of Northern Ireland*. Dublin: The Permanent Press.

Feldman, Allen. 1991. *Formations of Violence: The Narrative of the Body and Political Violence in Northern Ireland*. Chicago: University of Chicago Press.

Greer, John. E. 1985. "Viewing the Other Side in Northern Ireland: Openness and Attitudes to Religion among Catholic and Protestant Adolescents. *Journal for the Scientific Study of Religion* 24: 275–92.

Gurr, Ted R. and Barbara Harff. 1994. *Ethnic Conflict in World Politics*. Boulder: Westview Press.

Harris, Rosemary. 1972. *Prejudice and Tolerance in Ulster: A Study of Neighbours and Strangers in a Border Community*. Manchester: Manchester University Press.

Jackson, Harold and Ann McHardy. 1984. "The Two Irelands: The Problem of the Double Minority." London: The Minority's Rights Group.

Keogh, Dermot and Michael H. Haltzel, eds. 1994. *Northern Ireland and the Politics of Reconciliation*. Washington D.C.: Woodrow Wilson Center Press.

Koch, George. 1990. "The Price of Separation." *Alberta Report*, (March 17): 13.

LaPierre, Laurier. 1992. *Canada My Canada: What Happened?* Toronto: McClelland & Stewart.

Lipset, Seymour M. 1990. *Continental Divide: The Values and Institutions of the United States and Canada*. New York and London: Routledge.

MacLaughlin, James G. and John Agnew. 1986. "Hegemony and the Regional Question: The Political Geography of Regional Industrial Policy in Northern Ireland." *Annals of the Association of American Geographers* 76: 247–61.

McCann, Eamonn. 1974. *War and an Irish Town*. Harmondsworth: Penguin Books.

McGarry, John and Brendan O'Leary. 1995. *Explaining Northern Ireland: Broken Images*. Cambridge: Blackwell.

Mathieu, Jacques and Jacques Lacoursière. 1991. *Les mémoires Québécoises*. Sainte-Foy: Les Presses de L'Université Laval.

Miller, David. 1978. *Queen's Rebels: Ulster Loyalism in Historic Perspective*. Dublin: Gill and Macmillan.

Milner, Sheila H. and Henry Milner. 1973. *The Decolonization of Québec: An Analysis of Left-wing Nationalism*. Toronto: McClelland & Stewart.

Moxon-Browne, Edward. 1983. *Nation, Class and Creed in Northern Ireland*. Aldershot: Gower.

Murphy, Alexander B. 1988. *The Regional Dynamics of Language Differentiation in Belgium: A Study in Cultural-Political Geography*. Chicago: University of Chicago Press.

Northrup, Terry A. 1989. "The Dynamic of Identity in Personal and Social Conflict." In *Intractable Conflicts and their Transformation*, L. Kriesberg, T. A. Northrup, and S. J. Thorson, eds. Syracuse: Syracuse University Press.

O'Brien, Conor Cruise. 1986. "Ireland: The Mirage of Peace." *The New York Review of*

Books 33 (April): 23–33.

———. 1995. "Goodbye, Bill and Hello Again, IRA." *Irish Independent.* (December 10): 32.

O'Donnell, Edward E. 1978. *Northern Irish Stereotypes.* Dublin: College of Industrial Relations.

O'Dowd, Liam, Bill Rolston and Mike Tomlinson. 1980. *Northern Ireland: Between Civil Rights and Civil Wars.* London: CSE Books.

O'Leary, Brendan and John McGarry. 1993. *The Politics of Antagonism: Understanding Northern Ireland.* Atlantic Highlands, N.J.: Athlone Press.

O'Sullivan See, Katherine. 1986. *First World Nationalisms: Class and Ethnic Politics in Northern Ireland and Québec.* Chicago and London: University of Chicago Press.

Peritz, Ingrid. 1991. Anglo Separatists Surface Again. *Montreal Gazette* (April 20): 4.

Porter, John. 1965. *The Vertical Mosaic: An Analysis of Social Class and Power in Canada.* Toronto and Buffalo: University of Toronto Press.

Reilly, Wayne G. 1994. "The Management of Political Violence in Québec and Northern Ireland: A Comparison." *Terrorism and Political Violence* 6: 44–61.

Robert, Jean-Claude. 1975. *Du Canada Français au Québec Libre: Histoire d'un Mouvement Indépendantiste.* Paris: Flammarion.

Robinson, J. Lewis. 1989. *Concepts and Themes in the Regional Geography of Canada,* revised ed. Vancouver: Talonbooks.

Ross, Marc Howard. 1993. *The Management of Conflict: Interpretations and Interests in Comparative Perspective.* New Haven, Conn.: Yale University Press.

Rowthorn, Bob and Naomi Wayne. 1988. *Northern Ireland: The Political Economy of Conflict.* Cambridge: Polity Press.

Russell, Phillip H. 1992. *Constitutional Odyssey: Can Canadians Become a Sovereign People?* Toronto, Buffalo and London: University of Toronto Press.

Senehi, Jessica. 1996. "Language, Culture and Conflict: Storytelling as a Matter of Life and Death." *Mind and Human Interaction* 7(3): 150–64.

Smith, Anthony D. 1991. *National Identity.* Reno: University of Nevada Press.

Stewart, A. T. Q. 1977. *The Narrow Ground: Aspects of Ulster 1609–1969.* London: Faber and Faber.

Tajfel, Henri, ed. 1982. *Social Identity and Intergroup Relations.* New York: Cambridge University Press.

Taylor, Charles. 1993. *Reconciling the Solitudes: Essays on Canadian Federalism and Nationalism.* G. Laforest, ed. Montreal and Kingston: McGill University Press.

Todd, Jennifer. 1987. "Two Traditions in Unionist Political Culture." *Irish Political Studies* 2: 1–26.

Turner, John C. et al. 1987. *Rediscovering the Social Group: A Self-categorization Theory.* Oxford: Basil Blackwell.

Vallières, Pierre. 1971. *White Niggers of America: The Precocious Autobiography of a Québec*

"Terrorist". J. Pinkham, trans. New York and London: Monthly Review Press.

Varty, David L. 1991. *Who Gets Ungava?* Vancouver: Varty & Company Printers.

Volkan, Vamik D. 1988. *The Need to Have Enemies and Allies: From Clinical Practice to International Relationships*. New York: Jason Aronson.

Wallis, Roy, Steve Bruce and David Taylor. 1986. "No Surrender: Paisleyism and the Politics of Ethnic Identity in Northern Ireland." Belfast: Queen's University, Department of Social Studies, 1–35.

Watts, Ronald L. and David M. Brown, eds. 1991. *Options for a New Canada*. Toronto: University of Toronto Press.

Whyte, John. 1986. "How Is the Boundary Maintained between Both Communities in Northern Ireland." *Ethnic and Racial Studies* 9(2): 219–34.

―――. 1978. "Interpretations of the Northern Ireland Problem: An Appraisal." *Economic and Social Review* 9: 257–82.

―――. 1990. *Interpreting Northern Ireland*. Oxford: Clarendon Press.

Wright, F. 1988. *Northern Ireland: A Comparative Analysis*. Dublin: Gill and Macmillan.

Part 2

Conflict Resolution, Group Identity, and Human Needs

4

Understanding Protracted Social Conflicts: A Basic Needs Approach

Kathleen A. Cavanaugh

Introduction

THERE ARE CONFLICTING strains of analysis in the study of conflict. One theory, particularly strong amongst American sociologists, posits that conflict is dysfunctional. The task of these sociological thinkers is, therefore, to find the source of the defect and recommend ways it can be corrected. Sociologist Georg Simmel offers an alternative theory of conflict which was revisited some years later by Lewis Coser (1956). In their view, conflict is inextricably linked to all human interaction. The question becomes, therefore, not why conflict exists, but rather how to manage it.

If conflict underlies all human interaction then it follows that there must be a distinction between conflict and violence. Even without the visible expression of violence, conflict exists and may move from latent to an overt and violent state if certain triggers are activated. Recent events in the former Yugoslavia, Rwanda, and Burundi give weight to this interpretation. Such conflicts, which have been characterized as *protracted social conflicts*, are rooted in "religious, cultural or ethnic communal identity" (Azar 1990, 2). Precisely because these conflicts do not have an organic cycle, there is no clear starting or termination point (Azar 1990, 6). Protracted social conflicts may remain latent for substantive periods, emerging or reemerging as conditions allow. In the overt, violent stage, these conflicts have proven to be particularly intractable. As protracted social conflicts are easier to prevent than to resolve, understanding their genesis and process-related dynamics is fundamental.

Theories of conflict and causes of protracted social conflicts range from economic and rational choice interpretations to those that emphasize the psychological dynamics. Whilst not without merit, these explanations, which are often reductionist, generally fail to address the complexity and multiple causes of protracted social conflicts. Another approach to analysis of identity-related conflicts, most cogently argued by Burton (1987), emphasizes a needs-based approach to conflict analysis and resolution. According to this theory, conflict is rooted in the denial of basic human needs such as identity-recognition and security. The satisfaction of these needs must be, therefore, central to conflict management. According to Hoffman (1992), application of a basic needs theory to international conflict is problematic. However, when applied to protracted social conflict situations, the theory is particularly rich and useful.

Citing the limitations posed by current theoretical and applied approaches to the field of conflict analysis and management, Azar has developed an explanatory model for protracted social conflicts using a basic needs approach. Separating his model into three stages of development, Azar identifies the genesis, process dynamics, and outcomes unique to protracted social conflicts. The initial stage considers the communal composition and historical antecedents of protracted social conflict. Alone, these variables do not necessarily lead to protracted social conflict, but if present in conjunction with certain process dynamics, protracted social conflict is likely to emerge.

Critically engaging Azar's argument to an exploration of a substantive case study, this chapter will demonstrate that failure to satisfy basic needs criteria precipitated a crisis of legitimacy and contributed to the sociopolitical instability in Northern Ireland since 1968. Through application of Azar's framework to the Northern Ireland case, the purpose of this chapter will be to evaluate the efficacy of a basic needs approach to conflict analysis as well as its potential contributions to the theory of conflict management.

The Genesis of Protracted Social Conflict

In the debris of colonial rule in territories as disparate as Lebanon, Burundi, and Northern Ireland, the scenario is hauntingly familiar. Exogenous factors (a colonial legacy) combined with endogenous (historical social formation) factors engender the rise of multicommunal societies. These communities "are characterized by disarticulation between the state and society as a whole . . ." (Azar 1990, 7). A dominant group (often a remnant of colonial divide-and-rule tactics), exercising hegemonic control, emerges. Domination is often ensured by the subjugation of minority or subgroups (usually at the expense of the nation- and state-building process). To avert social conflict Azar (1990, 2) states that, "basic needs such as those for security, communal recognition and distributive justice" must be satisfied. When left unfulfilled, protracted social conflict is likely to emerge.

Systemic explanations of protracted social conflict subsume two sets of pre-conditions: the characteristics and composition of a society; and the historical antecedents that serve as a catalyst for politically activating communal groups. A society which experiences protracted social conflict will possess a multi or bicommunal composition. This composition may be the result of forced integration, or the incorporation of distinctive and antagonistic communities into one political unit.

Among the historical antecedents for protracted social conflict is a colonial divide-and-rule legacy. As a result of the colonization process, or through intercommunal struggle, an adversarial relationship between communities develops, and one or more dominant communal groups emerge and effectively co-opt the state machinery. Hegemonic control is exercised by the dominant political group(s) and the state remains unresponsive to the needs of minority or subgroups, thereby impeding the nation-state building process. Under basic needs theory, individual or communal survival is contingent upon satisfaction of three fundamental sets of basic needs variables: *acceptance needs* (recognition of communal identity); *access needs* (effective participation in society); and *security needs* (physical security, housing, and nutrition), henceforth referred to as basic needs criteria. The denial of physical and acceptance needs, per se, does not directly induce protracted social conflict. Rather it is the denial of the means to attain these needs, that is the *access* to social institutions, that prevents effective participation (political, social, and economic) in society. Effective participation may not be just an interest, but—along with communal recognition and physical security—a basic developmental need.

When needs are not met, grievances are usually expressed collectively. Groups that are, or perceive themselves to be, marginalized attempt to redress grievances through a variety of responses. The access the groups have to the economic decision-making apparatus determines the type of response employed. Thus Azar asserts (1990, 9) "participation in the economic decision making is, in turn, determined by the overall distribution of political power within the society." Grievances for the right to vote or to secure adequate housing, for example, may, if not redressed in a timely manner, soon envelop wider questions of the fairness and justice of the distribution of economic and political power.

Protracted social conflict may also result in countries where basic needs are not solely manifested in competition for physical resources or power. The denial of communal security, fair governance by ruling elites, and acceptance and recognition of cultural diversity (all basic to nation-state building) may also lead to protracted social conflict. Azar maintains that access to economic and political power is largely determined by the level of acceptance of each community within the larger social system. If the dominant political authority accepted and accommodated alienated communities, then grievances over economic and political power could be marginalized. However, often it is the refusal of one community to accept and respect the identity of the other that lies at the core of basic needs deprivation and blockage of effective societal participation. Recognition of communal identity, therefore, can also be understood as a basic need. Denial of this need can foster group cohesion within victimized communal groups and can work to promote collective violence if no other means of redress is available.

Regulation of social, political, and economic interactions is the role of the state. The state, in principle, is endowed with the power to ensure that basic needs criteria are met. If the state or dominant political authority falters in this role, then basic needs are not satisfied and another precondition for protracted social conflict has been met. However, it is not solely the role of the state which retards the nation-state building process and engenders (or prevents) protracted social conflict. Additionally, how a domestic agenda evolves and the type of state institutions developed are, according to Azar (1990, 11), "greatly influenced by the patterns of linkage with the international system." A territory may be economically dependent on an external power authority, thereby limiting regional autonomy. The state may also have a political and military client relationship in which an external power source provides protection for the client state (or territory) in return for the client's loyalty.

What Activates Protracted Social Conflicts?

Mobilization of marginalized minority groups occurs when individual victimization is recognized on a communal level. The mobilization of these groups as manifested in collective protest is often met by suppressive rather than accommodative measures by the dominant group. What may begin as a demand for fulfillment of one need can, if left unfulfilled, soon envelop a wider range of issues. This spillover effect may serve to mobilize a greater participation within the aggrieved group. The communal actions and strategies employed by the minority group may change to become more stringent or extreme, depending on the response of the political authority; civil disobedience may quickly turn to political violence.

Protracted social conflict can be resolved or kept latent if the state effectively intervenes to redress grievances, and attempts to satisfy basic needs during the initial stage. However, the politics of accommodation are rarely employed. Challenges to the authority of the state (or dominant communal groups) are often met by suppressive measures. Repressive state actions, in turn, may incite the marginalized minority community to employ equally hard-line tactics. If, as sometimes is the case, co-optive strategies are employed, they may serve to allay communal grievances. However, at this stage, co-option is often perceived by the minority community as merely a diverting tactic and is usually rejected. If attempts at co-option fail, the state (or dominant communal group) is then able to claim justification for implementing draconian measures which, in turn, may lead to greater tension and escalating levels of violence. If these measures fail, the political authority seeks to contain the conflict and, in doing so, may elicit external assistance using existing dependency or client ties.

In addition to communal and state actions, a conflict may be activated by what Azar terms its *built-in mechanisms*. These include both the history of experience between the groups (and the state or political authority, if separate) and the nature of communication between each conflicting communal group. If the conflict is based on collective identity and the fear of marginalization, then the perception of actions by both the state and opposing communal groups is pivotal. The demarcation between subjective and objective realities may become distorted. Reactions may be conditioned by fears and stereotyping. Segregation and polarization prevent intergroup communications, perpetuate communal fears and hostility, and serve to further solidify negative perceptions. Under these conditions Azar (1990, 15) states, "the worst motivations tend to be attributed to the other side. There is little possibility of falsification of belief, and the consequence is reciprocal negative images which perpetuate communal antagonisms and solidify protracted social conflict." Other researchers in the field concur. Both Mitchell (1981) and Burton (1987) argue that in the study of protracted conflicts, it is important to examine the role of perceptions, and the factors which contribute to the development of these perceptions including the history and nature of interaction among antagonistic communal groups.

What Are the Outcomes of Protracted Social Conflicts?

Once protracted social conflict has ensued, the society is likely to experience a deterioration of physical security and an underdevelopment of social, economic, and political institutions. Institutional deformity is likely to accompany the breakdown of socioeconomic and political institutions which become impotent and the social fabric of cross-community institutions may fray or disintegrate altogether. Cleavages between communities are cemented as polarization and segregation become institutionalized. A type of siege mentality develops. What may result, according to Azar (1990, 17), is the process of *psychological ossification*, which entails a perception within each community of collective victimization perpetrated by the other.

Finally, as a result of intercommunal mistrust, communities may turn to external actors for support. This serves to further economic dependency and client ties and abdicates internal social and political power and decision-making abilities.

Northern Ireland: A Case Study in Protracted Social Conflict

In Ireland, as in all democratic societies, issues of justice and of political legitimacy are interdependent. States exist, among other reasons, to arbitrate between citizens and dispense justice. The legitimacy of the state is measured, in part, by its ability to meet citizens' basic needs. Political legitimacy may be challenged and justice disputed if the state fails in this role or if the state machinery has been effectively co-opted by one or more dominant identity groups. In a study of inequality in Northern Ireland, Smith and Chambers (1991, 55) note: "Throughout the history of Ireland, questions of social justice have been intertwined with the conflict over the national question."

Others, like Kearney, contend that questions of social justice are not only intertwined with the national question but may very well be one and the same. Yet earlier social attitudinal research, coupled with a series of ethnographic studies undertaken by this author,[1] suggests that citizens evaluate issues of social justice separately from the national question. In a 1987 submission to the Standing Advisory Committee on Human Rights, the Policy Studies Institute stated (1987, paragraph 3.6): ". . . political and constitutional issues are not overwhelmingly the main frame of reference in which people locate the conflict. A substantial proportion of both communities think first and foremost in terms of social and economic conditions and the rights of citizens within Northern Ireland itself and not in terms of its relationships with larger political units."

On a communal level, therefore, many individuals locate the conflict in terms of basic needs' satisfaction within the existing state structure. While not abandoning nationalist aspirations, early civil rights initiatives led by National Unity (1959) and the Campaign for Social Justice (CSJ, 1964) sought reforms within a Northern Ireland framework. Issues of social justice remained at the core of subsequent civil rights endeavors led by the Northern Ireland Civil Rights Association (1967). Yet minority community demands for social and political equality were deemed suspect by the majority/unionist community. Unable to separate demands for social justice from a nationalist agenda, the civil rights movement was, from the onset, condemned as a front for the IRA. Unionists continued to see the Catholics as disloyal to the state and therefore undeserving of political and social equality (an opinion still reflected in social attitudinal and ethnographic studies). Reforms went unmet, violence escalated and, in 1971, internment was reintroduced. As O'Leary and McGarry (1993, 176) observe, "The radicalization of the minority community which preceded (but was dramatically enhanced by) internment allowed loyalist politicians (and some unionist commentators) to claim vindication: the Catholics had been republican all along."

Direct Rule, introduced in 1972, created a dual and often contradictory task for the British government, to provide just interim rule whilst concurrently endeavoring to divest itself of governmental powers. This dual role of both player and neutral arbitrator allowed, according to O'Leary and McGarry (1993, 183), the British government to "portray itself as an 'outsider' or 'insider' as the occasion demanded." The British government perceived the introduction of Direct Rule as "fundamentally reform[ing] the Northern Ireland State. From that point on, Miller (1993, 74) argues the causes of the conflict had been removed and any manifestations of unrest could only be explained as initiating from extremists." Yet, as O'Leary and McGarry (1993, 6) demonstrate, reforms, when applied, were limited and often contradictory. Much of the anti-discrimination legislation introduced "lacked teeth" and in some cases, advancements made through civil rights initiatives were actually compromised by subsequent reforms. As levels of violence directed against the state by the minority community continued to rise in Northern Ireland, draconian legislation was implemented unveiling the dilemma of Britain's player/neutral arbitrator role; measures enacted by the State under Direct Rule necessitated protection both for and then from the nationalist community.

Following Direct Rule, British government initiatives initially focused on internal power-sharing with domestic policies directed toward conflict containment. While questions of social and economic justice were sidelined, often imputed to the nationalist agenda, it is precisely in these issues that citizens in Northern Ireland continued to locate the conflict. This is not to imply that the amelioration of inequalities would result in conflict resolution. However, justification and rationalization of both nationalist and unionist intransigence on the national question have been wedded to demands for equality of opportunities, communal recognition, and security. As these needs are interdependent, deprivation of one need may impact other areas. While it is the national question which defines citizens' sense of political identity and community, (self-identification as either Irish nationalist or Ulster unionist), protracted social conflict in Northern Ireland cannot be understood without reference to equitable access to institutions of government, cultural tolerance, and acceptance of diversity. Examining the relationship among basic needs criteria moves us closer to understanding the causes and protractedness of conflict in Northern Ireland.

Access Needs

Distributive justice is dependent on access to social, political, and economic decision-making institutions. Within Northern Ireland, a sense of communal marginalization, increasingly felt by sections of both communities, is most often tied to issues related to fair employment, political and social empowerment, and legal justice. The difficulty facing a state whose very legitimacy is in question by one or more groups is that regardless of its role and the measurable degree of fairness applied, its practices are likely to be perceived as wrongful by the contesting community. The question of fair employment and human rights in Northern Ireland, therefore, can be as much about perceptions as about practice.

Controversy is rife (Osborne 1978, 1980; Miller and Osborne 1980; Smith 1987; Smith and Chambers 1991) regarding the extent to which religious discrimination, in and of itself, contributes to the employment differential. In a review of social attitudinal work on the question of fair employment, John Whyte (1991, 6) notes: "as a factor objectively differentiating the two communities, the economic gap is substantial, but it does not distinguish between them so sharply as some of the differences linked with politics and religion. As a source of perceptions differentiating the two communities, it is one of the most important in Northern Ireland."

The Fourth Report on *Social Attitudes in Northern Ireland* assessed communal perceptions of, amongst other factors, fair employment. When asked to indicate if the chances for securing employment were the same or different between Protestants and Catholics, 55 percent of Catholics, compared to only 32 percent of Protestants, felt that opportunities differed between the two communities. The disparity grew when 86 percent of Catholic respondents (compared to only 28 percent Protestant) indicated that the chances were greater for members of the Protestant community to secure employment (Gallagher, 1995, 24–25).

Interestingly, the percentage of Protestants who perceived that Catholics fared a greater chance of securing a position was nearly twice that obtained from a 1987 study undertaken by David Smith for the Standing Advisory Committee on Human Rights (Gallagher 1994, 39). This reflects the increasing number of Protestants who feel that fair employment legislation in Northern Ireland has actually facilitated reverse discrimination.

While Gallagher's study did not break down responses by socioeconomic class, Smith's earlier work surveyed attitudes toward employment among the working class. He found that while 64 percent of working class Catholics felt that Protestants were more likely to secure employment; only 2 percent of working class Protestant respondents agreed. Data collected during the authors' 1990 and 1994 participant-observer studies concur; whatever the realities of the employment situation, fact rarely dissuades or even impacts community perceptions. Azar (1990, 10) states that "*the ideal state characterized by a fair and just mode of governance [my emphasis] should be able to satisfy human needs regardless of commu-*

nal or identity cleavages, and promote communal harmony and social stability." When a state fails to fulfill (or be perceived to fill) this role, justice may be disputed and a crisis of legitimacy may ensue. Economic discrimination and the political marginalization of Northern Ireland's minority community were further coupled with endemic civil liberties and human rights abuse.

Northern Ireland's history is marked by fitful republican campaigns coupled with (later) civil unrest that has challenged both the authority and legitimacy of the state. Civil protests of the late 1960s turned to political violence inviting harsh and repressive state responses; a normalization of emergency was realized. Repressive responses by the state had two significant effects: they awoke and legitimized a previously dormant republican movement; and they served to further alienate and radicalize the Catholic community.

Emergency legislation in Northern Ireland was initially embodied in the Civil Authorities (Special Powers) Act (NI), which was introduced in 1922 and remained in effect until 1972. The Act provided the security forces with sweeping powers of search and seizure, arrest, and detention. Following a review by a government commission led by Lord Diplock in 1972, a series of recommendations was made culminating in the Northern Ireland (Emergency Provisions) Act (EPA); an infrastructure of emergency began. Many of the provisions of the repealed Special Powers Act were resurrected in the EPA. Under this legislation a system of trial without jury, commonly known as the Diplock Courts, was established. Subsumed under the EPA are sweeping powers of detainment, arrest, internment without trial, and the authority to proscribe organizations. Additional special powers were adopted under a series of Prevention of Terrorism Acts (PTA) first instituted in 1974. The most current PTA (1989) allows for detention for up to seven days, proscription of organizations, and for the execution of Exclusion Orders. Unlike the EPA, the PTA applies to all of the U.K. In 1990, the Police and Criminal Evidence (Northern Ireland) Order (1989) was adopted which addressed police powers. This was followed by the Northern Ireland Emergency Provision Act 1991 (extended 1996) which essentially readopted provisions from earlier PTAs, incorporated PTA provisions, and expanded special powers to include provisions for search and seizure, anti-racketeering, and the establishment of an independent assessor of military complaints.

Instituted initially as a temporary provision to respond to (arguably) a crisis of state, these emergency powers essentially became a permanent part of Northern Ireland's judicial process. From the perspective of the state, these provisions were (and continue to be) warranted to counter the use (or potential use) of political violence by paramilitaries. However, comparing the use of emergency powers under the PTAs with the record of violence, statistics reveal the number of persons detained under the PTA continued to increase despite a leveling in the record of violence.[2] This only reinforces accusations that detention under the PTAs serves as an information-gathering technique rather than (as intended) a due process mechanism.

Whatever the conditions or state justification for the necessity of these emergency provisions, however, it is clear that the use of emergency powers, together with the manner in which they were executed (and by whom), became as much a cause as a symptom of the protracted conflict. It is not merely that these emergency powers exist but that those empowered with their execution were, and continue to be, perceived by Catholics as biased and that when invoked these provisions weighed disproportionately against the minority community.

In 1993, Protestants and Catholics were surveyed to determine their perceptions of equalities of opportunities and fair application of the law. The survey revealed that significantly more Protestants than Catholics felt that legal justice in Northern Ireland was applied equitably. While both sides agreed that the courts treated those accused of non-terrorist activities evenly, only 53 percent of Catholics, compared to 79 percent of Protestants, felt that equal treatment was applied to those accused of terrorist offenses. Differences were most significant when questioned whether security forces treat both Protestants and Catholics equally: 73 percent of Protestant respondents, compared to 41 percent of Catholics, felt that the RUC (Royal Ulster Constabulary) treated the public fairly. Corresponding figures for the army were 71 percent of Protestants, compared to 42 percent of Catholics, and for the RIR (Royal Irish Regiment) 60 percent of Protestants, compared to 30 percent of Catholics (Gallagher, 1995, 23).

Given the largely sectarian nature of the security forces, unsurprisingly, Catholics perceive treatment by the security forces differently. The history of both the development and composition of security forces lends weight to Catholic perceptions of bias. According to the latest report of the Home Office Inspectorate of Constabulary, only 860 or 7.4 percent of 11,690 RUC officers are Catholic. The Catholic composition of the RIR is reported as 4 percent (McVeigh, 1995, 54).

The reasons for this are not surprising. The sectarian history of the security forces, coupled with the added security risks faced by Catholics, are obvious deterrents to greater Catholic participation. However, as McVeigh (1995, 59) has noted: "In the longer term, there is no doubt that the practice—intentional or otherwise—of arming one side of the population in Northern Ireland to police the other is inherently divisive. In a deeply divided society it reproduces and reinforces existing tensions."

While some researchers support RUC claims that sectarianism is not endemic within the police, others claim sectarianism is pervasive.[3] Whatever the realities, Catholics *perceive* the RUC to be inherently biased and essentially unreformable. This legacy tied to the development of early Irish police forces coupled with the distinctly Protestant composition of the RUC, now largely responsible for policing, has permanently alienated the Catholic population from the security forces in Northern Ireland. It has been suggested that the sectarian composition of the security forces has fostered a sectarianization of policing, policing in Catholic (particularly working class) areas allegedly differing from policing in Protestant districts. However, here, as in many other aspects of legal justice, the demarcation between fact and perception blurs. Yet, it is not merely legacies and perceptions that embitter relations between Catholics and the security forces. Without exception, during the course of the ethnographic studies carried out in a republican area of West Belfast, each respondent (formally or informally interviewed) had experienced some form of harassment. The high rate of unfavorable contact between the Catholic population and the security forces has two immediate effects: perceptions of an anti-Catholic bias among security forces are reinforced, and paramilitaries are legitimized, fostering further political instability.

Acceptance Needs

Identity is a process-related dynamic underpinning the activation and ossification of protracted social conflict. While other factors such as equitable access to political and economic forums and legal justice are integral to the conflict, symbiosis exists between these basic needs and identity which serves to reproduce the conflict over time.

Contemporary analysis of the conflict in Northern Ireland is likely to include reference to the concept of identity, that which is conflicting, lacking, or dependent on structural conditions. Protracted conflict in Northern Ireland is identity-driven and, as Horowitz (1985, 175–79) argues, based on the "fear of extinction." The communal identity of Irish nationalism stands in sharp contrast to Ulster unionism. While unionism seeks to *maintain* and strengthen an existing political order, nationalism's aspiration is to *create* a loosely visualized nation. As fulfillment of these objectives can only be achieved at the expense of the other, intergroup accommodation and acceptance of communal identities are prevented.

I conclude that within unionism, the fear of communal identity loss underpins unionist actions, prevents accommodation, and contributes to political undevelopment. Within nationalism, the demand for communal recognition and the inability to exercise cultural diversity within the existing state structure contributes to a sense of alienation from the state and precipitates a challenge to its authority.

Security Needs

Within Northern Ireland, the deprivation of communal recognition impacts a second basic developmental need, that of physical security. Subsumed under the concept of *physical security needs* is the fear of identity loss and betrayal. Results from the author's earlier studies clearly indicate that fear of communal identity loss affects perceptions of security, and an overall sense of communal well-being. These identity-activated fears engender group cohesiveness, forging a bond that exists regardless of underlying and, at times, significant differences on other issues.

According to Azar (1990, 2) within protracted conflicts, the perception of a threat to the communal identity, coupled with an increase in "internal repression, external intervention and manipulation of local grievances . . . ," is often accompanied by paramilitary organization. Azar (1990, 16) goes on to say that in societies experiencing protracted social conflict, citizens "become vulnerable to absorption in a violent war culture, further separating them from civil life." Results from interviews highlight the paradox in paramilitary support, with a sense of need for the boys to be ready and able when identity-related fears are activated, but with a rejection of the sectarian nature of paramilitary violence. I conclude that political violence is accepted and legitimized by the perceived collective victimization within both communal groups. Intracommunal inner policing is accepted, in part, as a result of the perceived absence of external safeguards. These perceptions allow for a collective rationalization for violence and have contributed to the protractedness of conflict in Northern Ireland.

Conclusion

Extensive ethnographic research on issues specific to Northern Ireland highlights the roles of perception and time in conflict analysis. The perpetuation of conflict over time produced concomitant shifts in issues, goals, and actors that, in turn, restructured and, in some cases, redefined the needs' base. While nationalist and unionist communities agreed on general basic needs criteria, differences emerged when evaluating factors impacting fair employment, equitable distribution of legal justice, and communal identity recognition. Conflicting communal perceptions of what constitute need fulfillment suggest that there may be, as Mark Hoffman (1992, 275) notes, a spectrum of need-fulfillment.

Critical engagement of Azar's model with a case study of Northern Ireland finds that a needs-based approach to conflict analysis provides a framework through which we can determine the genesis and identify the potential triggers of protracted social conflicts. Although additional factors revealed during data analysis—the role of perception, time, and the emergence of a hierarchy of needs—raise some questions regarding the efficacy of a needs based approach to conflict resolution, it should not be summarily dismissed. Instead, as Hoffman (1992, 275) argues, we should identify the place and role of needs-based third-party interventions in the context not only of a spectrum of third-party intervention, but viewing it as part of an interconnected process that includes more formalized negotiation processes.

Suggested Study Questions

1. According to basic needs theory, what fundamental needs are necessary for individual or communal survival?
2. How are needs which are not met likely to be expressed?
3. What factors tend to activate social conflicts?
4. What effect did the existence of a state of emergency regime have on community relations in the conflict in Northern Ireland ?
5. What other identity needs played a role in the Northern Ireland conflict?

Notes

1. Several ethnographic studies were conducted over a nine-year time frame in Northern Ireland. During this period, interviews were conducted with community and political leaders, paramilitary members and residents in several housing estates throughout Belfast. Additionally, two long-term ethnographic studies were conducted while residing within families in one nationalist and one unionist residential area. Field work was initially undertaken in 1985 and then revisited in 1990 and during the summer of 1994. These studies involved a combination of participant-observation and both formal and informal interviews. This chapter presents a summary of these findings. For full text see K. A. Cavanaugh, "Protracted Social Conflict in Northern Ireland: A Basic Needs Approach," Ph.D. thesis, London School of Economics and Political Science, University of London (1997).
2. See report of Amnesty International 1997; Human Rights Watch 1991.
3. See McMasterson 1993; Murray 1993 for contrasting views.

References

Amnesty International. 1997. *United Kingdom: Human Rights Concerns.* New York: Amnesty International.

Azar, Edward. 1990. *The Management of Protracted Social Conflicts.* Dartmouth: Dartmouth Publishing.

Boal, Fred W., Robert C. Murray and Michael Poole. 1976. "Belfast: The Urban Encapsulation of a National Conflict." In Susan Clark and Jeffrey Obler eds., *Urban Ethnic Conflict: A Comparative Perspective,* Comparative Urban Studies Monograph no. 3. Chapel

Hill, N.C.: Institute for Research in Social Sciences, University of North Carolina.

Burton, John W. 1987. *Resolving Deep Rooted Conflicts: A Handbook.* Lanham, Md.: University Press of America.

Coser, Lewis. 1956. *The Functions of Social Conflict.* London: Collier-Macmillan.

Darby, John. 1986. *Intimidation and Conflict in Northern Ireland.* Dublin: Gill and Macmillan.

Gallagher, A.M. 1994, "Community Relations." In *Social Attitudes in Northern Ireland: Third Report.* Peter Stringer and Gillian Robinson, eds. Belfast: Blackstaff Press.

———. 1995. "Equality, Contact and Pluralism: Attitudes to Community Relations." In *Social Attitudes in Northern Ireland: Third Report.* Breen et al., eds., 13–32.

Greenfeld, Liah. 1992. *Nationalism: Five Roads to Modernity.* Cambridge, Mass.: Harvard University Press.

Harris, Rosemary. 1972. *Prejudice and Tolerance in Ulster: A Study of Neighbors and 'Strangers' in a Border Community.* Manchester: Manchester University Press.

Hoffman, Mark. 1992. "Third-Party Mediation and Conflict-Resolution in the Post-Cold War World." In *Dilemmas of World Politics: International Issues in the Changing World.* New York: Oxford University, 272–75.

Horowitz, Donald. 1985. *Ethnic Groups in Conflict.* Berkeley: University of California Press.

Human Rights Watch/Helsinki. 1991. Human Rights in Northern Ireland. New York: Human Rights Watch.

Kearney, Oliver. 1988. *A Long Road to March.* London: Labour Committee on Ireland.

McVeigh, Robert. 1995. *It's Part of Life Here.* Belfast: Committee on the Administration of Justice.

Miller, David. 1993. "The Northern Ireland Information Service and the Media: Aims and Strategies and Tactics." In *Getting the Message.* London: Routledge.

Murray, Robert C. 1993. "A Hunt for an Alternative." In *Fortnight*, 316: 32–33.

O'Leary, Brendan and John McGarry. 1993. *The Politics of Antagonism: Understanding Northern Ireland.* Atlantic Highlands, N.J.: Athlone Press.

———. 1995. *Explaining Northern Ireland: Broken Images.* Oxford: Blackwell Publishers Ltd.

Smith, David and Gerald Chambers.1991. *Inequality in Northern Ireland.* Oxford: Clarendon Press.

Standing Advisory Commission on Human Rights. 1987. *Religious and Political Discrimination and Equality of Opportunity in Northern Ireland: Report on Fair Employment.* Belfast: HMSO.

Stringer, Peter and Gillian Robinson, eds. 1994. *Social Attitudes in Northern Ireland: 1992–1993.* Belfast: Blackstaff.

Sutton, Michael. 1994. *An Index of Deaths from the Conflict in Ireland: 1969–1993.* Belfast: Beyond the Pale Publications.

Whyte, J. 1991. *Interpreting Northern Ireland.* New York: Oxford University Press.

5

The Social Origins of Environmental Resource Conflict: Exposing the Roots of Tangible Disputes

Brian D. Polkinghorn

Introduction

AS THE TWENTIETH CENTURY comes to a close we are witnessing dramatic changes in many of the political systems and alliances that were set in place during the first half of the century. With the collapse of the Soviet Union as well as many other regimes throughout the world a new geopolitical order is developing that has fundamentally altered social structures, systems and institutions. One consequence of the rearrangement of political systems is that many conflicts once held in abeyance by old political alliances are now more free to express themselves (Huntington, 1996). Without external control or aid coming from allied countries a political vacuum is being filled by smaller scale internal conflicts waged largely by political minority groups. The move from bipolar to multipolar systems, which inherently tax the benefits that can be distributed, helps clarify the sources of state power, one of which is control of the environment and natural resources. More importantly, the conditions under which these conflicts have arisen in places such as Bosnia, Israel, and South Africa allow us to examine the dynamics of a new class of social conflict. As a result of this new found freedom by minority groups to express their concerns, researchers stand to learn a great deal about the sources of conflict as well as the mechanisms that contribute to conflict escalation and de-escalation. Conflict theorists and practitioners are in place to experience, first hand, a number of disturbing protracted social conflicts. There are numerous causes for these types of conflict—old historical rivalries, revenge, and fear to name a few. There are also tangible, present day conditions to consider too. With unequal standards of living existing between different groups we see the level of conflict and competition arising. Also, as rates of development continue to differ dramatically we are also seeing variations in the ways groups are choosing to engage in conflict. From a world systems approach these forms of developmental lag not only cause friction among nations but further lopsided power imbalances that inflame internal and external conflict. This phenomenon exists in every case comprising the present study.

How these issues of environment and identity are linked and translated into political models of governance and decision-making may well be rational, yet a sole emphasis on identity may be considered somewhat irrational in explaining all forms of intergroup conflict. As this chapter will demonstrate, what we are witnessing is a link between objective and technically negotiable items such as clean and accessible water and arable land with the subjective and nonnegotiable elements of communal identity, recognition, and autonomy. A balance sheet is becoming the major means of determining equitable distribution. By doing so, groups are effectively laying claim to territory and resources based largely on group affiliation and identity. In one sense, environmental resources conflict is a rich arena to test social conflict theory frameworks, construct a better understanding of conflict dynamics, and to search for links between political, psychological, and sociological conditions and frameworks. These conditions, when combined in some fashion, lead to predictable conflict dynamics. However, before going further, an examination of the author's assumptions is made so as to provide the readers a uniform platform upon which to place the data analysis.

Assumptions That Influence Environmental Conflict

The first assumption being made rests on the idea that protracted social conflict has often served a functional as well as normal role in human interaction and institutional development. This approach to conflict is embedded in Simmelian sociology (Coser 1956, 1973). In fact, people may actively engage in conflict to precipitate a social change. The second assumption is that environmental conflict occurs whether we want to recognize it or not. Even though some theorists state that a conflict must be perceived by all parties in order for conflict to arise, it is important to recognize the simple fact that the environment exists regardless of our level of perception. The author assumes that in many cases pure social constructionist thinkers, who present environmental conflict as originating strictly from the social realm, are mistaking the recognition of the external world with the ultimate understanding of it. There are ways to view environmental and natural resources conflicts which are formed largely from the study of the biological and physical spheres which is often taken for granted in protracted conflict settings. Finally, the last assumption is that there is an empirical reality to comprehend that is being labeled the physical and biological environments which we, in actuality, do not completely understand, so much so that when we experiment with them we sometime produce non-obvious results. This is not a social constructionist approach because it assumes that there are things we are not completely knowledgeable of or are incapable of comprehending that impact the way conflict eventually evolves.

Categorical Sources of Environmental Conflict

There are a number of patterns within the data[1] discussed below that expose some of the sources of environmental resources conflict. These patterns capture much of the reasoning behind disputants' behavior. Although this research does not fully determine which category is the primary motive for the construction and escalation of environmental resource conflict the findings tend to support Burton (1987) and Azar's (1990) theoretical framework regarding the deprivation of basic human needs. The next few sections, which constitute the bulk of the chapter, describe specific categories of data that are framed within basic human needs theory. More importantly, although the author advocates a systems approach, the data do not indicate that the participants recognize or utilize a systems approach to conflict analysis and resolution. This finding will be examined more closely toward the end.

Field Settings

The first setting is along the shores of the Mississippi River between Baton Rouge and New Orleans. Along this roughly one-hundred-mile stretch of the river lies a large number of historically African American communities. People within these communities and in adjacent rural areas have had to confront, over the last few decades, the development and subsequent invasion of agrochemical and petrochemical industries. A series of interviews with public opinion leaders in four communities located in close proximity to agrochemical and petrochemical plants was conducted between 1994 and 1996 to learn how and by what means these communities go about making claims of environmental damage and poisoning against chemical manufacturers. This setting also investigates how communities have managed to alter their tactics as a result of structural and systemic inequalities within the state and federal government. An examination is also made of the relationship between the social, biological, and physical spheres.

The primary focus of the conflict is on the contamination of these predominantly African American communities by agrochemical and petrochemical industries. The predominant focus and perception by members of these communities is on the lack of justice due to racism. Members of these communities feel as though the authorities are indifferent or hostile in helping find a remedy to their problems. Many people in these communities also see these large corporations being given unfair advantage by local authorities and state officials that allow them to continue to pollute and poison local residents.

The second setting is situated in an upper midwestern U.S. city. Like the first case it too focuses on environmental justice issues as they impact a predominantly African American inner city community. On a regular basis this community swells with seasonal American Indian people who contribute to a sense that minorities are being treated unfairly. Among the city's neighborhoods this one has the highest concentration of ethnic minority groups and is also the poorest. This case exposes how the community has effectively overcome the siting of a waste transfer station within their boundary by effectively presenting the conflict as a quality of life and self-determination issue rather than a sanitary, technical, or economic one. In addition, this case also focuses on the use of the media in creating environmental claims making. One important point is that the media was effectively utilized to thoroughly describe the process by which grounds are established for the development of a problem, including 1) the justification of the action to be taken, and 2) the decisions made on what actions should be undertaken. Interviews with the leading stakeholders, activists, and politicians, as well as popular press accounts and personal correspondence, constitute the bulk of the data sources.

The third setting centers on three South African squatter camps. One is located outside Durban, another just outside Cape Town, and the third in Soweto just outside Johannesburg. All three of these camps are located close to white suburbs or cities and have created tensions for people, regardless of race, living close to them. From a legal perspective these camps are unique because squatters rights in South Africa are powerful and allow people to occupy unused land even in cases where it may be owned by someone else. There is also a set of historical claims that makes these types of territorial and environmental cases difficult. On the one hand, legal ownership of the land is well documented. On the other, there is the influence of the former structure and system of apartheid that effectively eliminated the "Black spots" or African communities living on valuable land or near other resources. However, with a new government the conflict over land, water, farming, housing, and other basic human needs is now in full force. Squatter camps challenge old boundaries and have brought the issue of territorial control and freedom of movement to the forefront of political debate.

The fourth setting is a collection of numerous land disputes between Israeli and Arab communities inside Israel and the West Bank. The unique political nature as well as the relationship between the Israelis and Palestinians made the disposition of them hard to predict. One dispute deals with the siting of a water treatment plant and another with the location of a radio tower. The second dispute relates to Arab migration close to and inside of an Israeli community. Some call it "invasion" while others see it as free movement within their own territory. Charges of discrimination and delegating Arab citizens to second-class citizenship have substantially impacted how these problems have been framed and contested. However, during the last decade there have been a number of negotiated agreements over land use between Arab and Jewish communities that document the changing of attitude by the Israeli government toward Arab citizens.

The fifth setting centers on the control of land near the cities of Sarajevo and Mostar in Bosnia-Herzegovina. Control of the operation of hydroelectric power stations near Mostar and the placement of waste collection and incinerator units around Sarajevo are two of the many disputes that are pitting groups against one another. Ethnic identity is the determining force for many political decisions including those that relate to rebuilding, land use, and territorial control. The psychological status quo brought on by the war has created a sense, held by many people, that they are suspicious of others and feel the need to live with and be governed by their own kind. This thinking has severely influenced the reconstruction effort. It is not limited just to the spoils of rebuilding though. Fortunately, there is a centuries-old form of multicultural tolerance that still prevails in some parts of Bosnia that actively confronts those separatists intent on destroying the country.

Each of these five cases range from site-specific environmental and territorial conflicts to large-scale civil strife or low-grade civil war. Each case provides a common element in understanding the social origins of environmental conflict. Few of the cases take place in a peaceful context. Most can be seen within Galtung's (1996) "negative peace" framework in which fighting may be absent but structural and systemic violence continues. It is extremely important to also keep in mind that in South Africa, Israel, and Bosnia there have been huge migrations of refugees over time and that the consequences of such movement has made many internal disputes and conflicts even more complex. This is especially true in South Africa and Bosnia where the majority of citizens are now living in areas once controlled by others. The following discussion focuses on patterns and characteristics that link identity to how people struggle over basic human needs that are located in environmental, territorial, and natural resources.

How Participants Perceive Conflict

An examination of the data from each case study provides a good reason to explore the theoretical lens by which one analyzes peoples' perception of conflict. Perceptions play a role in the construction of conflict and how we interpret events. Perception, for many participants, is everything. Facts do not help them make decisions. One's attitude and thinking constitute the core of perception and are a source of conflict. The most striking is that many participants discuss their perceptions of environmental and natural resources conflicts in terms of social relations based on economic inequity, unequal treatment under the law based on race, ethnicity, and religion, or by deliberate acts of racism or genocide. In addition, there is a prevailing belief among the majority of participants that there are limits to resources; this has a powerful pull on their psychological disposition to consider many forms of conflict as acceptable routes to meeting or securing their needs.

In addition, perceptions of nature appear to be a function of the conditions that shape historical interpretations of intergroup relations. Those that are forced into poverty see the environment as a place where they live and how they manage to survive while those at the top have a tendency to see the environment as an economic resource; to keep the competition away they often resort to a "protection" attitude. However, it is hard for perceptions, which are interpretations of events, to completely replace those events. Many participants tend to "feel" or "think" about an issue when confronted with inconsistency between their ideas and other plausible interpretations. For instance, some concrete conditions that participants need to attend to partially include: Protection from industrial pollution in the United States; sanitation and housing in South Africa; physical security from military and terrorist acts in both the West Bank and Israel; or freedom of movement, security, and control of land in and around the cities of Sarajevo and Mostar. Yet, some participants do not perceive these things as legitimate issues for other people. It appears that the separation of "objective reality" from "subjective perceptions" and beliefs is one source of conflict for many participants. In essence, it should take all parties to recognize a contentious issue in order to create a conflict. Therefore, groups need to have their perceptions, attitudes, and beliefs recognized as legitimate. Otherwise, this will also become a source of tension and conflict. Perhaps instead of ignoring or denying others' perceptions we can develop some process by which to incorporate the meaning of perceptions, even if based on folklore and myth, into peaceful mechanisms which constructively attend to them. Indeed, the power of myth to shape perception is so strong in South Africa that government-sponsored groups are working on creating new common proactive social myths that are designed to be attached to all groups. By understanding the basis of perceptions we can get to the interests and needs of each group where the work of conflict intervention may commence. This helps to construct a setting that promotes more exchange and hopefully some long lasting, if not generational, shift in the way these groups relate.

Group Identity, Persecution, and Survival

One set of data patterns focus on both a strong sense of community based on identity and an almost paranoid focus on group survival. In societies where group cohesion and collaboration are the keys to its survival these relationships are the ultimate bond for the group. Although there are participants who stress only in-group cohesion, there are others who see security, survival, and recognition coming partially from cooperation with out-groups. Many U.S. and Bosnian participants stress independence from other people living in the same regions. The reasons are varied but the general idea running through their thinking is that as larger social settings become more organized and complex our social relationships that regulate interaction with physical and natural systems environments become more contentious. The demarcation between these groups goes directly toward some type of group identification. In most cases they are predictably such things as race, ethnicity, and religion. It is also readily apparent through these cases that our mastery over nature does not, however, guarantee social stability. As we become more independent in our individual lives we become more and more dependent on others to supply our basic human needs. As a result, cooperation with out-groups becomes necessary, yet there is also the inclination to struggle with them over natural resources and territorial control. A small number of participants see cooperation as a key ingredient but also see out-groups as competitors or enemies. It is a catch-22 scenario. This tension between increased cooperation, competition, and conflict is much easier to see in cases where a pre-existing tense relationship exists between the parties, as is the case in South Africa and Bosnia.

The underlying tension and struggle faced by various groups in each of these cases are extremely diverse in focus and intensity. However, all have an element of group identity which, when combined with resource scarcity and territorial control, becomes one of the defining factors in understanding how conflicts may unfold.

We can begin to make the link between perception and objective conditions by adopting Levine and Campbell's (1972) Realistic Group Conflict Theory (RCT) which sprung from work by conflict theorists such as Coser (1956) as well as a number of social psychologists. The basic propositions of Realistic Group Conflict Theory are: 1) real conflicts of interest and threats create the perception of threat, 2) real threat causes hostility, 3) real threat causes in-group solidarity and identity, and 4) real threats cause ethnocentrism. In every case in this study all groups demonstrate these patterns.

Ethnocentrism and nationalism are forms of power based on in-group identity that deliberately force others into subordinate positions. These forms of power, as described by participants claiming a minority status, are manifested by varying degrees of physical, verbal, mental, emotional, and psychological domination or violence. Yet, the data depict two unusual relationships between survival and persecution. The first is used to explain why groups are persecuting them. For instance, participants talk about Serbian nationalism, Afrikaner racism, Israeli discrimination, and racism in the U.S. as the source of their problems. The second more surprising pattern is the persecution complex that some participant's adopt so as to somehow justify their actions. Those people that participants see as oppressing them are "racists," "inferior," "animals," or somehow defective and in need of punishment, thus justifying their actions. Although the author is not clear on this line of thinking it might go something like this: if people treat us poorly because of their attitudes then that justifies our reasons to do to them what they have done or continue to do to us. Although these two points simply appear to be two sides to the same condition, it is interesting to note that no one appears to take responsibility for what they are doing. Out of all the interviewees some seem willing to take responsibility for their own actions. The rest seem to be so caught up in some macro power play that they see no need for self-control.

In the two cases from the United States there is clear evidence that African American communities are aiming to become self-reliant and maintain their independence while demanding to be treated equally in terms of access within the political system. The most important reason for self-reliance appears to center on the idea of community cohesion and trust. For instance, when asking questions about job opportunities at a local chemical company most interviewees claim there are none, that they are taken by people out of the area or the only ones available to local workers are usually unskilled and dangerous. Another reason for these communities to maintain a separate identity is due to its distrust of the political elements of Louisiana. In another example a clear distinction is seen in residents' perception of local agrochemical plants. Many see race as the major variable not only in the placement of the plant and the hiring of skilled and unskilled workers, but also as the basis for the intention to harm African American people.

When asked about non-African American residents living close to the plant and how they may be impacted by this arrangement, many interviewees do not consider them part of the larger problem or somehow discount their involvement as coincidental, thus reinforcing the idea that the major variable in the conflict is race.

Group identity also appears to have an element of pride. In the midwestern city case a local African American leader had this to say: "almost all of the two hundred odd businesses in this community are owned and operated by people from outside it. Of all the employees that these businesses have almost seventy percent come from outside the community. We are being sucked dry." Lack of employment, according to many interviewees, not only hurts self-esteem but racial pride. One woman states, "we have to succeed in our new enterprise to let the people of [this city] know we are capable and not stupid." Racial identity is deeply felt and measures to protect it can lead to either conflict escalation or conflict resolution.

Another pattern links race, community, and employment to environmental quality and human health. Information coming from one focus group led to the understanding that there is a clear theory to the siting of locally unwanted land uses (LULUs) such as the waste transfer station. The power vacuum created by lack of employment and the resulting lack of economic strength to fight such causes creates a situation wherein one of the unofficial criteria for siting LULUs is to find a location that will create the least resistance, such as poor neighborhoods where land is cheap and community resources are already scarce. Because of this, the communities' ability to organize and resist unwanted development is often weak.

These two cases link economics to identity as well as the resulting tension of environmental protection and human health to the need for efficiency, effectiveness, or profit. One model to explain this thinking about identity and environmental hazards follows this line of thinking: Economic stability and jobs cannot be presented without framing the discussion in terms of community development and longevity. Community development cannot be contemplated without some focus on the mental and physical health of the residents, which cannot be adequately grasped without focusing on diet, nutrition, and sources of illness. Sources of ill health from environmental hazards cannot be addressed without first contextualizing them into one of disproportionate impact based on race. Nor can environmental equity and justice be accomplished until the benefits and costs of industrial production are equally and fairly distributed. This means that minority residents need jobs to survive as well as some means to compete with others for benefits. If these conditions are not met then the group is being persecuted by not having fair access to benefits and being burdened with too many of the costs. And so the circle is made complete.

The South Africa data has many similarities to the two U.S. cases. However, there are a few unusual dynamics that greatly influence environmental resources conflicts. One is the amount and intensity of disputing among various African groups. The Afrikaner to African relationship, although still haunted by apartheid-induced systemic and structural violence, is more predictable, in the public spotlight, and generally understood. It is in interviews with Africans that some differences of opinion arise concerning the future economic and environmental health of the country. Various groups have different political, social, and cultural ideas on South Africa's future and group identity is paramount to conflict behavior. Indeed, few people express opinions that differ greatly from the group position. Another, more dramatic dynamic is the sudden shift in political power in South Africa. Many disenfranchised Africans now possess political dominance, which at least insures some form of survival. However, the vacuum that has resulted from the exodus of political, technical, and bureaucratic functionaries has produced a new set of role players who are bringing inexperience and new group animosities to the system. Some of the perceived results are: reverse political racism, favoritism based on tribal relations or animosities, which has resulted in white flight, fighting among new African political elites and a new set of technical elites, not yet capable of running the country as it had been.

From the qualitative data it is apparent that social issues are paramount, just as in the United States cases. However, because living conditions are so desperate the environmental condition of the poor has taken on a new and important political significance. What African American groups in the United States have been trying to establish in regards to environmental justice ideology and philosophy is being thrust to the political forefront in South African politics. All aspects of environmental resources distribution are directly connected to racial or ethnic identity. Job appointments, designation of new government-built, private, single-family homes, land distribution, and equitable distribution of social resources is based on racial and ethnic identity.

In Israel, however, both religious and national group identity are readily seen by most participants as the ultimate dividing line. In the siting of locally unwanted land uses such as water filtration plants, radio towers, or waste storage facilities, Israeli and Palestinian officials are also having to contend with international territorial issues. Theories of invasion and domination are so deeply held by some Palestinian participants that Israelis are considered dire enemies. Conversely, some Israeli participants are so adamant about occupying land that they will not stop their expansion efforts. Then there is a middle ground where many participants stand. Those in favor of continuing the peace process are also the ones whose identity, although strong, is not as much of a determining factor when it comes to environmental resource and territorial claims. Historically, the situation has been exacerbated by the claims by many groups over territory and resources in Israel or the occupied territories. The data also depict a sense that as territorial boundaries and subsequent power shifts occur there is a growing sense of uncertainty.

Bosnia is an unusual case in that the boundaries between it and Croatia are fluid and constantly being debated at the local level. Depending on who is being asked about boundaries you are likely to receive different answers. What is evident in the siting of new industrial facilities around Mostar and Sarajevo is the desire to have beneficial industry and jobs close by and pollution sources and undesirable jobs far away. International business plays a role in helping the Bosnian government in Sarajevo rebuild plants and its economic infrastructure. There is little conflict concerning this objective. However, new facilities need resources as well as locations to manage production and waste. This is where the data consistently show that conflict is on the rise. The data depict regional- and ethnic-based attitudes as major determinants of how people are likely to act on a given issue. Yet, ironically, there is also a strong sense of multiethnic nationalism among many urban dwellers. However, site selection for new industries is complicated not only by territorial claims by nations but also by ethnic identity.

In all these examples group identity is a means of creating physical and psychological boundaries aimed at not only enhancing the group's quality of life but its survival as well. This suggests that when groups, who may have long-standing adversarial relations, co-exist within a restricted environment then we may have the conditions that lead to the strengthening of in-group identity. Palestinian and Israeli people divide themselves into identity camps. Bosnians, while mainly of Slavic stock, are divided into Croatian (Roman Catholic), Serbian (Eastern Orthodox), and Muslim communities. More blatantly we see divisions in South Africa that focus more on differences than similarities. In all of these cases, identity influences how groups conflict. But what is most interesting to note is the nearly complete absence of anyone framing environmental and human health issues in a systems framework. All problems are addressed in a sociological framework so that the physical and biological systems are delegated to a second-level status to the social framing of the issues.

As for the impact conflict has on the physical and biological systems, the data are nearly silent. But it may not be unreasonable to suggest that many of these groups see their survival more in the context of intergroup struggle than in the larger context of a more encompassing ecosystems or holistic approach. Indeed, there is some evidence that a number of participants view the natural world as the prize for winning a social struggle.

Claims Making and Storytelling as Conflict Processes

Claims making is the process whereby groups attempt to create preset conditions before or during the struggle over scarce resources that eventually allow them to effectively assume some form of control. Among these case studies, moral claims are perhaps the most abundant type. Perhaps the best examples of claims making comes from the two cases in the United States. In these examples groups commonly depict the situation in the form of a story which is easy to follow. The story is framed within values and beliefs that are not only easy to understand but also that most people support. The story typically has a clear set of victims, villains, and consequences and is told in typical Western storytelling fashion. There is a beginning, when the problem arises and becomes identified. This is followed by the middle, when people take on the clearly understood roles of the victim and villain and a subsequent struggle ensues using these labels. In this case the victims continue to become ill and decide to further the struggle on their own once help is not forthcoming. And finally, there is the end where the struggle plays to some finale. It is the end that is so important to the claims maker. If the claim has been correctly constructed then the outcome should be the one that the group desires. Having established the story line and its consequences, what is left is only one or a few correct ways to solve the problem and thus successfully end the story.

In many of the towns along the Mississippi River the stories are similar. A generations-old community nestled along the river is invaded by an industry promising well paying and safe jobs and subsequent higher standards of living. The plant is built, yet of the few jobs that are offered most are low paying, unskilled, and typically revolve around the most dangerous functions of the plant. Slowly, children and women start becoming sick. Their illnesses are often dramatic, life changing or threatening, and leave the victim in a state from which they will not recover or may even die. As time passes, people who thought that they were experiencing something specific to themselves or their families learn of other similar stories. With this growing body of evidence citizens begin to suspect outside causes and usually focus their investigation on the local plant. A timeline is established wherein these severe illnesses are not prevalent, which is usually prior to the plant being located near them. It is only after the plant begins operation that these illnesses arise. Other links to these plants include: general proximity, worker health, and contaminated water, air, and soil which is traced, in some fashion, back to the plant.

In every setting people told similar stories, although not in the exact fashion just described. However, the process of storytelling helps people not only to convey clear evidence in a systematic way, but it also lends legitimacy in that a claim is established that anyone can understand. No elaborate use of scientific inquiry is needed to make the story any clearer, valid, or legitimate. In fact, for many of the participants such criteria seem to have little meaning or have somehow been shed and, indeed, in many communities science and technology are not fully trusted forms of knowledge transmission because they are often seen as devices that attempt to hide the obvious. In Bosnia science is seen a little differently but, in the end, the decision is usually approached through the use of such mechanisms as storytelling. In essence, the process of laying claim through storytelling is another means of conflicting.

Claims making, which partially focuses on capturing desirable roles within the conflict, also aids the construction of enemy images. For instance, if one group successfully lays claim to some issue based on their established publicly recognized role of the victim, then the resultant dynamic is that the other party or parties become, by default, the offender. Establishing a claim based on capturing roles and positions in which to bargain are seen in every single case and in every setting. Group identity is the primary role people choose to adopt and in some cases it is easy to establish a claim based on the role, while in others it may not be the case. However, this group-based conflict does not lend itself to individual cases where a person who has been victimized is denied the role, claim, and compensation. Likewise, someone can claim to be a victim based on group affiliation but not have been victimized. This is one problem with such thinking.

Claims making and storytelling are used to frame the way stakeholders want others to interpret the conflict and on what they consider to be important ways to view certain issues. In every one of the cases some form of claims making and storytelling that focuses on group differences is evident. How these contribute to conflict escalation are clarified when various groups deliberately search for means of gaining an upper hand in the conflict by pressing limited interpretations on how the conflict should unfold.

Symbolic Manipulation as a Form of Conflict and Control

Another category within the data is the idea of securing basic human needs through the transformation of tangible issues of conflict into purely symbolic struggles. It seems to be a slightly sophisticated procedure. Basically, symbolic struggles revolve not only around forms of information (e.g., science, technology, and law), but on how they are eventually interpreted. What appears to be a common factor in each of the cases is the need by most groups to create a set of symbols relating to the environment that revolve around two distinct characteristics. The first is a link between the physical environment and the group itself. Of all the case studies one in South Africa has the most interesting examples. White participants tend to view the squatter camp located in a ravine between two white suburbs as a wilderness buffer area that should be left alone, not occupied or developed for any reason under any circumstances. The "wilderness" interpretation may simply be disguised racism. However, before writing it off as such, the thinking by many Africans who live in the squatter camp provides insight on the issue of symbolic legitimacy of one's claim. African participants generally discuss the relationship of people to the land and nature in a more holistic way with many forms of integration between them. Thus, there can be no buffer between people and nature if people live within nature. This interpretation is in opposition to white symbolic interpretation of what wilderness or buffer zones mean. To many of the black African participants there can be no distinction between people and nature or wilderness.

The data also depict a common theme wherein groups tend to use some combination of their history and culture to create the symbols through which they create meaning. These symbols, as depicted in folklore and myths, help people construct meaning over the physical and biological environment, and understandably they typically differ in some way by group. As a result, how we relate to the physical and biological environmental spheres from a symbolic perspective can easily become a source of conflict. Therefore, it is likely that some forms of interaction between the social and the physical and biological spheres may invade another's symbolism and perhaps even impact on their need for recognition and an intact and respected identity. It is evident that people in all the case studies who have had their environment altered by war, invasion, pollution, or annexation typically feel physically and emotionally assaulted. More interestingly, their understanding of the world also somehow comes under attack. It is not merely a matter of taking one's land or destroying it, but also failing to recognize that groups have different ways of thinking about and interacting with their physical and biological surroundings.

Symbolism helps people to frame and make sense of complex relationships between groups and on occasion the "natural" world. It also ties the abstract to the real by involving people, in a personal way, with not only other members of their group but with other groups and the physical world. Symbolism is also a hidden language in conflict talk that is more often felt than expressed. In all of the cases symbolic conflict is a major component.

Examining Basic Human Needs Theory and Systems Analysis

In each of the settings for this study participants describe their problems in relation to how they relate to others. This necessarily brings up differences, some of which are clearly described in terms of identity that we recognize as one of the basic human needs described by Burton. In addition, recognition of a group's legitimate demands also fits into this theoretical framework. However, it is not completely clear that other differences are a contributing factor in how conflicts arise. The distinctions made between South African whites and tribal Africans brings to light differences about how people regulate their interaction between themselves and how they view nature.

In Israel, differences in the way groups treat the physical environment are also sometimes described in cultural beliefs that may provide other means by which to explore the sources of conflict. As for a systems approach, there is little evidence in the data to support it as a means of analyzing how people relate to each other and to the environment. This is not really a surprise. The author anticipated finding some evidence, perhaps directly from participants' comments or maybe indirectly through legal documents and press stories or through cultural norms and beliefs or even perhaps religious teachings. This is an important finding that may be partially explained by the relative deprivation many of the participants face, which explains that perhaps survival needs are more important. One participant sums it up this way: "the environment isn't even thought of when your children are hungry and sick." This understanding is important because, while the author might be thinking about rational models and frameworks, people living in these conditions tend to think in a completely different manner. We need to think of a research design that allows the researcher to manipulate the level of intergroup tension. This will allow us to better understand at what point a systems approach to conflict analysis and resolution, using basic human needs theory as the way to frame issues, is useful and where it is no longer a viable option. Perhaps a systems approach works only in the most placid of human environments and not when there is a great deal of tension and deprivation. This is one area where more research is needed.

Conclusion

It is practically impossible to think of deep-rooted protracted social conflict without observing that many sources are tied to unmet basic human needs. This study suggests that deeply held values and needs cannot be compromised or negotiated. What it does teach us is that more creative and integrative means must be found to protect and preserve the meeting of needs. This creates a difficult problem-solving endeavor though. Groups in conflict must learn to first understand the dynamics of their interaction and then the basic knowledge that allows them to identify common ground. This sounds easy but in each of the cases in this chapter only two groups, one in South Africa and one in the United States, have succeeded in reaching an agreement using this method. In all other cases, people continue to struggle in some way.

Environmental conflict does not exist in a social vacuum. In fact, it is most often framed strictly within a human relations perspective. In cases where violence and severe deprivation are not found, perhaps an emphasis on a systems or holistic approach can help people frame issues so they are all a part of a larger context where cooperation is the paramount mode of relating. In less protracted environmental conflicts, where the author has used basic human needs and systems analysis, there has been a tendency, through interest-based mutual gains approaches, to foster cooperation and reduce the tendency to escalate conflict. In addition, a holistic approach forces people to rethink their framework that fosters adversarial symbolic attacks, the primary task of claims making and blaming, the desires to construct desirable roles, and the whole process of conflicting. Until more research is conducted in this area we will continue to frame these problems in such ways that no matter how we go about solving such problems we are likely to obtain the wrong answers.

Suggested Study Questions

1. The deprivation of basic human needs or the struggle over scarce resources appear to be sources of conflict. Think of as many intergroup environmental conflicts as you can, write down the issues in conflict and see if they relate to human needs. Do any of the issues relate to "nature's needs"?

2. One of the findings of this study is that if the level of tension or stress is too high between conflicting parties then there is a tendency to not use a systems approach to framing the issues. What might explain why a systems approach may not be used?

3. List the number of identities you think you possess. Then rank them in order of those with which you feel most strongly connected to those with which you feel the weakest connection. Think of situations, either in your personal life or perhaps from a press story, where you feel you were somehow connected and try to determine what identity you associate with that connection. Are some identities more important to you than others? Are some worth protecting?

4. If someone makes a claim against your primary identity group that is based on an event happening centuries ago is the claim "legitimate"? Do people have a right to make such a claim? Do they have the right to put you in a position of defending yourself?

5. What types of data do people need to have in order to "win" an environmental conflict? List as many categories of data as possible. How do you compare and decide whose data are more valid? For example, is storytelling as "legitimate" as scientific data presentations?

6. If a systems approach is such a good way to frame and analyze environmental and natural resources conflicts why are so many of these cases seen as social relations problems?

Notes

1. A total of ten field research trips were conducted during a four-year period. One was to Louisiana, two to the upper midwest United States, two to South Africa, two to Israel and three to Bosnia. In each setting the data have been collected using a variety of quantitative and qualitative methods. The two case studies occurring in the United States rely primarily on exploratory personal interviews with members of local communities involved in a series of protracted social and environmental conflicts. This is supplemented by research conducted by the U.S. Environmental Protection Agency, private research groups, scholarly literature, archival data from personal libraries, court records, and popular press materials. In the international case studies the bulk of the descriptive qualitative and quantitative data come from personal interviews, survey research, e-mail exchanges, letters, and field notes taken in each of the settings. These data are supplemented by written materials coming from statistics and policy descriptions from governments, universities, the United Nations, the European Union, the Organization for Security and Cooperation in Europe, and from local and international press materials.

   Participants were chosen in the U.S. cases by interviewing people who have taken part in some public debate concerning environmental conflict in their communities. Using a snowball sampling technique, other participants were interviewed from numerous groups. For the international cases people were chosen because of their first-hand involvement.

References

Azar, Edward. 1997. *The Management of Protracted Social Conflict.* Dartmouth: Dartmouth Publishing.

Boulding, Kenneth. 1962. *Conflict and Defense: A General Theory.* New York: Harper & Row.

Burton, John. W. 1987. *Resolving Deep-Rooted Conflict: A Handbook.* Lanham, Md.: University of America Press.

Coser, Lewis A. 1956. *The Functions of Social Conflict.* New York: Free Press.

———. 1967. *Continuities in the Study of Social Conflict.* New York: Free Press.

Galtung, Johan.1996. *Peace by Peaceful Means: Peace and Conflict, Development and Civilization.* International Peace Research Institute, London: Sage Publications.

Huntington, Samuel P. 1996. *The Clash of Civilizations and the Remaking of World Order.* New York: Simon and Schuster.

Polkinghorn, Brian and C. Brannon Andersen. 1995. "Expanding the Role and Responsibility of Geoscientists to Environmental Justice Communities: Aiding in the Management and Prevention of Environmental Hazards," *Geological Society of America Abstracts and Publications,* Vol. 27, No. 2, October.

Wallerstein, Immanuel. 1974. *The Modern World System.* New York: Academic Press.

6

Constructive Storytelling in Intercommunal Conflicts: Building Community, Building Peace

Jessica Senehi

Introduction

IN JANUARY 1998, storyteller and theologian Megan McKenna opened a Hawaiian conference on sovereignty with the following story (McKenna 1997a): Two brothers were fighting over a piece of land, each believing that he was the rightful owner. A Rabbi was called to mediate, and each brother told his side of the story. After listening to them, the Rabbi said, "I now need to hear from the third party." He knelt down and put his ear to the ground.

This story questions assumptions about ownership and control. It makes me think about how the voice of the people on the ground level, so to speak, is often not heard by various elites. That is, the experience and knowledge of lay persons or disempowered groups are dismissed by decisionmakers and professionals. In societies throughout the world, as a result of colonization and modernization, indigenous knowledge and culture have been characterized as "folklore" and as inferior to "science" and "the arts." In this way, the intellectual, political, and cultural elite are able to own and control knowledge.

This story is an example of a medium that gives voice to persons at the grassroots level of society. Storytelling requires no special equipment or training: it can be utilized in almost any situation, even in conditions of dire oppression. "Short of killing its bearer, the human voice is irrepressible" (Scott 1990, 169). In the form of life narratives and testimonials, story is a means of reporting experiences and conditions that might be otherwise dismissed, denied, or misrepresented.

In only a few words that a child could understand, the above story creates a dramatic paradigm shift. As narrative, story is a particular kind of critical method that is able to give expression to metaphor, paradox, identity, and emotion. Story gets at subjectivity (Lane 1996). It articulates experience.

Interestingly, this story is about a conflict. There are two parties and a mediator. It starts out as a zero-sum conflict, but the mediator expands the pie. He does not make the dispute simpler, but makes it more complex. He does not answer questions, but raises more by turning the notion of ownership on its head. These new questions may inspire new solutions.

More interesting, this story is used in the context of talk about conflict. McKenna has chosen this story to open discussion on sovereignty in Hawaii—not simply as an entertaining rhetorical device. McKenna, who has two Ph.D.s and is a theologian, activist, and writer (e.g., McKenna 1997b; McKenna and Cowan 1997), has chosen storytelling as her primary title and primary method for effecting social change.

Thesis

Storytelling is the art of telling a story and includes all forms of shared oral (or signed) narrative, whatever the circumstances of the telling (Ryan 1995). Stories may be fictional tales or relate personal experiences. Storytelling is a process of cultural production. This process is a negotiation of meaning among culture, performers, and audience; storytelling is in a position of control in the social construction of meaning (Bauman and Briggs 1990).

Storytelling—like all cultural production—is a means through which community is constructed. Through stories, groups and societies create, recreate, and alter social identities, power relations, knowledge, memory, and emotion. Intercommunal conflicts—those conflicts defined in identity terms—involve structural issues. Because intercommunal conflicts come to be defined in identity terms and are often long-standing, they become encoded in all aspects of a community's culture. Thus, peace-building involves community-building in a way that is driven forward by the parties themselves and not imposed from above or without.

The thesis of this paper is that storytelling can and must be a significant part of this peace-building process. Stories are an important medium of culture to examine because stories are accessible and inclusive: no special equipment or training is required to be a storyteller, stories can be understood by persons of all ages and educational levels, and stories translate well across cultures. Understanding the role of storytelling in peace-building is significant for facilitating cultural spaces where people can participate in defining their communities, voicing their experience, healing from past conflict, and shaping their future.

Intangible Bases of Intercommunal Conflicts

Intercommunal conflicts are complex. Perhaps what most distinguishes them is their scope in time, space, and imagination. Intercommunal conflicts usually have a long history—from a half-century to two—although there may be periods or even centuries of peace in between outbreaks of violence.

Some scholars emphasize the material—or tangible—roots of intercommunal conflicts. They argue that identity is socially constructed and over time various identities emerge, become salient, and fade. They question why particular communal groups mobilize politically along identity lines at particular historical moments, and argue that this is largely due to groups being denied resources and security based on their identity. That is, conflict drives identity.

Others emphasize the intangible psychological, cultural, and moral roots of intercommunal conflicts. While they recognize that intercommunal conflicts have material bases that need to be addressed, they seek to explain the mistrust, emotions, and persistence that characterize these conflicts. That is, identity drives the conflict.

This analysis is based on the view that these tangible and intangible bases interdepend. "Structural violence" engenders "cultural violence," and "cultural violence" engenders "structural violence" (Galtung 1990). Inversely, improving the relationship between communities facilitates sustainable problem-solving, and successful problem-solving builds confidence and improves the intercommunal relationship (Kelman 1995, Rothman 1997). Thus, both the structural and psychocultural roots of conflicts must be critical foci of research and practice.

Protracted intercommunal conflicts play themselves out on multiple social planes: geographically, in the economic system, in politics, linguistically, in educational access and curricula, in religion, in cultural production, and even in recreational activities. The dynamics of conflict in these numerous social arena intersect and reinforce each other to perpetuate the conflict and the negative relationship between identity groups (Byrne and Carter 1996). An intercommunal conflict can become encoded in each group's identity and culture in an intensifying cycle of rigidification, separation, and distortion (Northrup 1991). The intercommunal conflict permeates social life.

To recognize the complexity of intercommunal conflicts is not only analytically accurate, but has tremendous practical implications. Conflicts' complexity is double-edged. Complexity contributes to the perpetuation and intractable nature of conflict. But simultaneously, these views suggest multiple arenas for intervention, multiple agents of intervention, and multiple intervention tasks in a dynamic process of social change (Kriesberg 1991). By naming in detail the ways that intercommunal conflicts are reinforced or perpetuated makes it possible for people at all strata of society to participate more consciously to determine their own culture, address critical concerns, and imagine modes of resolution.

We must examine the powerful economic, political, and social forces that shape persons' lives in ways that are often oppressive and dehumanizing. To ignore these factors is to attribute too much power to the individual or the local community and legitimize oppression and injustice. But we must also see persons as meaning-makers and agents in order to understand how social systems and identities are created, interpreted, accepted, resisted, and changed.

Here, I argue that storytelling may be a significant methodology for understanding and negotiating the intangible dimensions of intercommunal conflicts because storytelling is a means by which community is created and reproduced. Storytelling is a means through which individuals and groups define social identities, create shared knowledge, negotiate power relations, construct emotions, and educate new community members. Crucially, storytelling must not be a state-controlled process, but rather must be a democratic, grassroots cultural practice in order to promote peace-building, grounded in social justice.

Theory, Practice, and Power

Over the past several decades, influential thinkers from a variety of disciplines have problematized the relationship between knowledge and power. These theorists and practitioners have argued that lay persons, peasants, and other "unknowledgeable" groups are, in fact, knowledgeable and must be key resources in designing and implementing projects that structure their community and/or seek their personal development. The intervenor—whether therapist, educator, researcher, engineer, state bureaucrat, or conflict mediator—must not "work on," but rather work in partnership with the subjects of the intervention.

In 1942, Carl Rogers developed the idea of client-centered therapy, which placed power not in the mind of the therapist, but with the client. He wrote: "The aim is not to solve a particular problem but to assist the individual to grow, so that he can cope with the present problem and with later problems in a better integrated fashion" (Rogers 1942, 28). The role of the therapist is to facilitate, through dialogue, the client's making sense of her or his own experience and determining her or his future direction. This process must occur in the context of a therapeutic relationship characterized by unconditional positive regard, which allows the client to feel safe, valued, and to trust her or his own knowledge.

In 1970, in *Pedagogy of the Oppressed*, Brazilian educator Paulo Freire argued that the education system served as an instrument of oppression by creating a "culture of silence." He reframed the teacher-student relationship as interdependent and intersubjective. That is, students bring to the educational process important knowledge. The role of education should be to provide opportunities for teachers and students to work together through a dialogic process to critically examine and better their social situations and their lives. In this kind of an educational process, persons do not have the world explained to them, but rather become more able to interpret the world themselves. He wrote: "To exist, humanly, is to name the world, to change it" (Freire 1970, 69). Michel Foucault (1972) also challenged the authority of experts when he persuasively argued that knowledge is not "discovered," but rather is "produced" by the powerful "technologies" of the social system. Some discourses are seen as more legitimate or authoritative: mass media versus what has a lesser audience or no audience, discourses from within academia versus from without, and what the literary canon includes rather than omits. These privileged discourses are indices of power and may exclude or misrepresent the experience of many social groups, including communities of women, groups from the Third World, or the First World's poor (e.g., Gugelberger and Kearney 1991; Randall 1991).

In sociology, researchers began to explore how marginalized, stigmatized, and institutionalized persons and groups make sense of their lives, allowing these people some intellectual room to explain their perspective to the researcher and in this way have some access to the public transcript (e.g., Liebow 1967, Wiseman 1979, Solinger 1992). Feminist methodologists brought attention to the neglected needs of disempowered groups (such as women) by scientists and researchers when they asked, Who is the research for? (Harding 1987). In 1973, Tala Assad argued that colonial power relations were encoded in the discipline of anthropology, and by 1986, James Clifford stated that "no one can write about others any longer as if they were discrete objects or texts."

In the field of economic and social development, "appropriate technology" is the idea that the people being helped by development projects be partners in designing and implementing solutions to their problems. In an analysis of epic developmental failures of the past century, James Scott (1990) argues that the exclusion of local knowledge by the state's social engineers was a critical factor: "If I were asked to condense in one sentence the reasons for these failures, I would say that the progenitors of such plans regarded themselves as far smarter and farseeing than they really were and, at the same time, regarded their subjects as far more stupid and incompetent that they really were (343)."

Social interventions that treat the subjects of intervention as unknowing, interchangeable parts involve an "intellectual imperialism" that has several practical and ethical flaws:

1. The decisions of intervenors may be seriously ineffective or destructive.
2. The local knowledge is a valuable resource that remains inaccessible to the intervenor.

3. Cultural differences between the "experts" and "lay" persons may result in misunderstandings.

4. Skills and knowledge of indigenous persons or peasants may be permanently lost to the world when they are colonized or forcibly redirected by new systems.

5. These interventions may be more or less intentionally exploitative, benefitting one group at the expense of another.

6. Interventions may be based on unjust assumptions (e.g., racist or sexist) and therefore perpetuate inequality in ways of which the intervenor may be largely unaware.

7. To exclude people from participation in decisions that may disrupt their lives is dehumanizing, demeaning, and disempowering.

It is arguable that the discipline the least touched by these ideas is the one most explicitly concerned with power—political science. Increasingly, however, the traditional concepts of "high politics"—state power, state interests, and interstate diplomacy—are gradually accommodating more complex and dynamic paradigms emphasizing the role of a diversity of actors, including not only states, but also transnational organizations, nongovernmental organizations, regional groups, and individuals (Rasmussen 1997).

An emerging subfield, transformational politics, is seeking to develop a "politics of participation" by defining empowerment and examining the role of mid-level social organizations (Schwerin 1996; Woolpert et al. 1998). Much of this new thinking has grown out of the interaction between political science and the interdisciplinary conflict resolution field, which has been developing at an increasing rate since 1942 (Kriesberg 1997; Lederach 1997). The objective of the field of conflict resolution, which emphasizes both theory and practice, is to develop and implement ideas about how individuals and groups at odds can move effectively and in moral ways toward meeting their needs and achieving reconciliation.

That the power to transform intercommunal conflicts does not—and should not—reside solely in the state level is persuasively argued by John Paul Lederach (1996, 1997), professor of sociology and conflict studies at Eastern Mennonite University and director of the International Conciliation Service of the Mennonite Central Committee. While building on preexisting understandings of conflict intervention, Lederach's vision of peace education and peace-building involves a paradigm shift and a power shift. Lederach (1996, 1997) builds on the pedagogy of Freire and the ideas of applied technology to describe how conflict resolution training can build on the traditions of a particular community. Three ideas from Freire's pedagogy are fundamental: 1) education is never neutral and should empower students by developing their "awareness of self in context," 2) education is a mutual and interdependent process among educator(s) and students, and 3) people are key resources in this process and their everyday knowledge must be listened to and trusted (Lederach 1996, 24). That is, leaders and intervenors must put their ear to the ground.

Lederach (1997) applies these same principles to conflict resolution and describes a pyramid of conflict intervenors and intervention tasks that can be generally understood as involving top, mid-level, and grassroots leadership. Most relevant for this discussion, Lederach gives a compelling argument for how grassroots approaches can culminate from the local level. For example, in the case of the Somali conflict in the early 1990s, building on cultural traditions and guided by respected elders at the subclan level, agreement-building at local peace conferences over a period of several months established a framework for resolving substantive issues when top-down processes had failed (Lederach 1997, 52–53).

Clearly, there is an important role for a diversity of grassroots approaches in the resolution of intercommunal conflicts. These approaches are empowering to persons directly involved in the conflict and are a process of profound social change. Drawing on fifteen years of peace education and peace-building work throughout the world, Lederach (1997) reflects: "From personal experience I can attest to the fact that the process of advancing political negotiation at polished tables in elite hotels, while very difficult and complex in its own right, is both a more formal and a more superficial process than the experience of reconciliation in which former enemies are brought together at the village level" (55).

I emphasize this theory to open the reader's mind to the possibility that storytelling may be a significant methodology for addressing a subject as political and potentially destructive as intercommunal conflicts. That stories can be understood by the very young and persons considered to have cognitive deficits (McCabe and Peterson 1991) may make stories seem infantile and far afield from weighty matters. But I argue that stories' intellectual accessibility is a clue to stories' significance. Information necessary for survival and making society has to be able to be understood by and communicated by all members of the community. Also, this enables stories to be a critical medium for teaching children. Storytelling is a means of intergenerational continuity—or change. Storytelling is a cultural practice in all societies, and the ability to tell and understand stories and narrative is probably an innate human capacity.

Stories are also technically accessible; no special equipment or training is needed. In particular, because no special training or expensive equipment is required, access to storytelling is not restricted by economic class. In the restricted circumstances of slavery and oppression, storytelling can serve as a site of resistance and survival. James Scott (1990) describes how, in the United States, slaves used storytelling to encode instructions for escape to the North. Stories apparently innocuous to those in power can encode a subversive intent and relay different means to different persons within the same audience. This is not due only to story's accessibility but also its form. "Thus, it is the particularity and elasticity of oral culture that allows it to carry fugitive meaning in comparative safety" (162). Storytelling as the spoken narrative of life experiences has given a voice of resistance to whole groups otherwise excluded from the "authoritative" discourse of First World journalism, academia, and literature (Gugelberger and Kearney 1991; Randall 1991).

Except in these kinds of cases, storytelling is a process that is profoundly inclusive. Therefore it is a useful resource for intervening in conflicts and social life in ways that are sensitive to the issues of power raised in this section. As an intervention strategy, unless used in a top-down approach, stories usually reflect mutuality in the relationship between the teller and listener. While storytelling can be an intentional teaching strategy, stories are not didactic. They leave open the possibility of multiple interpretations. Through stories, it is possible to make a point while allowing the listener to save face. And stories are grounded in grassroots knowledge systems.

Building Community and Building Peace through Storytelling

It is a central tenet of the storytelling revival in the United States that storytelling builds community (McKenna 1997a; McKenna and Cowan 1997). Story is a means through which culture is constructed. Because intercommunal conflicts are encoded in culture, stories can be a means of intensifying or perpetuating the conflict (Senehi 1996). Or, stories can act as an avenue for social change and growth. Historical narratives, folktales, proverbs, jokes, songs, and life stories embody and transmit cultural identity and values. They represent a body of shared understandings to which persons are intellectually and emotionally committed. However, because they are accessible, flexible, and used contextually, stories and other popular expressive genres can be a means of reformulating cultural notions in order to comment critically and persuasively on community life.

In this section, I focus on some ways that storytelling builds community: by serving as a means for the social construction of identity, knowledge, memory, and emotion. All of these processes involve the negotiation of power relations within and among community groups. These processes are multiple and complex. My goal is not to pigeonhole the broad conceptions of storytelling or community-building. But I want to argue how these processes are related to intercommunal conflicts and the promotion of peace within and between communities. By peace, I do not necessarily mean the absence of conflict, but rather movement for inclusive participation in the making of society—that is, empowerment, democratization, and "positive peace" (Curle 1971). Ultimately, peace involves power relations characterized by shared power (Schwerin 1995).

While the process of storytelling is readily amenable to a cooperative paradigm, I do not believe that storytelling is peaceful in itself. Culture itself may be characterized as more or less violent. Such cultural violence both causes and is caused by structural inequality and its tragic effects or "structural violence" (Galtung 1990). Like any medium or tool, the effect of storytelling depends on how it is used. As Louis Kriesberg (1998) makes a distinction between destructive and constructive conflicts, I seek to identify in what ways storytelling can be constructive and a process of peace-building.

Identity

Storytelling is a process through which social identities are constructed. To say that community identity is socially constructed is not to suggest that identity is artificial and without inherent meaning or value. Collectivities may be seen to be legitimate, vital, and of inherent worth because they express the shared experience, values, and vision of a community (e.g., Williams 1982; Gurr 1993). A community is not a unitary subject and identity groups emerge and fade away, but group members are aware that they belong to a community conceived of as an entity moving through time.

In the case of long-standing intercommunal conflict, understandings of intergroup relations may be encoded in identity (Northrup 1989). Because stories encode group identity, stories can be a means through which intercommunal conflicts are perpetuated (Senehi 1996). A community's folk stories can encode highly negative images of the enemy (Volkan 1988, 1996). When there is social inequality among groups in a society, disempowered groups may not have access to dominant, powerful social institutions, and in this way their identity with the wider community is made invisible or threatened with erasure.

Storytelling can be a means of resistance and change to these dynamics. For groups threatened with cultural oppression or even erasure, storytelling and popular expressive traditions are a means through which the culture is kept alive and through which groups celebrate their survival and dignity. During decades of apartheid in South Africa, Xhosa oral historians and storytellers articulated various social and political arguments for the Xhosa people in order to inspire them to persist in their resistance to the state (Scheub 1995).

The construction of identities is intertextual and dominant discourses can be re-appropriated and used in new ways. While Bolivia's indigenous people are disenfranchised within the state, their culture and folklore is drawn on by the Bolivian state as a model of Bolivian identity. For example, migrant workers, recognizing the importance of a local festival, leveraged this cultural resource to strengthen community pride and assert their legitimacy within the nation (Goldstein 1998).

Workshops and long-standing dialogue groups involve intercommunity conversation and telling personal stories help individuals and communities identify common ground and their shared investment in problem-solving (e.g., Schwartz 1989; Rothman 1992; Kelman 1995). In an analysis of contemporary poetry and storytelling performance in Burundi, Rose Kadende-Kaiser and Paul Kaiser (1997) argue that this cultural practice could provide a means for developing a shared culture "as a necessary first step" in ending and recovering from the cycles of severe intergroup violence there.

Identity conflict does not have to be zero-sum; it is possible to expand the identity pie (Byrne 1997). Intercommunal peace-building involves meeting identity needs (Galtung 1990) and the need for recognition (Honneth 1996). Identity groups are recognized, valued, and share equal rights.

Knowledge and Cultural Memory

Language is society's most complex symbolic system. Language, narrative, and stories encode ways of seeing the world that facilitate shared understandings of experience and personal competency in social life. They form naturalized truths for a particular cultural community (Narayan 1989). Collectivities articulate a history, shared values, and a shared vision of the future through a group narrative.

Power and knowledge are inextricable. Dominant ideology that is produced by the powerful technologies of the mass media, the education system, and the high arts may make social inequalities appear natural. In this way social conflicts can be rendered less visible, and people may participate in the oppression of others and even in their own oppression in ways of which they are unaware. When a collective historical trauma or experience of violence is unacknowledged, this can be an obstacle to the traumatized group's healing and intergroup rapprochement. To dismiss or deny the knowledge and experience of a particular community is a form of silencing.

Historical narratives and stories do not mimic real events but rather impose an interpretation onto the world of real events (White 1981). These interpretations often, if not always, serve to justify the political structure in power, to mask inequality and past sins, and even foment hatred. Johan Galtung (1997) goes so far as to say that memories of past humiliations and past glories underlie paranoia and megalomania that characterize "pathological cosmologies" of whole civilizations. The danger of narrative is that it can generate sympathies with portrayals that demonize a certain group or misrepresent history. Present events from the point of view of an omniscient and unseen narrator, storytelling may disguise the fact that the story is constructed by a person who inevitably has a perspective and agenda. Narrative makes ideology appear natural.

But ideology is not dangerous in itself. A view of things drives all discourse and action. And dominant narratives are sometimes rejected or re-crafted. Storytelling and popular expressive traditions are a means by which people at the margins of the center of power appropriate language and articulate their knowledge.

For African Americans in the New World, efforts to maintain their culture were influenced "by everyday concrete realities which facilitated their clinging tenaciously to a value system both recognizable to them and alternative to that opposed to them" (Roberts 1989, 14). During the eighteenth and early nineteenth centuries when slaves were not allowed to learn to read and write, oral history was an important means of transmitting knowledge of their experience. Stories encoded important knowledge about survival.

Smadar Lavie (1990, 318) describes how stories among the South Sinai Bedouin focus on the strangeness of real life events: "Mzeina allegories, like all allegories, have a dialectical nature. They elevate, yet devalue, the immoral profane world of global politics by memorializing ordinary events as grotesque didactic tales emphasizing indigenous ethics and morality." For example, an Israeli minister lands a helicopter in search of a puppy. "He requests it not from the tribal dignitaries but from a crumpled little old woman, who cleverly takes advantage of this fortuitous event to bargain for some urgently needed water storage barrels for her community" (Lavie 1990, 316). Throughout the world and throughout history, groups in subordinate and vulnerable positions retell anecdotes where they are able to outsmart dominant figures at their own game. In sharing these tales, the group names an indignity and then recovers from it the only way it can, through wit.

Testimonial narrative, the recording of orally expressed live stories, can provide a voice for oppressed people's truth and, for Latin America, a discourse of resistance to the hegemonic discourse of the First World (Gugelberger and Kearney 1991). By recording oral life histories—a "practice of listening and telling"—some journalists and scholars are retrieving and recording a collective memory and identity as experienced by communities of women or in the Third World, previously misrepresented by U.S. mainstream media (Randall 1991, 105). Oral narrative has been a means of rediscovering and understanding the lives and viewpoints of African American women, usually absent in history and literature (Etter-Lewis 1991). The form of oral histories as narratives also get at the complexity of life experience that is difficult to articulate by means of the linear and dualistic reasoning of traditional scholarship.

People with common adversity can empower themselves by sharing their stories. Through small consciousness-raising groups, women (mostly middle-class white women) recognized that their experiences were not idiosyncratic but were shared by others. This led to a recognition of social forces that might be shaping these experience. Women saw themselves as connected in a common struggle and were able to mobilize for political and social change. The personal story became a group story.

Groups sharing a particular difficult experience may literally build a community base, power base, and knowledge base through sharing their stories (Plummer 1995). Community building in this sense is a means of empowering individuals and groups to address problems that previously were latent. Through the shared experiences expressed in stories, the group identity is created and the group knowledge is articulated. Individual experience becomes elevated to a group's shared experience, and in this sense means more than itself. This occurs in a social space where members' voices are dominant (that is, no longer silenced) and where they are free to analyze their social situation. As the narrative evolves from personal stories to a group story, the narrative gains potency. The personal becomes political. The new group narrative becomes a new framework for thought and blueprint for action.

Personal storytelling in a community context can also be a means of recovering knowledge about and healing from past intercommunal violence. In her research on a group of elderly Jews who lived together in a housing center and who had emigrated to the United States from Eastern Europe, Barbara Myerhoff argued that through a process of storytelling—telling stories from their life—the group accomplished their urgent mission to unload a "precious, unique cargo," which was "a set of memories of a culture and society extinquished during the Holocaust" (1992, 235). In the face of invisibility, impotence, and death, telling one's life story in a community context is a search for meaning: "Such remembered lives are moral documents and their function is salvific, inevitably implying 'All this has not been for nothing'" (240).

In South Africa, from April 1996 through July 1998, the hearings of the Truth and Reconciliation Commission (TRC) were a process of developing cultural knowledge in the aftermath of political and intercommunal violence. This process involved personal reports and related activities including theater. While the hearings were attended mostly by black South Africans, they were aired on national TV. Survivors were able to include their experience as part of the public record; Twenty-one thousand statements were recorded. The TRC received seven thousand applications for amnesty. They rejected forty-five hundred and granted 125. The material bases of the conflict were not ignored by the TRC, which resolved that big business will pay taxes to offset past poverty though a one-time levy of one percent of their capital.

Foucault (1972) forcefully argued that power precedes knowledge. What is important for peacebuilding is for all to have democratic access to this process. This may result in changes in how groups think about themselves, each other, and the world.

Emotion

Stories connect the mind and heart. Stories and cultural rituals such as community parades experienced from childhood may be connected with intense bonds of love that the child has for her or his caregiver(s) during the time of life when she or he is most helpless (Wadley 1994). Such storytelling is a process of political socialization and teaches about identity, power, and intergroup relations. Stories and rituals associated with identity and childhood bonds may provide existential meaning that could prove terrifying to question.

In cases of past intercommunal violence, cultural stories could be associated with painful memories of past loss and with fear of the future. Because of their emotional power, stories can be inflammatory. When political debates about present needs become associated with symbols of national identity, they become harder to challenge (Horowitz 1986). In times of fear and confusion due to social upheaval such as that fulminating in Yugoslavia beginning with the death Marhsall Tito in 1989, memories and fears of past intercommunal conflicts can be exploited (Volkan 1996).

But stories' ability to touch the heart may also make them a powerful tool for social change (Henderson 1996). Stories can exert moral pressure. Gandhi argued that to encourage personal transformation in others, reason alone is not the answer. "Nobody probably has drawn up more petitions or espoused more forlorn causes than I, and I have come to this fundamental conclusion that if you want something really important to be done you must not merely satisfy the reason, you must move the heart also" (cited in Barash 1991, 560).

Personal storytelling can put a human face on a problem. The process of listening to a story is one of identification. The listener stands in the teller's shoes.

Storytelling can be a means of retaining dignity and comfort for oppressed communities. No matter what the economic circumstances and even during severe oppression, groups can come together and enjoy storytelling and singing. This affirms the identity and dignity of the group. It brings relief and joy. Storytelling can also be a means of healing in the aftermath of intercommunal violence. Helen Bamber, who beginning in 1945 worked with victims of torture from all over the world for more than fifty years, describes torture victims' need to tell their stories in complete detail over and over again, to "vomit" out the stories of their appalling experiences (Belton 1999). In a Tanzanian camp for Rwandan refugees where refugees were told not to discuss their experiences, women cured their insomnia by telling the stories of the atrocities they had experienced to a "story tree" (Anderson and Foley 1998).

Storytelling connects people in ways that bring individuals and groups affirmation and pleasure. U.S. Storyteller Bill Harley states that even more profound than stories' role in education or protest, is the joy experienced in the storytelling interaction. In 1996, at the Jonesborough Storytelling Festival in Tennessee, storyteller Kathryn Windham characterized the sharing that occurs during storytelling as "love."

Intercommunal conflict thrives on and engenders feelings of shame, anger, fear, and profound despair. Peace building involves a healing from past intercommunal violence. Peace building is a movement toward respect, trust, and joy.

Storytellers

In the United States, since the early 1970s, there has been a self-conscious storytelling renaissance. Storytellers tell stories in a wide variety of public settings: educational settings, arts venues, business contexts, therapeutic settings, hospitals, prisons, places of worship, parks, and housing developments. Every year in the United States, there are more than a hundred storytelling festivals.

Unlike most other performance artists, such as actors and classical musicians, storytellers are far freer to choose material that is meaningful to them. Many storytellers have developed unique projects. In St. Louis, January Kiefer and Blake Travis have developed story-based workshops that address race relations. Minnesota farmer Michael Cotter traveled to New Jersey to help twenty-two AIDS patients tell their personal stories, which were recorded and edited for a video documentary. In 1994, Gladdys and Truman Coggswell, who participate in the St. Louis storytelling festival, established an annual storytelling festival in northern Missouri emphasizing African American traditions. The Liz Lerman Dance Exchange works with communities to interpret their histories through dance and story. Retired engineer Mel Hatcher leads storytelling programs for children in inner-city Detroit Schools.

In 1992, Ellen Munds established Stories, Inc., a not-for-profit organization in Indianapolis to provide a variety of storytelling events for the city—the first and only organization of its kind. Her goal is for Stories, Inc., to be thought of in the same way as the local theater company, museum, and orchestra. Munds is also introducing storytelling programs with explicit social goals, for example, community-building and healing.

In this chapter, I have sought a theoretical rationale for why storytelling is relevant to intercommunal conflicts and their resolution in order to bring attention to the importance of the work of contemporary storytellers. Throughout the U.S. and the world, storytellers use stories in intentional ways to promote desired personal and social change. Their projects may provide important models for ways in which intercommunal relationships can be improved from the grassroots level.

Conclusion

Stories operate in the world and get results. Stories shape our understandings of the past, tell us who we are, and provide a vision of the future. Because they define our communities, they provide a rationale for collective action. Stories have "narrative potency" (Raheja and Gold 1994). Peace building may require voicing or re-imagining our stories.

However, our stories, voices, imagination, and power are constrained. Stories operate within a context of ideological, economic, and power constraints. Peace building requires facilitating social spaces where people can voice their experience, develop shared understandings, and build trusting relationships. Throughout history, storytellers have served as community leaders, memory-keepers, cross-cultural ambassadors, consciousness-raisers, and mediators (e.g., Hale 1998). In contemporary contexts throughout the United States and the world, people who embrace the label of storyteller are using stories in numerous creative ways toward goals of promoting personal and social change. We must seek to recognize, amplify, encourage, and facilitate their efforts to promote cross-cultural understanding and build peaceful communities.

Suggested Study Questions

1. Why is storytelling an important facet of grassroots peace building?
2. How can storytelling be a means for enhancing participatory democracy?
3. How can storytelling be a potent means of transformation that gets results in society?
4. Is it possible to use storytelling to remember and affirm past tragedies and achievements across divides without perpetuating a sense of victimization or triumphalism that exacerbates conflict? If so, how?
5. What kinds of storytelling programs can you envision that could promote cross-cultural relations?

6. How can we develop theoretical ideas about the relationship between storytelling and conflict resolution?

References

Anderson, Herbert and Edward Foley. 1998. *Mighty Stories, Dangerous Rituals: Weaving Together the Human and the Divine.* San Francisco: Jossey-Bass.

Assad, Talal, ed. 1973. *Anthropology and the Colonial Encounter.* Atlantic Highlands, N.J.: Humanities Press.

Barash, David P. 1991. *Introduction to Peace Studies.* Belmont, Calif.: Wadsworth.

Bauman, Richard and Charles L. Briggs. 1990. "Poetics and Performance as Critical Perspectives on Language and Social Life." *Annual Review of Anthropology* 19: 59–88.

Belton, Neil. 1999. *The Good Listener: Helen Bamber, A Life against Cruelty.* New York: Pantheon.

Byrne, Sean. 1997. *Growing Up in a Divided Society: The Influence of Conflict on Belfast Schoolchildren.* Cranbury, N.J.: Associated University Presses.

Byrne, Sean and Neal Carter. 1996. "Social Cubism: Six Social Forces of Ethno-territorial Conflict in Northern Ireland and Quebec." *Journal of Peace and Conflict Studies* 3(2): 52–71.

Clifford, James. 1986. "Introduction: Partial Truths." In James Clifford and George E. Marcus, eds. *Writing Culture: The Poetics and Politics of Ethnography,* 1–26.

Curle, Adam. 1971. *Making Peace.* London: Tavistock.

Etter-Lewis, Gwendolyn. 1991. "Black Women's Life Stories: Reclaiming Self in Narrative Texts." In Sherna Berger Gluck and Daphne Patai, eds. *Women's Words: The Feminist Practice of Oral History.* New York and London: Routledge.

Freire, Paulo. [1970] 1993. *Pedagogy of the Oppressed.* New York: Continuum.

Foucault, Michel. 1972. *The Archaeology of Knowledge and the Discourse on Language.* New York: Pantheon.

Galtung, Johan. 1997. "Is There a Therapy for Pathological Cosmologies?" In Jennifer Turpin and Lester R. Kurtz, eds. *The Web of Violence: From Interpersonal to Global.* Urbana: University of Illinois Press, 187–206.

Galtung, Johan. 1990. "Cultural Violence." *Journal of Peace Research* 27(3): 291–305.

Goldstein, Daniel. 1998. "Performing National Culture in a Bolivian Migrant Community." *Ethnology* 37(2): 117–32.

Gugelberger, G. and M. Kearney. 1991. "Voices for the Voiceless: Testimonial Literature in Latin America." *Latin American Perspectives* 18: 3–14.

Gurr, Ted Robert. 1993. *Minorities at Risk: A Global View of Ethnopolitical Conflicts.* Washington, D.C.: United States Institute of Peace Press.

Hale, Thomas A. 1998. *Griots and Griottes: Masters of Words and Music.* Bloomington: Indiana University Press.

Harding, Sandra, ed. 1987. *Feminism and Methodology.* Bloomington: Indiana University Press.

Henderson, Michael. 1996. *The Forgiveness Factor: Stories of Hope in a World of Conflict.* London: Grosvenor.

Honneth, Axel. 1996. *The Struggle for Recognition: The Moral Grammar of Social Conflict.*, Joel Anderson, trans. Cambridge, Mass.: MIT Press.

Horowitz, Donald. 1985. *Ethnic Groups in Conflict.* Berkeley: University of California Press.

Kadende-Kaiser, Rose M. and Paul Kaiser. 1997. "Modern Folklore, Identity, and Political Change in Burundi." *African Studies Review* 40(3): 29–54.

Kelman, Herbert. 1995. "Informal Mediation by the Scholar/Practitioner." In Jacob Bercovitch and Jeffrey Z. Rubin, eds. *Mediation in International Relations.* New York: St. Martin's Press, 65–96.

Kriesberg, Louis. 1998. *Constructive Conflicts: From Escalation to Resolution.* Lanham, Md.: Rowman and Littlefield.

Kriesberg, Louis. 1997. "The Development of the Conflict Resolution Field." In I. William Zartman and J. Lewis Rasmussen, eds. *Peacemaking in International Conflict: Methods and Techniques.* Washington, D.C.: United States Institute of Peace, 51–80.

Kriesberg, Louis. 1991. "Formal and Quasi-Mediators in International Disputes: An Exploratory Analysis." *Journal of Peace Research* 28(1): 19–28.

Lane, Belden. 1996. Personal communication, May 8.

Lederach, John Paul. 1997. *Building Peace: Sustainable Reconciliation in Divided Societies.* Washington, D.C.: United States Institute of Peace.

Lavie, Smadar. 1990. *The Poetics of Military Occupation: Mzeina Allegories of Bedouin Identity under Israeli and Egyptian Rule.* Berkeley: University of California Press.

Lederach, John Paul. 1996. *Preparing for Peace: Conflict Transformation across Cultures.* Syracuse, N.Y.: Syracuse University Press.

McCabe, Allyssa and Carole Peterson, eds., 1991. *Developing Narrative Structure.* Hillsdale, N.J.: Lawrence Erlbaum.

Liebow, Elliot. 1967. *Tally's Corner: A Study of Negro Streetcorner Men.* Boston: Little, Brown.

McKenna, Megan. 1997a. Personal communication, December 10.

McKenna, Megan. 1997b. *Rites of Justice.* Maryknoll, N.Y.: Orbis.

McKenna, Megan and Tony Cowan. 1997. *Keepers of the Story: The Sacraments and Liturgy as Ethical Imperatives.* Maryknoll, N.Y.: Orbis.

Myerhoff, Barbara. 1992. *Remembered Lives: The World of Ritual, Storytelling, and Growing Older.* Ann Arbor: University of Michigan Press.

Narayan, Kirin. 1989. *Storytellers, Saints, and Scoundrels: Folk Narrative in Hindu Religious Teaching.* Philadelphia: University of Pennsylvania Press.

Northrup, Terrell A. 1989. "The Dynamic of Identity in Personal and Social Conflict." In Louis Kriesberg, Terrell A. Northrup and Stuart J. Thorson, eds. *Intractable Conflicts and Their Transformation.* Syracuse, N.Y.: Syracuse University Press, 55–82.

Plummer, Ken. 1995. *Telling Sexual Stories: Power, Change and Social Worlds.* London: Routledge.

Raheja, Gloria Goodwin and Ann Grodzins Gold. 1994. *Listen to the Heron's Words: Reimagining Gender and Kinship in North India.* Berkeley: University of California Press.

Randall, Margaret. 1991. "Reclaiming Voices: Notes on New Female Practices in Journalism." *Latin American Perspectives* 18: 103–113.

Rasmussen, J. Lewis. 1997. "Peacemaking in the Twenty-First Century: New Rules, New Roles, New Actors." In I. William Zartman and J. Lewis Rasmussen, eds. *Peacemaking in International Conflict: Methods and Techniques: Methods and Techniques.* Washington, D.C.: United States Institute of Peace, 23–50.

Roberts, John W. 1989. *From Trickster to Badman: The Black Folk Hero in Slavery and Freedom.* Philadelphia: University of Pennsylvania Press.

Rogers, Carl R. 1942. *Counseling and Psychotherapy.* Boston: Houghton Mifflin.

Rothman, Jay. 1997. *Resolving Identity-based Conflicts in Nations, Organizations, and Communities.* San Francisco: Jossey-Bass.

Rothman, Jay. 1992. *From Confrontation to Cooperation: Resolving Ethnic and Regional Conflict.* Newbury Park, Calif.; London; New Delhi: Sage Publications.

Ryan, Pat. 1995. *Storytelling in Ireland: A Re-awakening.* Londonderry, Northern Ireland: The Verbal Arts Center.

Schwerin, Edward W. 1995. *Mediation, Citizen Empowerment, and Transformation Politics.* Westport, Conn.: Praeger.

Scheub, Harold. 1996. *The Tongue Is Fire: South African Storytellers and Apartheid.* Madison: University of Wisconsin Press.

Schwartz, Richard D. 1989. "Arab-Jewish Dialogue in the United States." In Louis Kriesberg, Terrell A. Northrup and Stuart J. Thorson, eds., *Intractable Conflicts and Their Transformation.* Syracuse, N.Y.: Syracuse University Press, 180–209.

Scott, James C. 1998. *Seeing Like a State: How Certain Schemes to Improve the Human Condition Have Failed.* New Haven, Conn.: Yale University Press.

Scott, James C. 1990. *Domination and the Arts of Resistance.* New Haven, Conn.: Yale University Press.

Senehi, Jessica. 1996. "Storytelling and Conflict—A Matter of Life and Death." *Mind and Human Interaction* 7(3): 150–64.

Solinger, Rickie. 1992. *Wake Up Little Susie: Single Pregnancy and Race before Roe v. Wade.* New York: Routledge.

Volkan, Vamik. 1996. "Bosnia-Herzegovina: Ancient Fuel of a Modern Inferno." *Mind and Human Interaction* 7(3): 110–27.

Volkan, Vamik. 1988. *The Need to Have Enemies and Allies: From Clinical Practice to International Relationships.* New York: Jason Aronson.

Wadley, Susan Snow. 1995. Personal communication, May 22.

White, Hayden. 1981. "The Value of Narrativity." In W. J. T. Mitchell, ed. *On Narrative.*

Chicago: University of Chicago Press, 1– 23.

Williams, Colin, ed. 1982. *National Separatism.* Vancouver: University of British Columbia.

Wiseman, Jacqueline P. 1979. *Stations of the Lost: The Treatment of Skid Row Alcoholics.* Chicago: University of Chicago Press.

Woolpert, Stephen, Christa Daryl Slaton and Edward W. Schwerin, eds. 1988. *Transformational Politics: Theory, Study, and Practice.* Albany: State University of New York.

7

Peace Building in Identity Driven Ethnopolitical Conflicts

Ho-Won Jeong

Introduction

THE GROWTH OF NATIONALISTIC manifestations stems from an awareness of distinctive national identities and a perception of the incompatibility of interests. Recent ethnic struggles between Tutsi and Hutu in Rwanda and Burundi, between Serbs, Croats, and Muslims in the former Yugoslavia, and between Catholics and Protestants in Northern Ireland can be characterized by identity driven conflicts. The issues of peace building in divided societies have to deal with such questions as how social values can be negotiated in a large social framework.

Understanding identity needs to be juxtaposed in a late modern condition in which universal subject positions do not exist any longer. Instrumental solutions to ethnopolitical conflict does not provide strategies for how social relations can be transformed in identity politics. After critically assessing neoliberal approaches to peace building in divided societies, this chapter conceptualizes late modern conditions of ethnic conflict, illustrates identity politics at the margins, and explains the political economy of identity reconstruction.

The Management of Ethnopolitical Conflict

Ethnic groups can remain passive and unmobilized for a long period of time. Owing to the combined phenomena of rising expectations and relative deprivation, a sense of entitlement rises faster than is fulfilled for ethnic groups. The presence of grievances leads to the mobilization of resources for collective action. Mobilization by one community may activate responsive countermobilization by others. Other ethnic groups which demand cultural rights and autonomy status can be seen as a threat to the expectations or interests of the other community.

Various types of structural and procedural arrangements can be made to control ethnic conflict. If interethnic conflict is attributed to a rational pursuit of organized group interests, parties are helped to recognize shared interests in survival and long-term prosperity. Defining an ethnic agenda may be articulated in the way changes would be made within the existing system. Peaceful coexistence can be achieved by negotiation, accommodation, and compromise resulting from hard bargaining through political processes that may not eliminate conflict, but prevent the competition from erupting into destructive violence.

In many ethnic conflicts, situations are more complicated to be resolved in a rational manner. The commitment to a nation can be mutually incompatible with loyalty to the state. The self-assertion of ethnic groups has been made in various forms, ranging from the demand for cultural autonomy (the practice of ethnic religion, and the education of ethnic languages and history) to political organization and struggle for an independent political status. Some national groups that lack sovereign territory fight to create a new state.

Ethnic boundaries do rarely coincide with the territorial frontiers of a state. The case of a single state inhabited by one nation is quite exceptional. State boundaries were often fixed by artificial political changes which are associated with the efforts to satisfy dominant political interests. The frontiers of many Eastern European states were imposed by the post World War I and II settlements. The postcolonial independence of many African and Asian states led to the mix of many ethnic groups which, in some cases, have been traditional rivalries. Thus, many states are comprised of diverse national groups. In other cases, one national group is scattered among several states, as exemplified by Kurds and Tutsis.

Different patterns are observed in managing ethnopolitical conflicts. Genocidal measures were taken against Ibos in Nigeria, Southern blacks in Sudan, Kurds in Turkey, Iraq, and Iran, Tibetans in China, Timorese in Indonesia, and Crimean Tatars and Chechyen-Ingush during the Stalinist period of the Soviet Union. Many post-colonial states attempted to coercively integrate a polyethnic society into a territorial nation state system. Ethnocide is the outcome of the coercive attempt for national integration.

In Israel, a sizable Arab minority is absorbed into a state dominant identity. On the other hand, significant levels of cultural and political autonomy have been granted to diverse ethnic groups in Switzerland, Belgium, Luxembourg, and other small Western industrialized countries. Other countries such as Canada and the former Soviet Union adopted a federation of national republics to satisfy the demand for autonomy.

Peace Building in a Neoliberal Political Model

Most debate on structural arrangements for peace building focused on the formation of a new civil society. Political development is associated with the growth of a more powerful central government which is able to reshape ethnic loyalties, individual identity, and group structures. National commonalities are emphasized at the expense of subnational identities. Social, psychological, political, and economic relations need to be changed in the efforts of national capacity building.

The establishment of modern, bureaucratic, centralized states embodies the territorial concept of nationality. The creation of modern nations has often been assisted by the process of state building. New institutions, laws, social programs, and economic policies of the state are designed to create an alternative locus of belongings and a new center for loyalty. New material conditions are based on the mobilization of goods and people at a national scale. Ethnic conflict can be managed by expanding economic resources and the recognition of civil rights into a pluralistic political system.

In a neoliberal model of peace building, the state is a logical form for resolving ethnic conflict. Civic nationalism is adapted to promote such universal principles as individual civil liberty and rights to a property ownership. Ethnic differences can be managed in a functionally sophisticated division of labor. The destructive potential of ethnic diversity has to be controlled by setting up the rules of the game.

Civic identities coincide with societal structures in which rewards are given according to universal and objective criteria of individual achievement and performance. New civic identities are organized on the basis of high degrees of specialization and role differentiation. Social mobilization creates conditions for individual identification along professional lines and status.

Institutional and legal frameworks of modern states are reinforced by industrialization, economic, social, and political mobilization. A modern political process exerts a strong centripetal pull. Ethnic groups are integrated into a large national society by the state. Social differentiation shifts an individual status away from the smaller, ascriptive communities to larger, functionally oriented societies centered around personal merits and performance.

Civic identity is protected in a unified legal code of common rights and duties. Rights and status in a modern state derive from citizenship. These civic identities and universalistic norms are embedded in laws, state institutions, mass cultural bases, and communication networks. Separate nationalities can be allowed to coexist with a single citizenship. The delegitimation of discrimination is critical in accommodating the demands of those with a minority status.

The reconstruction of state institutions is designed to promote a single political culture through public mass education and socialization. If individuals are related to a state, ethnic differences are integrated into a civic identity. The needs and aspirations of individuals would replace ethnic values. The process of new identity formation is associated with the creation of a national political center.

Democracy is seen as a means to promote civic identity which offers an alternative to ethnic identification. The behavior of groups is controlled by incentives and sanctions from both state institutions and international donors. Concessions can be made in response to desires for greater local autonomy. Some functions can be decentralized, and a certain level of cultural pluralism encouraged as long as they do not threaten national identity.

In case religious and cultural divisions are deep, polyethnic claims can be legitimized and incorporated into a consociational model of state building. National doctrines may be made compatible with cultural pluralism and ethnic grievances can be managed by the equitable sharing of power and wealth. Thus, problems with dominant relations in ethnically heterogenous societies can be addressed within the existing framework of multinational states. Switzerland maintained political unity with a clear sense of historical destiny despite linguistic, religious, and economic divisions.

Dual identities can be comprised of a territorial state identity and a cultural identity. The political sentiment contained in national identity would not be undermined by a lack of cultural homogenization. The aspirations for separate ethnopolitical identity are controlled through a universalistic system of reward and guarantee of equal civil rights. Thus, in the creation of a national identity, ethnic identity is recognized only as a linguistic or ethno-regional category.

Regional autonomy can be maintained through such procedures as proportionality or minority guarantees. Consensual adjustment is essential in the normal and ongoing pursuit of group interests. In consociational democracy, power-sharing schemes complement intragroup dynamics as well as the patterns of group relationships. Conflict between ethnic groups can be made diffuse by internal politics within each ethnic group which is fragmented along class, ideological, and other lines.

However, a modern state is based on a fragile construction of civic identity never to be acquired, especially in antagonistic material conditions. Identities built around the state, as observed in the recent crisis of Indonesia, can be destabilized or unraveled by economic recession and the intervention of external market forces. Stable alliances for power sharing are weakened, as economic decline undermines a hegemonic state form. Collective state identities do not permanently curb ethnic cultural values and promote a sense of security and stability.

Stability in ethnic relations would not be offered by the rules of games in democracy unless there is a significant level of consensus on both political and cultural foundations of the state. The constitution of collective identities is based on the assumption that clearly differentiated positions can be compromised (Mouffe 1994, 109). This is not an easy task when multicultural issues need to be confronted with particularism in the resurgence of exclusive ethnic identity. The reconstruction of identities has to consider the political as a domain of power struggles and competition for social hegemony. This is not captured in the liberal, rationalistic, and individual conceptions of democracy (Mouffe 1944, 107).

Ethnic Politics in Late Modern Conditions

Inherent contradictions exist in a neoliberal model of peace building in divided societies. Its unproven utility directly derives from historical assumptions behind the political and ideological victory of a Western pluralistic political system over a socialist one. The nature of peace building in the periphery is interpreted in terms of the need to maintain stability and predictability in a hegemonic and neoliberal political economic order. However, it ignores late modern social conditions which can be characterized by alienation and marginalization in a changing cultural matrix of globality.

Ethnic relations are reflected in the reproduction of material and symbolic forms of life. Cultural marginality is an essential feature in ethnopolitics. "In many societies, the state is an instrument of domination by privileged ethnic groups who engage in a form of cultural despotism" (Laclau 1996, 35). Popular mobilization is based on the movements of subjugated people against dominant ethnic groups and ruling elites of alien states. The protest is directed against the existing distribution of power within the polyethnic state, and its systematic exclusion of certain ethnic categories.

Multiethnic polities have been a norm across time and places. In the prevailing expectations of modernization, ethnic identities are gradually eroded as individuals are incorporated into a common, secular culture rather than depending on traditional social structures. National economic integration in a free market economic order is associated with the universal and timeless culture of globalization. However, modern societies are often psychologically inhospitable and unsatisfactory. Ethnic time and place of origin in a cognitive map provide a means for new interpretations of identities and self-assertion.

The invention of national identities has not transformed those foci of identification which states failed to eradicate. Political and economic integration is not always successful in penetrating into regions with low levels of social mobilization. Central institutions insulate rather than integrate peripheral cultures. Ethnicity is no longer supposed to demarcate people in the public sphere but only in private aspects of their lives. However, universalistic criteria of inclusion for citizens are quite often not applied to those who are aliens.

Thus, the instability of post-colonial states has promoted a heightened sense of ethnic identity. Conflicts of marginalized groups with states and other communities have resulted from a wider self-awareness and a sense of social and economic status. Despite integrative forces, ethnic attachments and traditional social structures have not completely been wiped out in the peripheries due to inefficient and ineffective state mechanisms.

In the state hegemonic system, an ethnic hierarchy is anchored in the forms of a cultural division of labor. The encroachment by the center precipitates conditions for center-locality conflicts in which the issues of language, education, and religion are the basis for ethnic mobilization. National insurrection by those who seek to become a sovereign entity is sparked by cultural thrust of separate identities. Ethnic sentiments can be mobilized in the discursive practice of everyday life. In postnationalist politics, cultural conceptions of ethnicity take place through a mutual labeling process between the subject and others.

A postmodern cosmopolitan culture carried out by mass media and telecommunications does not fill the void in ethnic group identification. Whereas the global cultural forms are indifferent to place or time, the new cosmopolitanism is inherently eclectic and in motion with its shape constantly changing. This process does not lead to the formation of a coherent self. The meanings of a particularistic identity are made more salient in a local space. Every human being is enmeshed in cultural conventions. The search for a stable identity requires a new vantage point of reference. Ethnopolitical identity still plays an important role in maintaining group unity and cohesion as opposed to postmodern and universalistic cultural forms.

In late modern conditions, ethnic politics can be characterized, therefore, by the assertion on the part of "others" protesting their subordination or exclusion by the state. During the crisis the central sphere especially is not open to everyone through civil roles and functions. The goal of cultural politics for the marginalized is that emancipation must be achieved by liberation from the domination hidden in the state's universalistic norms.

Consequently, violent ethnic identification derives from the failure of fully constituting any identity. Violence is generated by the modern contents of identity which are subject to contestation and antagonism. In violent practice, the identities of others can be perceived to be a threat to the survival of the self.

Political Economy of Identity Reconstruction

Ethnic boundaries are maintained and reinforced by a collective sense of selfhood in the identity poles of enactment and reception. In a premordialist argument, the possibility for identity reconstruction does not exist since ethnic affiliation and identity are chosen by birth (Barth 1969). People are socialized into their ethnic identity from infancy. The sense of belonging is attached to ascriptive characteristics. Since ethnic identity is not an individual choice, sociocultural incentives, values, and sanctions relevant to shaping individual identity are not rendered salient in group formation.

Ethnicity has also been considered as a self-concept derived from a culturally coherent and insulated environment. Cultural markers serve for internal cohesion as well as differentiation from other groups. Such cultural elements as custom, language, class, gender, territory, language, and race strengthen the internal logic of ethnic ideology which center a collective sense of selfhood (Laclau 1996, 30).

In recent scholarly studies, ethnic identities are treated more often as fluid, socially constructed rather than assumed to be fixed or given (Smith 1996). Identity is established through boundary functions of group formation (Barth 1969). Particular claims for group rights and privileges are inherent in identity politics. Given their contingent and adaptive nature, identities can be reinvented and reconstructed.

Discourse is constitutive of identities. Group boundaries are always renegotiated, especially in situations where identities need to be reconstructed. The functions of a nation-state not only lie in demarcating territorial boundaries but also in maintaining discursive authority. Hegemony is established through the practices and processes which assign meanings to social realities.

The process of locating individuals within social formations takes not only cultural but also material forms. The material world is not completely isolated from symbolic values and expressive signs. Most importantly, "the ethnic function of constructing a collective identity may be dictated by the material conditions in which the ethnicizing function is realized" (Wilmsen 1996, 6).

Ethnic relations are reconfigured by social change associated with a development process. The uneven wave of economic development creates material divisions and deepens cultural differences. Thus, the political and economic positions of the groups cannot be ignored in identity construction. More specifically, "the essence of ethnic existence lies in differential access to means of production and rights to shares in production returns" (Wilmsen 1996, 5).

In the mobilization of ethnic groups in a postcolonial political context, ethnic competition is expressed in material forms as much as in symbolic forms. Ethnic politics reflects mechanisms of power relations and the distribution of economic resources. Ethnic organizations are exposed to an uneven process of economic development, often fueled by increased competition. In that sense, ethnic association and mobilization are affected by the modes of modernization and development. Economic situations influence the forms of ethnic co-operation and competition; economic contraction generates new tensions in existing ethnic relationships.

Postmodern ethnic relations are constructed upon the power of representations which allow the maintenance of boundaries between self and other. Institutional and procedural engineering of ethnic conflict management do not seriously count social, cultural contacts in reducing communal strife. The ability to establish and police boundaries is crucial for a hegemonic order and peace. In order to clearly delineate the boundaries between order and disorder, a state promotes a particular identity and culture. From the viewpoint of the marginalized, ethnic relations can be recreated by the acceptance of or resistance against dominant cultural forms imposed by states.

Identity construction and reconstruction may reflect a dialectical integration of conditions of inequality within an arena of social power and subjective classification on a stage of social practice. Existential and experiential realities may be reified into a sociocultural premise for inequality (Wilmsen 1996, 6). Identity formation is constituted in particular ideologies within the framework of political struggle. In a hegemony model, elites impose their agendas on subordinate groups through the agency of an ideological state apparatus (Lather 1994, 114). Critical narratives illuminate the way power shapes the social world, and any peace process.

Marginal zones are not represented in an institutionalized peace building process. Women, children, and other underprivileged groups do not have the resources to mobilize themselves, nor have they the capacity to raise their voices in an official negotiation process. However, a hopeful sign still remains that there is no margin without capacity to resist a hegemonic power structure. Invisible forms of resistance may take a cultural character. Violence, for example, did not prevent tribal elders and women in Somalia and Liberia from playing an important role in the reconstruction of their communities. Groups in a peripheral position may also use newly constructed ethnic forms as an internal rationale in overcoming marginalization. In a discursive practice, the self does not exist outside a particular discourse. In order to change dominant relations, the assumptions of a universal subject position have to be challenged and deconstructed. Ethnic positions of subordinate groups can be reformulated within a cultural imagination.

The challenge for peace building remains to find a negotiated order in a world of contradictions. The pragmatic solutions have to emerge in the real world where social experiences are heterogeneous and discontinuous. "Unitary meaning is temporary and only held in place by force before it drifts away in a never-ending web of other texts" (Deetz 1994, 194). Consensus does often reflect a hidden order of oppression rather than reveal the emancipatory capacity of the marginalized.

Political agency is situated in a social space of identity reproduction. Autonomy needs to become a principle of her or his existential being—more than an ethical imperative for the individual, but not just a political ideal to be invoked in times of danger or crisis. Opportunities for empowering formerly repressed identities are provided by a receding influence of dominant identity forms. New subject positions can be facilitated by the deterritorialization and dislocation of people in a postnational identity space.

Multiple identities are generated in the period of social transition. The existence of multiple subject positions enables the marginalized to question the foundations of oppressive institutions and practices. The social function of ethnicity is about the maintenance of a group identity which is inscribed by the division between inside and outside. The contingent base of discursive resources is ascribed to the institutional incapacity to generate shared experiences among diverse types of actors in a changing environment. The subject could be claimed as an agent in its struggle against dominant relations. Shared meaning arises out of constitutive practices of the search for identity. Human subjectivity is contextualized in the socially, and historically structured world. Since the subject is not represented by a single signifier, the need to fulfill the true identity would never be satisfied. The constitution of identity for the marginalized takes place on the residue of resistance against a dominant political and economic order. Securitized identities, exclusive to a specific group, derive from the efforts to create an autonomous community.

In a postcolonial discourse, positions of marginality can be used to launch an attempt to subvert a hegemonic state form. Political means of resistance can be found in an informal political process. Multi-party systems, to be created after elections, are less important than cultural autonomy. Culture can be interpreted as energy to motivate the marginalized to search for a new means for empowerment and self-reliance in their local space. The emphasis on local forms of culture and political relations would be helpful in inventing non-hegemonic political entities which would allow peaceful coexistence between diverse ethnic communities.

In conclusion, ethnic identification is formed in relation to the outside world. The subject positions are structured in multiple individual histories of ethnic groups. Ethnic identity is constructed externally as well as internally. One of the most important elements in peace building for fractured societies, therefore, is the creation of a new political process which securitizes new identities without threats to others.

Suggested Study Questions

1. How are civic and ethnic identities constructed?
2. How can ethnic conflict be managed?
3. In what ways is identity politics important in understanding peace building?
4. What are some of the social functions of ethnicity?
5. How do economic conditions influence ethnic relations?

References

Barth, Fredrik. 1969. *Ethnic Groups and Boundaries.* Boston: Little, Brown.

Deetz, Stanley. 1994. "The New Politics of the Workplace: Ideology and Other Unobtrusive Controls." In *After Postmodernism: Reconstructing Ideology Critique.* Herbert W. Simons and Michael Billig, eds. London: Sage Publications, 172–99.

Laclau, Ernesto. 1996. "Universalism, Particularism, and the Question of Identity." In *The Politics of Difference: Ethnic Premises in a World of Power.* Edwin N. Wilmsen and Patrick McAllister, eds. Chicago: The University of Chicago Press, 45–58.

Lather, Patti. 1994. "Staying Dumb? Feminist Research and Pedagogy with/in the Postmodern." In *After Postmodernism: Reconstructing Ideology Critique.* Herbert W. Simons and Michael Billig, eds. London: Sage Publications, 101–132.

Mouffe, Chantal. 1994. "For a Politics of Nomadic Identity." In *Travelers' Tales: Narratives of Home and Displacement.* George Robertson, ed. London: Routledge, 105–113.

Smith, Anthony D. 1996. "Culture, Community and Territory: The Politics of Ethnicity and Nationalism." *International Affairs* 72(3): 445–58.

Wilmsen, Edwin N. 1996. "Introduction: Premises of Power." In *The Politics of Difference: Ethnic Premises in a World of Power.* Edwin N. Wilmsen and Patrick McAllister, eds. Chicago: The University of Chicago Press, 1–24.

Part 3

Strategies and Techniques in Conflict Resolution and Reduction

8

Yugoslavia, What Went Wrong? Constitutional Development and Collapse of a Multiethnic State

Mitja Zagar

Introduction

WHEN WE THINK OF the former Yugoslavia in the 1990s we usually remember the tragic images of the war in Croatia and Bosnia-Herzegovina that were broadcasted throughout the world. The former Yugoslavia and, especially, Bosnia-Herzegovina have become synonyms for ethnic conflicts and war, ethnic cleansing, atrocities, and war crimes. The outbreak of conflict in Kosovo has further confirmed this view and reinforced the traditional perception of the Balkans as the region of political, military, and social instability.

Indeed, it might well be said that the Yugoslav crisis has come full circle. It was often said that the Yugoslav crisis had begun in Kosovo and that it would end there. Developments in Kosovo in 1999 (for example, intensified repression and "ethnic cleansing" of Albanians in Kosovo, armed resistance of Albanians, NATO attacks on the FRY (Former Republic of Yugoslavia), the refugee crisis, international intervention in Kosovo, the return of Albanian refugees to Kosovo, the exodus of Serbs and Roma/Gypsies from Kosovo, etc.) are marking, no doubt, an important turning point in this crisis that might determine its resolution.[1] I do not agree with those who claim that the international intervention in Kosovo (in combination with the Dayton Peace Accords) will end the Yugoslav crisis. It could contribute to the redefinition or end of the FRY, it will increase autonomy (and independence) of Montenegro and Kosovo, and it will weaken the ruling Milosevic regime in Serbia and FRY. Nevertheless, these developments in Kosovo alone are unlikely to remove Milosevic from power. A concerted action of the political opposition in Serbia is required for the successful realization of this goal. Even in this case, one could not exclude the escalation of conflicts and the possibility of a civil war in Serbia, especially considering the strength of Milosevic's police. From the perspective of the region, one could not exclude the possible spillover effect of problems and conflicts in Kosovo and in other countries. No doubt, long-term projects for economic and social development, foreign investments, and the assistance and active role of the international community will be important also for the prevention of the escalation of (ethnic and other) conflicts in Albania, Bosnia-Herzegovina, Macedonia, Montenegro, Sandzak/Sandjak, and Serbia.

It is, then, extremely ironic that until the 1980s the former Yugoslavia was cited as a successful multinational state that had managed to establish good (inter)ethnic relations. Even its citizens did not perceive Yugoslavia as a divided society or a fractured state. It did not match the typical model of a divided society that pictured a bicommunal society characterized by protracted conflicts between two distinct—ethnic, linguistic, religious, etc.—communities. Ethnic relations in Yugoslavia seemed good despite substantial ethnic diversity. Those ethnic conflicts that escalated occasionally in some regions were resolved successfully and in a peaceful way. The federal constitution officially recognized the multinational nature of the federation and proclaimed the principle of equality of all "Yugoslav nations and nationalities." Aware of the permanent danger that nationalism and nationalists represented for this multiethnic country, the ruling Yugoslav regime had long fought nationalism

Nevertheless, the former Yugoslavia collapsed and disintegrated in a tragic war. What went wrong? Why did it happen? Were such developments unexpected? Why did the Yugoslav constitution and political system fail to prevent or resolve ethnic conflicts? Why were the existing Yugoslav regime and the international community unable to prevent the tragic developments? These are a few of the questions frequently asked in this context. This chapter is an attempt to answer some of them and explain what actually happened. It focuses on the constitutional development of Yugoslavia and analyzes the evolution of the constitutional regulation of ethnic relations. This analysis provides the framework for the presentation of some aspects of the Yugoslav crisis in the 1980s and the early 1990s. The concluding section presents some lessons that could be learned from these tragic experiences.

Yugoslavia: Geographic, Political, Historic, and Demographic Context

Located in the southeast of Europe, the former Yugoslavia was considered a Balkan country, although not all its parts belong to the Balkan peninsula geographically.[2] As a communist country it was considered politically a part of Eastern Europe after World War II, although it did not belong to the Soviet bloc. After the break with Stalin and the Soviet Union in 1948, Yugoslavia developed a nonaligned foreign policy. It was one of the founding members and leading countries of the nonaligned movement established in Belgrade (Yugoslavia) in 1961. The nonaligned movement attracted several Third World countries advocating a "third way" characterized by the equidistance from the Eastern and Western military and political blocks. Because of its nonaligned foreign policy, Yugoslavia was often viewed as a "grey zone" in between the East and West.

The territory of the former Yugoslavia shared the region's turbulent history. The Balkan peninsula—a natural bridge between Asia and Europe—has been a crossroad of different religions, cultures, and civilizations from prehistoric times. Frequent migrations of peoples have continually changed the ethnic composition of the region. As "new historic peoples" have come to the region, the "old population" has moved to remote areas where they have often managed to preserve their language, culture, and identity. South Slavs would settle in the territory of the former Yugoslavia in the sixth and seventh centuries. The division of the Roman Empire in the fourth century A.D. established a borderline, which to a considerable extent still exists, in the territory of what is today Bosnia-Herzegovina. After the schism in 1054 A.D., this border divided two Christian cultures: the Roman Catholic culture in the West and the Orthodox culture in the East.

The invasion of the Ottoman Turks in the fourteenth and fifteenth centuries would bring the Islamic religion and culture to this region. Although Islam dominated Eastern culture for five centuries, it did not eliminate Orthodox Christianity. While the relatively tolerant attitudes of the Ottoman Empire enabled the coexistence of several specific—ethnic and regional—Islamic and Orthodox cultures, it did not eliminate occasional conflicts. Rebellions against Ottoman rule in the nineteenth century ultimately eroded the Ottoman Empire and enabled the creation of new Balkan states, including the Kingdom of Montenegro and the Kingdom of Serbia, while Northern and Western parts of the former Yugoslavia remained within Austria-Hungary until the end of World War I.[3]

The region's turbulent history has also contributed to the specific ethnic structure of the population and to the existing ethnic and cultural diversity in every part of the former Yugoslavia. As tables 8.1 and 8.2 illustrate, the ethnic makeup of the population has been changing constantly in the history due to historic migrations of peoples, wars, changed administrative and political borders, natural disasters, and especially in the last hundred years, economic migrations.

The disintegration of the former Yugoslavia and war in the 1990s changed the ethnic structure in this territory again. As with every war, it interrupted traditional patterns of ethnic relations and changed perceptions. After this war, almost everyone forgot that ethnic relations in this territory had traditionally been good. Although some small-scale and low-intensity ethnic conflicts always existed (as in every multiethnic environment), major and violent ethnic conflicts within the local population did not arise until World War II and the war in the 1990s.

Constitutional Development of the Former Yugoslavia

The constitutional development of the former Yugoslavia is usually divided into two main periods: 1) the period of the monarchy until World War II, and 2) the period of the federal republic after World War II.

The first period began with the formation of the Kingdom of Serbs, Croats, and Slovenes after World War I. Its unitary and centralized political system did not reflect the incredible cultural, ethnic, and regional diversities in the country. Instead of recognizing the existing cultural and ethnic diversity, the Yugoslav constitution-makers decided to limit these differences by creating a new ethnic and national identity. The Constitution of the Kingdom of Serbs, Croats, and Slovenes of 1921 introduced a new concept of "one (Serbian-Croatian-Slovenian) nation of three names" (*troimeni narod*) consisting Montenegrin or Bosnian Serbs with specific historic features. The introduction in 1929 of a new official name, "The Kingdom of Yugoslavia," reinforced the unitary system and the goal of creating a new "Yugoslav nation." The Constitution of the Kingdom of Yugoslavia of 1931 forbade any political association on "religious, tribal (ethnic), or regional" grounds, thereby substantially restricting political rights, including rights to association and to gather, and freedom of speech. The only trace of linguistic or ethnic pluralism in this Constitution was the definition of the official "Serbian-Croat-Slovene" language based on the recognition of the existence of, at least, three different languages.[4]

Although the constitutions of 1921 and 1931 proclaimed democratic principles and human rights, their provisions were seldom realized. Several constitutional provisions were ignored or even invalidated by subsequent legislation. Additionally, the work of the democratic institutions was often paralyzed. The underdeveloped unitary monarchy dominated by the king could not be classified as a democratic state by any standards. Non-Serbian citizens became increasingly dissatisfied due to a number of factors, including the denial of the existence of ethnic pluralism, Serbian domination and expansionism, economic and social crises, restricted human rights and curtailed democracy, centralism and unitarism. Demands for the development of democracy; ethnic and social equality; social, economic and political reform; decentralization and broad autonomy; and the establishment of federalism were ignored by the ruling estab-

Table 8.1   The Percentage Share of the Total Population by Major
Ethnic Groups in Yugoslavia according to Official Censuses, 1948–91

Population/Year	1948	1953	1961	1971	1981	1991*
Croats	24.0	23.5	23.1	22.1	19.8	19.1
Macedonians	5.1	5.3	5.6	5.8	6.0	5.8
Montenegrin	2.7	2.8	2.8	2.5	2.6	2.3
Muslims	5.1	5.9	5.2	8.4	8.9	9.6
Serbs	41.5	41.7	42.1	39.7	36.3	36.0
Slovenes	9.0	8.8	8.6	8.2	7.8	7.4
Albanians	4.8	4.5	4.9	6.4	7.7	9.1
Bulgarians	0.4	0.4	0.3	0.3	0.2	0.1
Czechs	0.2	0.2	0.2	0.1	0.1	0.1
Germans	0.4	0.4	0.1	0.1	0.0	0.0
Hungarians	3.2	3.0	2.7	2.3	1.9	1.6
Italians	0.5	0.2	0.1	0.1	0.1	0.1
Jews	-	0.0	0.0	0.0	0.0	-
Roma (Gypsies)	0.5	0.5	0.2	0.4	0.7	0.8
Romanians	0.4	0.4	0.3	0.3	0.2	0.2
Russians	0.1	0.1	0.1	0.0	0.0	-
Ruthenians	0.2	0.2	0.2	0.1	0.1	0.1
Slovaks	0.5	0.5	0.5	0.4	0.4	0.3
Turks	0.6	1.5	1.0	0.6	0.5	0.5
Vlach	0.7	0.2	0.1	0.1	0.1	-
Regional Identity	-	-	-	0.1	0.1	-
Undeclared	-	-	-	0.2	0.2	-
"Yugoslavs"	-	-	1.7	1.3	5.4	3.0
TOTAL (in %)	100.0	100.0	100.0	100.0	100.0	100.0

Sources: Stanko Culjic. 1989. Narodnosna struktura Jugoslavije i tokovi promjena (The Ethnic Structure of Yugoslavia and the Trends of Changes), No. 108, Ekonomski institut Zagreb, Zagreb; Svein Mønnesland. 1992. Før Jugoslavia og etter: Nye stater – gamle nasjoner; Sypress Forlag, Oslo; Statisticki bilten (Statistical Bulletin – Federal Statistical Office), Br./No. 1295, Savezni zavod za statistiku, Beograd. Note: Data for 1991 are very uncertain and should be considered provisory information.

Table 8.2 Languages, Alphabets, and Religion of Major Ethnic Groups in the Former Yugoslavia

Ethnic Group (Nation, Minority)	Language	Alphabet (Script)	Typical Religion
Croats	Croat (Croatian)	Latinic	Roman Catholic
Macedonians	Macedonian	Cyrillic	Orthodox
Montenegrins	Serbian	Cyrillic/Latinic	Orthodox
Muslims (Bosnians)	Serbo-Croatian (Serbian, Croat)	Latinic	Islam
Serbs	Serb (Serbian)	Cyrillic	Orthodox
Slovenes	Slovene (Slovene)	Latinic	Roman Catholic
Albanians	Albanian	Latinic	Islam/Roman Catholic
Hungarians	Hungarian	Latinic	Roman Catholic
Roma (Gypsies)	Roma languages/ dialects	Latinic	mostly Christian
Turks	Turkish	Latinic	Islam

Sources: Stanko Culjic. 1989. *Narodnosna struktura Jugoslavije i tokovi promjena* (The Ethnic Structure of Yugoslavia and the Trends of Changes), No. 108, Ekonomski institut Zagreb, Zagreb; *Statisticki bilten* (Statistical Bulletin – Federal Statistical Office), Br./No. 1295, Savezni zavod za statistiku, Beograd.

lishment. Instead, the official ideology of kinship of the Yugoslav population, and repression, provided for the necessary cohesion.

An attempt to recognize the existing ethnic diversity and to decentralize the country was the establishment of "Banovina of Croatia" (Banovina Hrvatska) in 1939. "Banovina Croatia" included most territories where Croatians formed the majority of the local population. It was established through a special decree issued by the vice-regency based upon the constitutional provisions for a state of emergency, that is, without the cooperation of parliament. This decree was the realization of the so-called Cvetkovic-Macek Agreement on mutual cooperation and sharing of power between the ruling Serbian and Croatian elites.[5] It was the result of an awareness among national elites that ethnic differences would not disappear, and that a new Yugoslav national identity would not be created easily. This agreement assured a special position of Croatia and Croats, but it also emphasized the equality of Serbs, Croats, and Slovenes in the common state. The agreement anticipated wide autonomy and elements of statehood for ethnically defined "Banovina Croatia."[6]

The controversial formation of "Banovina of Croatia," on the one hand, began decentralization in the highly centralized Kingdom of Yugoslavia, which could have laid the foundations for the different treatment and official recognition of ethnic diversity. On the other hand, it did not start democratization. Rather, it was an exclusive deal between two hegemonic ethnic elites that assured their domination and introduced a kind of dualism, thereby placing other ethnicities in an inferior position. The decree on the formation of "Banovina of Croatia" was probably issued in a constitutional way under provisions on a state of emergency that entitled the vice-regency to issue special orders. These special orders then had to be confirmed by the People's Assembly, but it has never confirmed the special decree on the formation of "Banovina of Croatia." Namely, the assembly was dissolved and the new elections did not take place until the beginning of World War II.[7]

This war ended the first phase of the constitutional development of the former Yugoslavia. The existing centralized, unitary, and undemocratic political system did not provide the necessary cohesion and failed to mobilize people of different ethnic origin for the defence of the country. The institutions of the Kingdom of Yugoslavia, including its army, disintegrated within a few days of the attack on Yugoslavia in April 1941, thereby exposing the fragility of Yugoslavia's political system. The four-year occupation saw (different) divisions of the territory among aggressors, the rise and fall of Croatian and Serbian puppet states, destruction, and casualties. During the war, however, the National Liberation Movement, which was an important part of the anti-Nazi coalition, united all patriots regardless of ethnic origin or political affiliation and successfully liberated the country. Although the Communist Party of Yugoslavia (CPY) and its legendary leader Josip Broz Tito led and dominated resistance to the Nazis, the National Liberation War was above all a struggle for ethnic survival and liberation. The National Liberation Movement was by its nature multiethnic. Not only did it recognize and respect the existence of ethnic diversity, it was organized as a coalition of national liberation movements built on the federal model. It proclaimed principles of equality, equal cooperation, "brotherhood and unity of all Yugoslav nations."

World War II would, however, also lead to the first major violent ethnic conflict in this territory. The main protagonists of this ethnic war were Serbian Chetniks (*cetnici*) and Croatian Ustashe (*ustashe*). Chetniks considered themselves to be the "king's army in Yugoslavia" and operated mostly in Serbia, Montenegro, and Bosnia-Herzegovina. Ustashe were the political and military arm of the Croat puppet state—the Independent State of Croatia. Both armed formations helped in the administration of occupied territories and collaborated with German and Italian occupiers of Yugoslavia in the fight against partisans. Usually, they did not fight each other directly. They terrorized local populations, mostly because of their ethnic or religious origin, but also because of their political affiliation. Ustashe tended to terrorize the Serbian and Orthodox population, while Chetniks terrorized Croatians and the Catholic population. Both exterminated their political opponents and terrorized Gypsies (Roma) and Jews.[8]

When the Constituent Assembly passed the Constitution of the Federal People's Republic of Yugoslavia (FPRY) in January 1946, the second phase in the constitutional development began formally. Nevertheless, some important developments had taken place already during World War II and immediately after it. The Antifascist Council of National Liberation of Yugoslavia (AVNOJ), as the supreme authority of the Yugoslav National Liberation Movement comprised of representatives of all national liberation movements, established the Democratic Federal Yugoslavia (DFY) in November 1943. The decree stated that the common resistance of liberation movements of all nations secured the material, political, and moral conditions for the "creation of the future brotherly, democratic, federative community of our nations" built upon the "democratic federative principle of a community of equal nations." DFY was defined as a state established "on the basis of every nation's right to self-determination including the right to secession or union with other nations." The federation ensured "full equality of its five nations, Serbs, Croats, Slovenes, Macedonians, and Montenegrins or the national states of the peoples of Serbia, Voivodina (Vojvodina) and Sanjak (Sandzak), Croatia, Slovenia, Bosnia-Herzegovina, Macedonia, and Montenegro, respectively," and excluded "every possibility of domination, privileges, or majorization of one nation to the disadvantage of another, or one federal state to the disadvantage of another." Additionally, "all national minorities in Yugoslavia" were ensured national and minority rights by a special decree.[9]

The Constituent Assembly was elected immediately after World War II to determine the form of government and adopt a constitution. Its bicameral structure reflected the federal structure of the country. The Federal Chamber was a house of representatives where one representative was elected per forty thousand voters. The Chamber of Nations represented federal units and the ethnic plurality of the Yugoslav community. This chamber was to ensure equality of nations (and nationalities) and federal units in the drafting and adopting of the new constitution.[10] The Constituent Assembly passed the Declaration on the Proclamation of the FPRY on November 29, 1945. This declaration determined the republican and federal form of government.

Following the Soviet example, the Constitution of the FPRY established a fairly centralized Soviet-type federal model and a one-party political system known as a "people's democracy." Nevertheless, the constitution took into account achievements of the National Liberation Movement. Despite fears of possible disintegration, the constitution defined "the Yugoslav federal republic" as a "community of equal nations, which, on the basis of their right to self-determination, including the right to secession, expressed their will to live together in a federative state." As in most federations, the People's Assembly (parliament) had two chambers that were equal in their competencies. In this manner, the constitution guaranteed a balance between the democratic rule of the people and the equality of the federal units and nations. The Federal Chamber was a traditional house of representatives and the Council of Nations represented federal units. Regardless of size, each Constituent "People's Republic" (PR)—Bosnia-Herzegovina, Croatia, Macedonia, Montenegro, Slovenia, and Serbia—elected thirty representatives to this chamber. As parts of the PR of Serbia, the Autonomous Province (AP) of Voivodina elected twenty representatives and the Autonomous Region of Kosmet-Metohia (Kosovo) elected fifteen representatives to the Council of Nations. In addition to the equality of nations and federal units, the constitution proclaimed "the right to cultural development and free use of their language" for all national minorities.[11] Neither the federal constitution nor the Constitution of the PR of Serbia defined Serbia as a federation, although it included the AP of Voivodina and the AR of Kosmet-Metohia which were guaranteed autonomous rights and were directly represented at the federal level.[12] This additional representation of Serbia in the federal Assembly should have strengthened the position of Serbia in the federation, but it held little weight considering the centralized political process and the power of the federal leadership and CPY at the time.

Formally, the constituent republics restricted their sovereignty only by transferring to the federation, through the federal constitution, certain rights. Competencies of the federation resembled those in other federations, but in practice most relevant political, economic, and social issues were decided at the federal level. In the years immediately following World War II, communist ideology dominated all spheres of everyday life. The existing political monopoly of power of the CPY considerably reduced the constitutionally provided autonomy of nations and PRs. Continuing its prewar orientation, the CPY insisted on ethnic equality and protection of minorities. The official ideology declared that the national liberation and "socialist revolution" had resolved all ethnic and other social conflicts. Consequently, the constitution did not include provisions on the management and resolution of conflicts. The CPY and President Tito performed these functions informally when needed—which continued until the 1980s.

After the initial fascination with the Soviet Union, Tito's government would break with Stalin in 1948.[13] The constitutional law of 1953 introduced self-management, and substantially changed the existing political system. It was expected that the introduction of social self-management would eventually eliminate all social conflicts. The new self-managing system was to replace traditional political institutions and enable full direct social, economic, and political participation in the development of the country. The slogan "Factories to Workers!" was realized by the election of workers' councils in all factories, and the same organizational concept was to be introduced in all other spheres of life. In this context, the constitutional law abolished the Council of Nations as an independent chamber of the federal assembly, replacing it with the Chamber of Producers. The Council of Nations, as a kind of "half-chamber" with very restricted competencies, became a part of the Federal Chamber. Representatives in the Council of Nations were elected by the Assemblies of the republics and the Assemblies of the autonomous province and the autonomous region.[14]

A year later, the next constitutional law changed the political system and further reduced the role of the Council of Nations, which remained a part of the Federal Chamber. This constitutional law provided for the calling of a special session of the Council of Nations upon the request of its members, but such a session has never been convened.[15] Self-management was developed as an alternative to the Soviet model of development and to Soviet ideology. The formal introduction of self-management in different spheres of economic and social life and the transformation of the "people's democracy" into a new self-managing system demanded a different role from the CPY. The CPY renamed itself the League of Communists of Yugoslavia (LCY) at its Seventh Congress in Ljubljana in 1958 to stress its new role in the self-managing society. Although its political and ideological monopoly was, to a large extent, preserved and many of the changes made to differentiate the LCY from Soviet-type communist parties were largely cosmetic, the LCY was, nonetheless, quite different from traditional communist parties. The political reforms introduced by the LCY opened the door to gradual democratization. The new LCY program adopted at this congress elaborated the policy and role of the LCY in different fields. It stressed the importance of the principle of self-determination of nations for the existence of the Yugoslav federation. Principles of equality and the "brotherhood and unity of the Yugoslav nations," and the assurance of adequate social status for ethnic minorities were declared the bases for the regulation of ethnic relations. The LCY was aware of the importance of stable ethnic relations. The program criticized nationalism, stressing its potential destructive powers in a multiethnic society. Nationalism was defined as "the remains of bourgeois nationalism," incompatible with self-management and democratic socialism. In the utopian view of the LCY, self-management would resolve all conflicts, including ethnic conflicts, thereby surpassing the conflicting class society.[16]

The Constitution of the Socialist Federative Republic of Yugoslavia (SFRY) of 1963 was based on the ideology of social self-management. It introduced the system of "socialist democracy" based on integrative social self-management, and changed the official name of the country to stress these developments. Although Yugoslavia was still defined as a multinational federation, the class component of the federation clearly prevailed over the ethnic component in the constitution. The federal constitution defined the six Socialist Republics (SR) as "state socialist democratic communities, based upon the power of working people and self-management" with their own constitutions, which had to comply with the principles of the federal constitution. Instead of different status for autonomous units, the constitution outlined the equal status of two Autonomous Provinces (AP), Kosmet-Metohia and Voivodina. They were defined as sociopolitical communities within Serbia. The Council of Nations, which was to reflect a pluralistic ethnic structure and to assure equality among federal units and ethnic communities in the federal parliament, was still a "sub-chamber" of the Federal Chamber in the five-chamber Federal Assembly. Its competencies were very limited.[17]

Besides the general provisions on equality of languages, alphabets, and nations, the constitution guaranteed the rights of members of each nation to be educated in their own language in the territory of another republic.[18] The Constitution also guaranteed the rights of national minorities to education in their own language. Other minority rights were regulated by the Constitutions and laws of the SRs. The term "nationality" was employed instead of the term "national (ethnic) minority" to express the new ethnic policy that established these minorities as equal communities. These changes actually improved the situation of ethnic minorities in the former Yugoslavia.

In response to different problems in ethnic relations, the competencies of the Council of Nations were strengthened later in the 1960s. Amendment I, implemented in 1967, assured the equality and influence of nations, nationalities, the SRs, and the APs. It entitled the Council of Nations to deal with all matters related to the equality of republics, nations, and nationalities, or related to the constitutionally guaranteed rights of the republics. This chamber became equal to the Federal Chamber within the framework of its competencies.[19]

During the 1960s, a new round of federal constitutional reforms was launched. Amendments VII, IX, and XII of 1968 defined the Chamber of Nations as the first chamber of the Federal Assembly and significantly strengthened its competencies. The Chamber of Nations independently dealt with matters of equality of the republics and the autonomous provinces and other matters of common interest. As an equal chamber (to the Chamber of the Working Communities), it decided at all instances when two-chamber decision-making was constitutionally anticipated in the Federal Assembly. In accordance with the specific procedure determined by the standing orders of this chamber, if ten representatives of this chamber so demanded, the Chamber of Nations could deal with any issue related to the equality of the republics, nations, nationalities, or with any issue which involved encroachment upon the constitutional rights of the republics and autonomous provinces. Each Republic Assembly elected twenty representatives to the Chamber of Nations, and each Assembly of the AP elected ten representatives.[20] Amendment XVIII outlined the significance of the socialist autonomous provinces (SAP) of Voivodina and Kosovo within the SR of Serbia for the realization of national equality and for the integral development of self-management. The rights and duties of the SAP and competencies of its bodies were determined by its Constitutional Law in compliance with the federal and Serbian republic constitutions. Additionally, Amendment XIX granted the right to use minority languages in dealing with public institutions and in public activities, in accordance with the Constitutions and laws of the republics.[21]

Contrary to the expectations of the ruling regime, the introduction of self-management did not eliminate social conflicts. The system of self-management was very complex, thereby limiting popular participation in decision-making. Based on the ideological presumption that Yugoslavia was—or was soon to become—a conflict-free society, the political system did not develop adequate democratic mechanisms for the management and resolution of conflicts. Problems in ethnic relations and occasional nationalistic excesses persisted throughout the 1960s and 1970s. Nationalism escalated especially in Croatia, but it also grew in other parts of the country. Considering its potential destructive power, nationalism was declared the main danger for the existence of the multinational Yugoslav federation. The leaders of Croatia, Slovenia, and Serbia were replaced on the pretext of their nationalism (in combination with so-called liberalism). Lacking adequate constitutional and legal mechanisms for the management of ethnic relations and conflicts, President Tito and the communist leadership employed informal methods to handle these problems. The leadership hoped that further decentralization and the introduction of certain confederal elements into the Yugoslav federal system would prevent possible ethnic conflicts. Influenced by problems in ethnic relations, constitutional amendments in the late 1960s increased the autonomy of SRs and SAPs and stressed the importance of ethnic pluralism. However, this process of decentralization and democratization did not substantially reduce the actual power of the federal center nor that of the LCY.[22]

The 1974 Constitution of the SFRY continued the decentralization and democratization process launched by the Constitutional Amendments of the 1960s. It emphasized ethnic and social pluralism and—to a certain degree—enabled its manifestation in the political system. The Yugoslav leadership believed that further decentralization of the federation would enhance the equality of nations and federal units and reduce the possibility of ethnic conflicts. The Constitution of the SFRY defined the SRs as "states based on the sovereignty of the people and the power of and self-management by the working class and working people." SRs were defined simultaneously as states and as "socialist, self-managing communities of the working people and citizens and of nations and nationalities having equal rights." The idea was that self-management would slowly transform the existing models of alienated nation-states with their monopoly of power, into self-managing communities based on the initiative and participation of the people. The hope was that self-management would eventually eliminate the traditional nation-state. The SAPs within the SR of Serbia were not defined as states, but as "autonomous, socialist, self-managing democratic sociopolitical communities" which were to provide for ethnic equality and for the preservation of ethnic plurality of these communities. Nevertheless, the SAPs were defined constituent elements of the Yugoslav federation and the constitution provided for a direct representation of SAPs in all major federal institutions.[23] Again, the constitution did not define Serbia formally as a federation, although Serbia included autonomous provinces which held that status of constituent elements of the Yugoslav federation.

Both chambers of the Assembly of the SFRY reflected the concept of parity to ensure the greatest possible measure of equality of the constituent federal units. The Federal Chamber was defined as a House of Representatives to which each SR (irrespective of its size and number of voters) elected thirty delegates and to which each SAP elected twenty delegates. The Chamber of the Republics and Provinces represented federal units. The assembly of each republic was assigned twelve delegates, and the assembly of each SAP eight delegates. The delegates elected to the Chamber of the Republics and Provinces retained their position in the respective republic or province assembly. The federal constitution defined which matters had to be decided on the basis of the consensus in the Chamber of the Republics and Provinces. In these matters, the members of this chamber from a certain SR or SAP voted in unison. If a consensus was not reached, the decisions could not be adopted, unless the issue required urgent measures, but even these could not be adopted for longer than one year. A form of minority veto was given to the SRs and the SAPs to ensure their equality.

To ensure the equality of all federal units (republics and autonomous provinces), nations, and nationalities, the parity structure was implemented in other federal institutions—such as the Presidency of the SFRY, the Federal Supreme Court, the federal Constitutional Court, etc. The federal and ethnic structure was to be considered also in the federal government called the Federal Executive Council.

The constitutional reform of 1974 strengthened the autonomy of federal units and introduced a concept of shared sovereignty, thereby introducing certain traditional confederative elements into the system. Republics were constitutionally defined as nation-states of constituent nations which were based on the sovereignty of the people. As federal units they did not have international independence and legal personality, but they were given all other attributes of statehood. They had their republic constitutions that determined their political systems, coats of arms, national anthems, national official languages, republic holidays, specific educational systems, and programs. Autonomy and independence of the republics were formally limited only by the constitutional principle that the constitutions of republics should not contradict the federal constitution. Nevertheless, the constitutions of the republics introduced only a limited number of specific features into their respective systems.[24]

The federal constitution determined the specific constitutional status of SAPs. Their primary role was to assure ethnic equality and to preserve ethnic plurality. Although they were not defined as states, they were constituent elements of the Yugoslav federation with substantial autonomy and direct representation in federal bodies, in addition to the equal representation which Serbia enjoyed. When the constitution was drafted, there was criticism that such arrangement could favor Serbia within the federation. The Serbian leadership, however, insisted on such an arrangement.

Regardless of the formal decentralization introduced by the constitution, the Yugoslav federation was still rather centralized in the beginning of the 1970s. The LCY dominated political processes and life; its monopoly of power was not questioned. Nevertheless, the introduction of the federal, republic and provincial constitutions started the gradual process of (formal) decentralization in Yugoslavia which gradually increased the actual autonomy and influence of federal units, including that of the autonomous provinces which would become important independent players at the federal level in the 1980s, as their interests often conflicted with the interests of Serbia. The Serbian leadership responded by complaining that the increased autonomy of the provinces placed the republic in an inferior position in the federation. They claimed that Serbia was unable to control its own affairs and entire territory.

Beginning in the 1980s, the Serbian leadership, unhappy with the existing situation and constitutional arrangements, began to demand the introduction of policies and institutional reforms that would assure the influence and control of the Serbian government over provincial affairs.

The late President Tito and the LCY had played the central role in political processes and had been the main integrative factors in the Yugoslav federation in the 1970s. Their actual role and influence enabled them to resolve all conflicts, although the constitution—based on the official ideological presumption that Yugoslavia was a conflict-free society, and that the system of self-management assured the necessary cohesion—did not create any political institutions and procedures for the management of conflicts. After the death of President Tito and the disintegration of the LCY in 1990, there was no political institution that could have assumed the functions of President Tito and the LCY in the management of conflicts and in assuring the necessary cohesion within Yugoslavia. This deficit became particularly evident in the late 1980s when the economic, political, and social crisis in the former Yugoslavia deepened. The existing system was unable to deal with the crisis and the ruling regime initially blamed the inadequate realization of the existing constitutional system for all problems.[25] When it recognized the need to reform the existing political system in Yugoslavia, the consensus of all federal units necessary to amend the federal constitution no longer existed. Two opposing concepts for political reform of the federation had emerged by the late 1980s that made global political reform impossible. The first concept advocated further decentralization and increased autonomy of federal units, while the second concept called for a strong and centralized federation.

The adoption of Constitutional Amendments in 1988[26] represented a compromise, but was ultimately a solution that failed to resolve the major problems of the day. Nevertheless, these amendments enabled further democratization, multiparty elections, and the introduction of certain limited economic and political reforms. The economic and political reforms proposed by the federal government of Prime Minister Markovic soon failed, however. There was neither the political consensus nor the public support necessary for successful political and economic reform.

In the period from 1989 to 1991, all attempts to reform the existing political system failed. The proposals advocated by the federal institutions of Serbia and Montenegro to centralize the existing federal system and substantially increase the competencies of federal institutions did not find the necessary support.[27] The proposal to introduce asymmetrical federalism, which would have allowed for different political systems within Yugoslavia, and the proposal of Slovenia and Croatia for a confederal Yugoslav union were also rejected.[28] Conflicts between the "centralists" and "decentralists" that had existed throughout the existence of Yugoslavia escalated in the late 1980s. They finally paralyzed the existing political system in the beginning of the 1990s.

The Constitutional Collapse of the Yugoslav Federation

With the existing system unable to deal with the growing crisis, little could be done to disguise or address the economic, social, and political differences in Yugoslavia. Political systems of individual federal units began to reflect these differences and the political concept desired by their political leadership. Differences further increased with the introduction of political pluralism and a multiparty system and were reflected also in the constitutional reforms within federal units. Constitutional reforms in republics and autonomous provinces in the period from 1989 to 1991 substantially exceeded the traditional task of the harmonization of the constitutions of the federal units with the amended or new federal constitution.[29] The new constitutions in Serbia and Croatia and the amended constitution of Slovenia introduced new constitutional systems in respective republics, reshaped the federation, and changed relations at the federal level, although there were no new formal changes to the federal constitution.

In September 1990, prior to the first multiparty elections, Serbia became the first Yugoslav republic to adopt a new constitution. Although this constitution introduced formally the multiparty political system, it actually consolidated the political power of Slobodan Milosevic, the Serbian communist leader.[30] The Constitution of the Republic of Serbia introduced the (semi)presidential system, thereby replacing the former assembly system. It essentially diminished the autonomy of both autonomous provinces and abolished their constitutions. Additionally, it abolished the presidencies of both provinces, and changed the name of the autonomous province of Kosovo to the Autonomous Province of Kosmet and Metohia. Formally Serbia retained minority rights which were already in force.[31] However, minority rights recived less protection due to the reduction of the autonomy of the provinces. Although the Serbian constitution encroached upon the Constitution of the SFRY (1974), Serbia maintained that the federal bodies should not be changed and that the autonomous provinces, now controlled by Serbia, should remain represented in the federal bodies, thereby ensuring Serbian control over these bodies. Although Serbian proposals to centralize the federation dominated by the LCY had failed, at that point Milosevic still hoped to become a leader at the federal level who would replace the late President Tito.

The Constitution of the Republic of Croatia was adopted after the multiparty elections[32] in December 1990, while Croatia was still a constitutive part of the SFRY. This constitution introduced the multiparty political system and a specific variant of the (semi)presidential system.[33] However, it aggravated relations with Serbs in Croatia who were treated as a national minority. Rebellious Serbs in Croatia—supported by the leadership of Serbia—demanded the status of a constituent nation and rejected their new status. These conflicts resulted in the civil war (1991–92) and the temporary division of the country. During the war in Croatia, the Croatian Parliament (Sabor) passed a special constitutional law on human rights and freedoms and on special rights of ethnic minorities. In addition to certain traditional minority rights, minorities were given the right to special cultural autonomy. Their proportional participation in the representative bodies was assured, with the possibility of founding of local communities and regions with special autonomous status.[34]

Slovenia chose to reform its political system by amending the republic constitution of 1974. Almost a hundred amendments adopted by the republic assembly from 1989 to 1991 introduced political pluralism, furthered political and economic democratization, strengthened the republic's autonomy, reinforced Slovenia's right to self-determination, abolished the communist political ideology in the Preamble, and changed the official name of the Socialist Republic of Slovenia to the Republic of Slovenia. This gradual constitutional reform enabled a peaceful political transition, and political and social stability. The Constitution of the Republic of Slovenia was adopted in December 1991 when actually the SFRY no longer existed.[35]

The formal international recognition of the disintegration of the SFRY came in January 1992, when the European Union (including some member states) and a number of other states recognized the independence of Slovenia and Croatia.[36] Practically speaking, the federal system collapsed by 1991 as a consequence of the paralysis of federal institutions caused by growing political conflicts and inability to find a compromise.

What Went Wrong?[37]

The combination of several internal and external—social, cultural, economic, political—factors, including the deterioration of ethnic relations, contributed to the collapse of the Yugoslav federation. The process of the disintegration of Yugoslavia had already started in the 1980s and intensified in the beginning of the 1990s. The inability of the existing constitution and regime to deal with the crisis and provide the framework for the democratic management of conflicts played a significant role in this context. I believe that especially the following issues were important from the perspective of ethnic relations and conflicts:

1. Societies developed different—traditional and new, formal and informal— mechanisms for the management and resolution of conflicts that are normal phenomena in every plural society. As traditional mechanisms are some-

times undemocratic and often incompatible with political systems introduced by modern (nation-)states, these states try to replace them with new apparently more democratic mechanisms. When these democratic mechanisms fail, states then resort to repression. The absence of adequate mechanisms for the management and resolution of conflicts—no doubt—contributed to the tragic development in the former Yugoslavia. Varying substantially from the region to region, traditional mechanisms for the management of ethnic relations and resolution of conflicts had provided for good ethnic relations, peaceful coexistence, cooperation, and relative social stability, although often they were not democratic. As in many places in the world, the "new" states abolished several traditional mechanisms for the resolution of conflicts in this territory and often abolished mechanisms introduced by previous states. As already mentioned, the LCY and President Tito had resolved conflicts in an informal way when needed. These informal mechanisms disappeared with the death of President Tito and dissolution of the LCY. The consensus needed for the introduction of new adequate—formal and informal—mechanisms for the management of conflicts no longer existed in Yugoslavia at that point.

2. Lacking formal mechanisms for the resolution of conflicts, the existing constitutional system failed to perform its main function: It did not ensure the social stability and peace necessary for the long-term existence of every state. The existing constitutional and political system no longer corresponded to the social reality. Specific and often conflicting interests of federal units produced conflicts at the federal level that paralyzed the federation by 1990.

3. The traditional conflict between "decentralists" and "centralists" in Yugoslavia appeared again as the conflict between two incompatible political concepts of the future development. The leadership of Slovenia and later Croatia advocated decentralization of the federation, stronger autonomy of federal units, democratization and the introduction of market economy, and the multiparty political system. On the other side, the leadership of Serbia and Montenegro demanded the strong, centralized federation and the restoration of the political monopoly of the LCY. The still-communist leadership of both republics also used ethnic identity to mobilize public support for their policy. In this context, people saw the political conflict between the political leadership of Slovenia and Serbia as an ethnic conflict between Serbs and Slovenes, which resulted in Serbia even in the (economic) boycott of goods produced in Slovenia at the end of the 1980s. The growth of Serbian expansionist nationalism in the beginning of the 1990s and the

escalation of conflicts increased the support for decentralization of the federation in Croatia, Macedonia, and Bosnia-Herzegovina. As it turned out, neither of the options prevailed. Escalating conflicts paralyzed the existing constitutional system, rendering it incapable of coping with the crisis.

4. The process of democratization in Yugoslavia proceeded at a different pace in each federal unit in the late 1980s. It resulted in the creation of political parties, the formal introduction of a multiparty system and the first multiparty elections in all republics in 1990. The international community and public that supported democratization in Yugoslavia saw multiparty elections as a necessary precondition and the only way to realize democracy. Reformers and political opposition in Yugoslavia shared this view. They were not aware of the possible consequences of multiparty elections in a multiethnic environment with limited or no democratic political traditions. Additionally, the situation differed from republic to republic. In an environment without multiparty political traditions, politicians and political parties used ethnicity and reinterpreted ethnic myths to mobilize people for their political programs. Ethnic affiliation and nationalism became important political factors. The use of nationalism and historic and ethnic myths contributed to the transformation of political conflicts into ethnic conflicts and to their escalation. In Croatia and Bosnia-Herzegovina this led to a tragic ethnic war.

5. Although the international community did not pay much attention to the former Yugoslavia after the collapse of the bipolar international system, it has been an important factor in the Yugoslav crisis. Lacking a coherent approach to the crisis, it sent mixed signals and did not act until it was too late. The proponents of centralization—federal institutions and especially the army—interpreted the support of the international community for the territorial unity and integrity of Yugoslavia as the approval for the intervention in Slovenia that demanded democratic political reforms, a decentralized federation, stronger autonomy, and independence of federal units. On the other hand, the international community's support for democratization and multiparty elections encouraged democratic political reforms in Slovenia and political opposition in other parts of country. Unaware of the possible consequences of multiparty elections in a multiethnic environment without democratic traditions, the international community did not expect tragic developments and insisted on measures that could have prevented the escalation of conflict.

Conclusion: The Lessons of Yugoslavia

The former Yugoslavia is an example of how inefficiently managed social and political conflicts in a multiethnic country could be transformed into violent ethnic conflicts. These ethnic conflicts destroyed the multiethnic federation and triggered the ethnic war in Croatia and Bosnia-Herzegovina.

Analyzing the constitutional development of the former Yugoslavia from the perspective of ethnic relations, this chapter has presented only a few aspects of the Yugoslav crisis. Obviously, the existing federal constitutional system failed to resolve the crisis. Lacking adequate mechanisms for the management and resolution of ethnic and other social conflicts, this system did not prevent the escalation of conflicts. It did not provide an adequate formal framework for the democratic management and resolution of conflicts and crisis.

Historic experiences have shown that constitutions and legal systems can be successful in resolving internal conflicts only if they are accepted, followed, and supported by the people. The state needs the cooperation of (networks of) individuals, associations, organizations, and institutions that constitute a civil (civic) society. They are essential for the success of mechanisms for the prevention, management, and resolution of ethnic and other social conflicts. The success of these mechanisms improves if every escalation of conflicts is detected very early and is immediately being dealt with appropriate measures. We can expect the (active) participation of people in social and political processes only if their interest for the participation and common action exists. The absence of such an interest and nonexistence of centripetal forces at the federal level were the key reasons for the collapse of the Yugoslav federation. The central task of a successful policy in every state should be the mobilization and promotion of the interest for the common existence within the state. Such an interest can only be built if the state enables the realization of specific and common interests of people and communities.

I would especially like to stress the important role of education and mass media in this context. Not only should they provide the necessary information on ethnic diversity, knowledge about "others," opportunities for meetings and cooperation, education and training for the management of ethnic relations and conflicts, etc., they should especially work on the promotion of the "ideology" of cooperation. Principles of tolerance, coexistence, and cooperation should—at least—supplement and in many cases replace the prevailing practice of competition in multiethnic and other plural societies.[38]

Suggested Study Questions

1. To which part of Europe did the former Yugoslavia belong geographically?
2. Describe the ethnic structure of the population of the former Yugoslavia.
3. What was the Yugoslav Idea? Did it exist before the Yugoslav state? If yes, how did it influence the creation of the Yugoslav state?
4. The constitutional development of the former Yugoslavia is usually divided into two main stages. Define these phases and describe their characteristics. How many constitutions were passed in the first and how many in the second phase of development?
5. When did the first large-scale violent ethnic conflict occur in the territory of the former Yugoslavia? Who were the protagonists of this ethnic conflict?
6. In your view, which factors did play important roles in the escalation of the Yugoslav crisis and conflicts? How does a political conflict become an ethnic conflict?

Notes

1. See, for example, Noel Malcolm, *Kosovo: A Short History* (New York: New York University Press, 1998). This book is (in my opinion) the best and most up-to-date account about the history of this region. For a chronology of events see Brana Markovic, *Yugoslav Crisis and the World: Chronology of Events, January 1990–October 1995* (Belgrade: Institute of International Politics and Economics, 1996).
2. The Balkan Peninsula is defined geographically by the lower Danube and Sava rivers (to the north), by the Adriatic Sea and Dinara Mountains (to the west), the Ionian Sea (to the southwest), the Mediterranean Sea (to the south), the Aegean Sea (to the southeast) and by the Black Sea (to the east). Geographically Slovenia, Croatia (north of the Sava river, peninsula Istria) and Voivodina (the northern province of Serbia) do not belong to this region. Nevertheless, the traditional political definition of the Balkans included Albania, Bulgaria, Greece, Rumania, the former Yugoslavia, and the European part of Turkey. Slovenia, and sometimes Croatia, as two successor states of the former Yugoslavia, are nowadays excluded from this political region. The name of the peninsula and one of its mountain-chains derives from a Turkish expression for mountains—"Balkan."
3. See Richard Crampton and Ben Crampton, *Atlas of Eastern Europe in the Twentieth Century* (London and New York: Routledge, 1997); Charles Jelavich and Barbara Jelavich, *The Establishment of the Balkan National States, 1804–1920*, Vol. 8 of *A History of East Central Europe* (Seattle: University of Washington Press, 1977). For different accounts see also Ivan Ninic, *Migrations in Balkan History* (Belgrade: Serbian Academy of Sciences and Arts, Institute for Balkan Studies, Prosveta/Santa Barbara: University of California, Department of History, 1989); L. S. Stavrianos, *The Balkans since 1453* (New York: Rinehart & Comp., [1958]); Yuri Stoyanov, *The Hidden Tradition in Europe: The Secret History of Medieval Christian Heresy* (London and New York: Penguin, 1994).

4. On the Constitution of the Kingdom of Serbs, Croats, and Slovenes of (June 28) 1921 (also called "St. Vitus Constitution"—*vidovdanska ustava*), the Law on the Name and Division of the Monarchy into Administrative Regions of (October) 1929 that introduced the new official name "The Kingdom of Yugoslavia," and the Constitution of the Kingdom of Yugoslavia granted by King Aleksandar in 1931 in the Serb-Croat language see Branko Petranovic, Momcilo Zecevic, eds., *Jugoslovanski federalizam: Ideje i stvarnost, Tematska zbirka dokumenata, Prvi tom 1914–1943* (Yugoslav Federalism: Ideas and Reality, Thematic Collection of Documents, Vol. I, 1914–1943) (Beograd: Prosveta, 1987).

5. Yugoslav Prime Minister Dragisa Cvetkovic, the leading Serbian politician at the time, and Vlatko Macek, president of the Croatian Peasants' Party (Hrvatska Seljacka Stranka – HSS) and leader of "The Peasant Democratic Opposition," signed this agreement (Sporazum Cvetkovic-Macek) on August 23, 1939.

6. For the Serb-Croat text of the agreement see Branko Petranovic, Momcilo Zecevic, eds. (1987), *Jugoslovanski federalizam: Ideje i stvarnost, Tematska zbirka dokumenata*, Vol. I., 508–510.

7. See, for example, Joze PIRJEVEC, *Jugoslavija, 1918–1992: Nastanek, razvoj ter razpad in Titove Jugoslavije* (Yugoslavia, 1918–1992: The Formation, Development and Downfall of Karadjordjevic's and Tito's Yugoslavia) (Koper: Zalozba Lipa, 1995), 93, 100–102.

8. See, for example, Eric Hobsbawm, *The Age of Extremes: A History of the World, 1914–1991* (New York: Vintage Books, 1996 [1994]), 170; Janko Pleterski, *Narodi, Jugoslavija, revolucija* (Nations, Yugoslavia, Revolution) (Ljubljana: CZDO Komunist – TOZD Komunist/Ljubljana: Drzavna zalozba Slovenije, 1986), 299–323.

9. The Second Conference of AVNOJ, held in Jajce (Bosnia-Herzegovina) on November 29–30, 1943, adopted the "Decree on the Formation of Yugoslavia on the Basis of Federative Principle" that established the DFY. For the Serb-Croat and Slovene texts of this and other documents of the Conference see Branko Petranovic and Momcilo Zecevic, eds. (1987), *Jugoslovanski federalizam: Ideje i stvarnost, Tematska zbirka dokumenata*, Vol. II., 791–801; *Prvo in drugo zasedanje AVNOJ; 26. in 27. novembra 1942 in 29. in 30. novembra 1943* (The First and the Second Conference of AVNOJ: November 26–27, 1942, and November 29–30, 1943) (Ljubljana, Komunist, 1973). (Citations from the decree translated by M. Zagar.)

10. See *Zakon o ustavotvorni skupscini* (The Law on the Constituent Assembly), *Sluzbeni list DFJ/Uradni list DFJ* – Official Gazette of the DFY, No. 63/1945. This law determined that each of the six federal units, irrespective of its size, elected twenty-five representatives to the Chamber of Nations, whereas citizens of Voivodina elected fifteen, and citizens of Kosmet and Metohia (Kosovo) ten. Additionally, it regulated the procedures for decision-making and the required majority for the adoption of decisions.

11. See the 1946 Constitution of the FPRY. For the Serb-Croat text of this constitution with commentaries, see *Novi ustavi: Zbirka ustava donetih posle drugog svetskog rata* (New Constitutions: A Collection of Constitutions, Adopted after the WW II)

(Beograd: Arhiv za pravne i drustvene nauke, 1949), 11–40, 155; Branko Petranovic and Momcilo Zecevic, eds., *Jugoslovanski federalizam: Ideje i stvarnost, Tematska zbirka dokumenata, Drugi tom: 1943–1986* (Yugoslav Federalism: Ideas and Reality, Thematic Collection of Documents, Vol. II.) (Beograd: Prosveta, 1987), 234–44.

12. Article 13 of the Constitution of the PR of Serbia of 1947 stated that the AP and AR had autonomous rights, ensured by the Constitution of the PR of Serbia in accordance with the Constitution of the FPRY. It also outlined that each autonomous unit had its own autonomous statute, sanctioning its autonomous rights. These autonomous statutes had to be submitted to the People's Assembly of the PR of Serbia for verification. See Branko Petranovic and Momcilo Zecevic, eds. (1987), *Jugoslovanski federalizam: Ideje i stvarnost, Tematskazbirka dokumenata, Vol. II.*, 245–46.

13. See Eric Hobsbawm (1996), *The Age of Extremes: A History of the World, 1914–1991*, p. 396–97; Joze Pirjevec (1995), *Jugoslavija, 1918–1992: Nastanek, razvoj ter razpad Karadjordjeviceve in Titove Jugoslavije*, 171–218.

14. The Federal Chamber was elected by voters in general elections. They elected one representative per sixty thousand voters (Article 26). People's representatives, standing for the Council of Nations, were elected in such a way that each Republic's Assembly elected ten representatives, the Autonomous Province's Assembly 6, and the Assembly of the Autonomous Region 4 representatives (Article 27 of the Constitutional Law). See *Ustavni zakon o temeljih druzbene in politicne ureditve FLRJ in o zveznih organih oblasti* (Constitutional Law on the Foundations of the Social and Political Regulation of the FPRY and on the Federal Authority Bodies), *Sluzbeni list FNRJ/ Uradni list FLRJ* – Official Gazette of the FPRY, No. 3/1953.

15. See *Zakon o spremembi 45., 46., 47., 48., in 2 odstavka 51. clena ustavnega zakona o temeljih druzbene in politicne ureditve FLRJ in o zveznih organih oblasti* (Law on the Changing of the Articles 45, 46, 47, 48 and Paragraph 2 Article 51 of the Constitutional Law on the Foundations of the Social and Political Regulation of the FPRY and on the Federal Authority Bodies), *Sluzbeni list FNRJ/Uradni list FLRJ* – Official Gazette of the FPRY, No. 13/1954.

16. See *Program Zveze komunistov Jugoslavije, sprejet na 7. kongresu ZKJ* (The Programme of the LCY: Adopted at the 7th Congress of the LCY) (Ljubljana: Komunist, 1978), especially its section "Federation and Relations between the Nations of Yugoslavia," 157–66.

17. See *Ustava SFRJ* (The Constitution of the SFRY), *Uradni list SFRY* – Official Gazette SFRY, No. 14/1963.

18. Paragraph 3 of Article 42 introduced an exemption to the principle of equality of languages and scripts of the nations of Yugoslavia: In the Yugoslav People's Army only the Serb-Croat language was used at the level of command, in military education, and in the administration.

19. See Amendment I (1967) of the Constitutional Amendments to the Constitution of the SFRY of 1963, *Uradni list SFRJ* – The Official Gazette of the SFRY, No. 18/1967.

20. The Chamber of Nations with 140 representatives was the largest of the chambers of

the Federal Assembly, which had 120 representatives each.

21. See Constitutional Amendments VII, IX, XII, XVIII, and XIX (1968) to the Constitution of the SFRY, 1963, The Official Gazette of the SFRY, No. 55/1968.

22. Historian Dusan Bilandzic claims that as early as the beginning and mid-1960s the late Yugoslav President Tito and Edvard Kardelj expressed their fear that ethnic conflicts and aggressive nationalism in Yugoslavia could endanger its very existence and cause the destruction of the multinational state. The solution was sought in decentralization and even confederalization of the state, in order to ensure greater autonomy and independent development for each republic. See Dusan Bilandzic, *"Tito je jos 1962. predvidio raspad Jugoslavije: Nekrolog SFRJ"* (Tito foresaw the decomposition of Yugoslavia already in 1962: Necrology to the SFRY) – in *Slobodni tjednik* (Zagreb: September 5, 1992), 10.

23. See *Ustava Socialisticne federativne republike Jugoslavije* (Constitution of the SFRY) (1974), *Uradni list SFRJ* – Official Gazette SFRY, No. 9/1974, and corrections in No. 11/1974. Official English translation: *The Constitution of the SFRY (With Constitutional Amendments I–VIII of 1981)* (Belgrade: The Assembly of the SFRY, 1981).

24. See *Ustav SFRJ, Ustavi socijalistifkih republika i pokrajina, Ustavni zakoni, Registar pojmova* (The Constitution of SFRY, Constitutions of SRs and SAPs, Constitutional Laws, [Legal] Glossary) Zbirka propisa (Beograd: Prosveta, 1974).

25. See *Kriticna analiza delovanja politicnega sistema socialisticnega samoupravljanja* (Critical Analysis of the Functioning of the Political System of Socialist Self-Management) (Ljubljana: Zvezni druzbeni svet za vprasanja druzbene ureditve, Delavska enotnost, 1985).

26. See *Amandmaji IX–XC* – Amendments IX-XC (1988) to the Constitution of SFRY (1974), *Uradni list SFRJ* – Official Gazette SFRY, No.70/1988.

27. The Presidency of the SFRY prepared a proposal for the reform of the federation based largely on the Serbian concept of a centralized federation, although the Presidency's proposal was not as radical. This proposal, supported by federal institutions, including the federal army, was supported by Serbia, which hoped to take control over the federal institutions on the basis of this proposal. (See "A Concept for the Constitutional System of Yugoslavia on a Federal Basis" (1990), *Review of International Affairs*, Vol. XLI, No. 974, Belgrade, November 5, 1990, 15–18.)

28. See the proposal for "A Confederate Model Among the South Slavic States" by the Presidency of the Republic of Croatia and Presidency of the Republic of Slovenia, Zagreb, and Ljubljana, October 4, 1990, in *Review of International Affairs*, Vol. XLI, No. 973 (Belgrade: Assembly of SFRY, October 20, 1990), 11–16.

29. These differences among constitutions of SRs and SAPs grew with the adoption of constitutional amendments and new constitutions 1989–91. (See Mitja Zagar, *"Primerjalna analiza amandmajev k ustavam SR in SAP iz leta 1989 v primerjavi z ustavo SFRJ (1974) in ustavnimi amandmaji (1981, 1988): Primerjava amandmajev k ustavi SFRJ (1988) z amandmaji k ustavam SR in SAP iz leta 1989"* (Comparative analysis of amendments to constitutions of SRs and SAPs of 1989 in comparison with the Constitution

of SFRY of 1974 as amended in 1981 and 1988: The comparison of the amendments to the Constitution of SFRY of 1974 adopted in 1988 with the amendments to constitutions of SRs and SAPs adopted in 1989) (Ljubljana: Predsedstvo SRS, October–November 1989).)

30. Slobodan Milosevic, who by 1988 had captured his political power in Serbia by replacing the existing independent leadership in both autonomous provinces, was elected President of Serbia. He served for two consecutive terms in this office and was later elected President of the Federal Republic of Yugoslavia, which includes Serbia and Montenegro.

31. See *Ustav Republike Srbije* (Constitution of the Republic of Serbia), *Sluzbeni list RS* – Official Gazette of the Republic of Serbia, No. 1/1990.

32. After the first multiparty elections in the early Spring of 1990 the previous political opposition—the Croatian Democratic Union (HDZ – Hrvatska demokratska zajednica)—came to power in Croatia. Its leader, Franjo Tudjman, became the president of the Republic of Croatia with extensive competencies.

33. See *Ustav Republike Hrvatske* (Constitution of the Republic of Croatia), *Narodne novine RH* – Official Gazette of the Republic of Croatia, No. 56/1990.

34. See *Ustavni zakon* (The Constitutional Law on Human Rights and Freedoms and on the Rights of Ethnic and National Communities or Minorities in the Republic of Croatia), *Narodne novine RH* – Official Gazette of the Republic of Croatia, No. 65/1991.

35. See *Ustava Republike Slovenije* (The Constitution of the Republic of Slovenia), *Uradni list Republike Slovenije* – Official Gazette of the Republic of Slovenia, No. 33/1991. The official English translation of the constitution was published in the Fall 1992: Constitution of the Republic of Slovenia, *Casopisni zavod Uradni list Republike Slovenije*, Ljubljana 1992.

36. The Constitution of the Republic of Macedonia (1992), the Constitution of the Federal Republic of Yugoslavia (1992), and the Dayton Constitution of Bosnia-Herzegovina (1995) were adopted later.

37. For a more detailed personal account on the Yugoslav crisis and the analysis of the collapse of ex-Yugoslavia see Mitja Zagar, "Yugoslavia: What Went Wrong? Constitutional Aspects of the Yugoslav Crisis from the Perspective of Ethnic Conflict" in Metta Spencer, ed., *The Lessons of Yugoslavia*, Research on Russia and Eastern Europe Series, Volume Two (Canada: JAI Press, forthcoming). For accounts of different authors see the books listed as the suggested readings.

38. These principles should be considered when the process of democratization starts in a certain plural environment. Namely, democracy is not just competition and the rule of a simple majority but also cooperation and the protection of minorities. In this context, we need to reconsider also the introduction of multiparty elections in ethnically plural societies where no political traditions exist. The introduction of multiparty elections might require several long-term activities, education, and effective mechanisms for the democratic management of possible conflicts.

References

Banac, Ivo. 1993. *The National Question in Yugoslavia: Origins, History, Politics,* 2nd ed. Ithaca, N.Y.: Cornell University Press.

Bilandzic, Dusan. 1985. *Zgodovina Socialisticne federativne republike Jugoslavije: Glavni procesi* (The History of the Socialist Federal Republic of Yugoslavia: Main Processes), 3. izdanje (Third edition), Skolska knjiga, Zagreb.

Cviic, Chrisopher. 1991. *Remaking the Balkans.* New York: Council on Foreign Relations Press.

Clissold, Stephen, ed. 1960. *A Short History of Yugoslavia from Early Times to 1966.* Cambridge: Cambridge University Press.

Denitch, Bogdan. 1990. *Limits and Possibilities: The Crisis of Yugoslav Socialism and State Socialist Systems.* Minneapolis, Minn.: University of Minnesota Press.

———. 1994. *Ethnic Nationalism: The Tragic Death of Yugoslavia.* Minneapolis, Minn.: University of Minnesota Press.

Djilas, Aleska. 1991. *The Contested Country: Yugoslav Unity and Communist Revolution, 1919–1953.* Cambridge, Mass.: Harvard University Press.

Djordjevic, Dimitrije, ed. 1980. *The Creation of Yugoslavia, 1914–1918,* London: Clio Books.

Jovan Djordjevic, Jovan. 1980. *Ustavno pravo* (Constitutional Law). Beograd: Savremena administracija.

Gellner, Ernest. 1983. *Nations and Nationalism.* Ithaca and London: Cornell University Press.

Glenny, Misha. 1990. *The Rebirth of History: Eastern Europe in the Age of Democracy.* London: Penguin Books.

Hobsbawn, Eric J. 1990. *Nations and Nationalism since 1789: Programme, Myth, Reality,* Cambridge: Cambridge University Press.

Hoptner, J.B. 1962. *Yugoslavia in Crisis, 1934–1941.* New York and London: Columbia University Press.

Horowitz, Donald L. (1985), *Ethnic Groups in Conflict.* Berkeley: University of California Press.

Jelavich, Barbara. 1983. *History of the Balkans.* Cambridge: Cambridge University Press, vol.1: *Eighteenth and Nineteenth Centuries* & Vol. 2: *Twentieth Century.*

Jelavich, Charles and Barbara Jelavich. 1977. *The Establishment of the Balkan National States, 1804–1920,* Vol. 8 of *A History of East Central Europe.* Seattle: University of Washington Press.

Lucarelli, Sonia. 1995. *The International Community and the Yugoslav Crisis: A Chronology of Events,* EUI Working Paper RSC No. 95/8 (March 1995), Robert Schuman Centre, European University Institute, Florence.

Magas, Branka. 1992. *The Destruction of Yugoslavia: Tracing the Break Up, 1980–1992.* London: Verso.

Mønnesland, Svein. 1992. *Før Jugoslavia og etter: Nye stater – gamle nasjoner.* Sypress Forlag, Oslo; *Statisticki bilten* (Statistical Bulletin – Federal Statistical Office), Br./No. 1295, Savezni zavod za statistiku, Beograd 1982.

Montville, Joseph V. *Conflict and Peacemaking in Multiethnic Societies,* Lexington, Mass. and Toronto: Lexington Books.

Petranovic, Branko and Momcilo Zecevic, eds. 1987. *Jugoslovanski federalizam: Ideje i stvarnost, Tematska zbirka dokumenata, Prvi tom 1914–1943* (The Yugoslav Federalism: Ideas and Reality, Thematic Collection of Documents), Prosveta, Beograd; *Prvi tom, 1914–1943 (Vol. I, 1914–1943); Drugi tom: 1943–1986 (Vol. II, 1943–1986).*

Pirjevec, Joze. 1995. *Jugoslavija, 1918–1992: Nastanek, razvoj ter razpad Karadjordjeviceve in Titove Jugoslavije* (Yugoslavia, 1918–1992: The Formation, Development and Downfall of Karadjordjevic's and Tito's Yugoslavia), Zalozba Lipa, Koper.

Poulton, Hough. 1991. *Balkans: Minorities and States in Conflict.* Foreword by Milovan Djilas, Minority Rights Group. London: Minority Rights Publications.

Ramet, Pedro. 1984. *Nationalism and Federalism in Yugoslavia, 1963–1983.* Bloomington: Indiana University Press.

———. 1985. *Yugoslavia in the 1980s.* Westview Special Studies on the Soviet Union and Eastern Europe. Boulder and London: Westview Press.

Rusinow, Denison, I. 1977. *The Yugoslav Experiment, 1948–1974.* Berkeley: University of California Press.

Rusinow, Denison I., ed. 1988. *Yugoslavia: A Fractured Federalism.* Washington, D.C.: The Wilson Center Press.

Statisticni godisnjak Jugoslavije. 1988. (The Statistical Yearbook of Yugoslavia – 1988), Year XXXV, *Savezni zavod za statistiku,* Beograd, 1988.

Minority Rights Group. 1989. *World Directory of Minorities.* London: Longman International Reference.

Zametica, John. 1992. *The Yugoslav Conflict: An Analysis of the Causes of the Yugoslav War, the Policies of the Republics and the Regional and International Implications of the Conflict.* Adelphi Paper 270, The International Institute for Strategic Studies – IISS/Brassey's, London.

Zagar, Mitja. 1994. "Nation-States, Their Constitutions and Multi-Ethnic Reality: Do Constitutions of Nation-States Correspond to Ethnic Reality?" *The Journal of Ethno-Development,* Vol. 3, No. 3: 1–19.

———. 1995a. "Constitutions in Multi-Ethnic Reality." *Gradiva in razprave/Treatises and Documents,* No. 29–30, Institut za narodnostna vprasanja/Institute for Ethnic Studies, Ljubljana, 1994/1995, 143–64.

———. 1995b. "*Nekaj hipotez o kvadraturi kroga: Ustava SFRJ in proces osamosvajanja Republike Slovenije – Etnicna dimenzija osamosvajanja Slovenije*" (The Constitution of the SFRY and the Struggle for the Independence of the Republic of Slovenia: Ethnic dimensions of the independence) *Gradiva in razprave/*Treatises and Documents, No. 29–30, Institut za narodnostna vprasanja/Institute for Ethnic Studies, Ljubljana, 231–60.

9

South Africa's National Peace Accord and Laue's Developmental Vision for Community Conflict Intervention

George J. McCall and Miranda Duncan

Community Conflict Intervention and the Just Social System

COMMUNITY CONFLICT INTERVENTION (CCI) is not merely the application of techniques of mediation and conciliation to community-level disputes. What most distinguishes community conflict intervention from (or within) the broader field of conflict resolution are 1) its consideration of a wider spectrum of conflict roles and outcomes, and 2) the centrality of a "social change toward justice" orientation.

In any one conflict, it is typical that some intervenors are advocating for a particular party, other intervenors are advocating for a particular outcome, and yet other intervenors are advocating for a particular process to be employed in conducting the conflict (Laue 1978, 1981a). Emphasizing that negotiation plays a particularly vital part in all social conflicts, and that a just, proper, and effective negotiation process requires adequate representation of all parties, community conflict intervention does in practice focus on the key role of negotiation-process advocates, or mediators. Here, mediation is viewed not as a means of social control, of settlement, but rather as a means of social change (Scimecca 1987). That is, by empowering all parties within the negotiation process, the power structure of the community may be altered (Laue 1971, 1977) and a just solution may emerge; "true substantive justice will flow from the procedural safeguard of proportional empowerment" (Laue and Cormick, 1978, 220).

Social change toward justice thus becomes the proper general goal for intervenors in community disputes. Justice is the ultimate social good. The just social system would be one in which power (control of decisions) is diffused, decision-making is participatory, accountability for decisions is visible, and resources are adequate and equitably distributed. Justice can only result from the continuous interplay of individuals and groups adequately empowered to represent their own interests, with a minimum of superordinate umpiring to prevent power concentrations and, therefore, abuses (Laue and Cormick 1978, 219–20).

On the Road to a Just Social System?

In his classic article assessing "The Future of Community Conflict Intervention," James H. Laue acknowledged the three directions CCI (and its vision of the just social system) logically might take: 1) gradual decline; 2) continuation of its previous, somewhat bumpy trajectory; or 3) a dramatic take-off. He both hoped and believed that this third—"developmental"—track would prove to be the best-fit model.

By the "developmental track" Laue meant not only the cumulative and continuous development of the theory and practice of community conflict intervention narrowly defined, but the diffusion of its ethos across the institutions of civil society. A critical mass of citizens and organizations would demand access to collaborative procedures in which all parties could effectively express their interests and participate in shaping outcomes. In response to such popular demand, many private- and public-sector agencies would routinely and continuously fund a wide variety of such forums. In effect, collaborative conflict resolution would have become institutionalized (at least as an available alternative) within virtually every sector and arena of conflict. Weighing various concrete factors favoring and threatening that scenario, Laue concluded that:

If the field of community conflict intervention is to take the developmental track in the 1980s, I believe three major needs must be addressed: (a) adaptation of mediation and other techniques to pre-crisis, preventive, and policy-making uses; (b) thorough exploration of the relationships of conflict intervention at the community and national levels with that at the international level; and (c) establishment of a broadly-respected clearing house or umbrella function for the field (Laue 1982, 61–69).

Did the field successfully address those three major needs? And did community conflict intervention indeed "take the developmental track" in the 1980s?

Looking back now from the vantage point of the late 1990s, the scorecard for the U.S. in these respects seems to us a bit muddled. Although CCI clearly did not just fade away, like a passing fad (the scenario of decline), neither did

CCI attain the degree of intellectual synthesis and critical mass required for that dramatic take-off envisioned in the scenario of cumulative and continuous development of the field. Certainly, some dramatic advances—the Hewlett university centers, the National Institute of Dispute Resolution (NIDR), the Negotiated Investment Strategy, the Conflict Clinic, the Institute for Conflict Analysis and Resolution, to name just a few—were achieved, many of them through visionary funding by the Hewlett Foundation, Ford Foundation, the Kettering Foundation, and individual philanthropists. Conversely, just as Laue had feared, synthesis and critical mass were seriously hindered by other factors, both internal and external to the field.

Rather than the CCI evolving into a discipline or profession of "conflict resolution," various existing disciplines and professions developed their own conflict resolution subfields, thus hindering that bringing together of people and approaches required for intellectual synthesis.[1] External factors—particularly the "New Federalism" of the Reagan and Bush administrations, that Laue had so strongly feared—prevented the achievement of critical mass, by undercutting federal leadership in the field through altering jurisdictional relations (partially offset by the concomitant rise of state offices of mediation), fiscally crippling extant federal programs (Community Relations Service, Federal Mediation, and Conciliation Service, the neighborhood justice centers program), and effectively hobbling new federal initiatives that those administrations could not block (United States Institute of Peace, the Dispute Resolution Act of 1980). In Laue's analysis, critical mass will have been achieved only when "Cooperative and equitable dispute resolution . . . is viewed as a necessary service and is supported by permanent endowments from the private sector as well as ongoing public resources" (Laue 1982, 65). Whether either of these two criteria were met in American society during (or since) the 1980s seems quite debatable, nor does the subsequent development of American CCI strike us as having become "truly cumulative, continuous and directional" (Laue 1982, 63).

A much closer fit, we contend, was the astonishing and scarcely anticipated development of CCI in South Africa during the early 1990s. In the remainder of this chapter, we examine how that country's National Peace Accord did effectively address all three of the needs identified by Laue and so achieved that dramatic take-off which he labeled the developmental track.

South Africa's National Peace Accord

If CCI as a discernible field can indeed be dated to the American civil rights era (McCall 1995), its emergence in South Africa must be said to have lagged considerably. Though infamous as a deeply divided society, South Africa experienced tight state controls over many foreign innovations (such as television) with potential for disturbing the precarious political balance achieved by the apartheid regime.

As in the U.S., the evolution of CCI in South Africa proved discontinuous and episodic. During the national wave of popular unrest inspired by the Soweto uprising of 1976, a handful of progressive, religiously based fellowship centers across South Africa began to respond to requests to intervene in local community conflicts. In 1980, one of these (the Centre for Intergroup Studies [CIS], at the University of Cape Town) "decided to focus its research on the theory and practice of mediation" (Salem 1994, 12; Hare 1983). During the next and greater wave of popular rebellion in 1984–85, CIS began to offer major training programs in negotiation and mediation, and spun off the Independent Mediation Service of South Africa to mediate and arbitrate labor disputes. Significantly, these efforts, like others scattered across the country, directly involved American and British experts.[2] Mediation began to acquire a measure of popular respect and interest, not only from some notable successes in the labor field, but also from the efforts of the Commonwealth's Eminent Persons Group (van der Merwe 1989, 99). Before the end of the decade, a national association of practitioners and scholars had emerged: the South African Association for Conflict Intervention (SAACI).

An important countervailing factor, however, was the militancy of the anti-apartheid movement. Negotiation and collaboration were considered virtually dirty words. Yet, all the while, a common realization was developing (backstage, among the various political elites) of the necessity for a negotiated settlement rather than an armed victory (Mandela 1994; Sparks 1995).

When that unspoken reality finally became public, through the new State President F.W. de Klerk's famous "Red Friday" address to the South African parliament in February 1990, many NGOs and universities responded immediately by organizing new and exciting programs of CCI—the Community Dispute Resolution Trust, the African Centre for Constructive Resolution of Disputes, the Community Conflict Resolution Service, the Institute for the Study and Resolution of Conflict, to mention only a few.[3]

At that time, however, it must be emphasized that the political elites who promulgated the new doctrine of negotiated settlement were certainly far out in front of their followers. With the unbanning of leftist parties, the release of Nelson Mandela and other political prisoners, and the return of political exiles, lower-ranking players were simply caught unprepared. In the high-stakes scramble for power, the actions of these lesser leaders often actually promoted political violence—which till then had been largely confined to the province of Natal, but now became essentially national in scope. Absent any tradition of political tolerance, South Africa's negotiated transition to democracy was rapidly foundering on the shoals of aggressive political violence—violent confrontations surrounding rallies, marches, and political funerals; openly conducted large-scale attacks by supporters of one political organization on territories dominated by one of its rivals; and intimidation through proclamation of well-defended "no-go areas." Various bilateral peace agreements—between the government and the African National Congress (ANC), between the ANC and the Inkhata Freedom Party(IFP)—negotiated by the highest party leaders, immediately proved unenforceable and ineffective. Many analysts argued that only a broad, multiparty peace accord stood any chance of effectiveness.

By the beginning of 1991, various societal elites sought desperately to broker such a multiparty accord. The church elite, the progressive element of the business elite, and the state elite each undertook separate attempts, all of which failed miserably. It was only when church and business leaders joined in a more politically balanced cooperative effort that a truly broad-based peace meeting could be organized. From that June 22 meeting emerged "a structured process that would bind parties to an agreement providing a framework for ending the violence" (Gastrow 1995, 27). That sometimes frantic, often creative structured process culminated in a National Peace Convention on September 14, bringing together for the first time the national leaders of virtually every political group (including the government), to sign the National Peace Accord (NPA).

Perhaps the first consensual document to have been produced in South Africa, the NPA was a high-profile social contract to honor—and to jointly enforce—a common code of political conduct calculated to minimize political intimidation and violence.[4] Indeed, because the security forces were widely regarded as a part of that problem, the NPA spelled out a special code of conduct for the South African police calculated to reinforce De Klerk's edict of political neutrality and to promote sound police practices. The NPA drafters attempted (but did not meet the deadline) to formulate a similar code for the South African Defense Forces. Nevertheless, both the police and the military were clearly expected to participate in Peace Accord structures at every level.

To the national elites, this peace accord was principally a step necessary to taking the next steps in the negotiated transition to democracy (Haysom 1992; Friedman 1993). Their attention turned immediately to Codesa, a forum for the first constitutional negotiations. To lower strata, however, the NPA was a matter not of symbolic politics but of realpolitik; in many localities, its implementation was, quite literally, a life or death concern.

Predictably, implementation of the document—roughly cobbled together and never fully drafted—proved problematic throughout. Some provisions were never implemented, and none without considerable difficulty and travail. The

NPA itself had spelled out a multipronged, multilevel structural arrangement for the joint enforcement of the new codes of conduct. Political muscle was to be provided by the overarching National Peace Committee (NPC), comprising one or two senior representatives from each of the thirty-six signatory organizations. The factfinding function was assigned to two types of new structures: a judicial Commission of Inquiry for the Prevention of Public Violence and Intimidation (with a mandate to conduct inquiries at national, regional, and local levels, and reporting directly to the State President), and specially appointed Justices of the Peace (to operate at the local level to investigate complaints pertaining to public violence or intimidation). Designated to serve the justice function were two other types of new structures: these same Justices of the Peace (empowered to take action in urgent local cases), and special criminal courts (to deal with unrest-related cases, cases of public violence, and cases involving political intimidation). The function of socioeconomic reconstruction was to be served by establishing local subcommittees on socioeconomic reconstruction and development (responsible to an NPC subcommittee), envisaged to operate hand-in-hand with local dispute resolution committees to facilitate development of a community's economic and human resources and to initiate reconstruction projects.

Of all the structures prescribed to pursue these three key functions, only the Commission of Inquiry (better known as the Goldstone Commission) was ever appointed—and it actually antedated the Peace Accord by several months! Still, the Commission was seen as perhaps the most credible body in South Africa at that time (indeed, its inclusion in the NPA amounts to its endorsement by the signatories), and its inquiries played a crucial role in shaping public discourse. Otherwise, factfinding, justice, and socioeconomic reconstruction remained in quite short supply.

The actual work of the NPA centered, then, almost exclusively on its order function. Peripheral to that function was the Police Board, not implemented until 1992 and in any case intended as only advisory to the minister of law and justice. What became familiarly known to South Africans as "the Peace Accord structures" was its multitiered system of dispute resolution committees (later relabeled as peace committees).

The head and the heart of this system was the National Peace Secretariat (NPS)—a far smaller, essentially full-time, multiparty body which was responsible to the NPC, funded by the Department of Justice, and charged to establish and coordinate regional and local dispute resolution committees. Membership of these regional dispute resolution committees (RDRCs) was to include regional leaders of political organizations, churches, trade unions, business and industry, local and tribal authorities, and the security forces. RDRCs were to inform and advise higher peace structures, guide and monitor local committees, settle disputes, and combat violence and intimidation. Local dispute resolution committees (LDRCs) were to create trust and reconciliation among grassroots leaders and security forces; liase with police to ensure that meetings, rallies, and marches could be held peacefully; and settle community disputes through mediation and negotiation.

The process to settle the composition of the NPC and NPS required two months of delicate political balancing. Once established, the NPS divided the country into eleven regions, and tackled immediately the two most violence-racked regions (KwaZulu-Natal, and the region around Johannesburg). By the time that Parliament managed to formalize the design of the NPA through the Internal Peace Institutions Act in July 1992, the NPS had already organized an RDRC in most of the regions as well as several dozen LDRCs. By the end of 1993, DRCs had been established (and trained) in all eleven regions and in about 250 communities. Paid staff numbered 239, supplemented by some 8,500 volunteers. These DRCs handled hundreds of conflicts over highly divisive issues, and thus contributed substantially to maintaining a degree of grassroots stability sufficient to sustain the process of constitutional negotiations well into its third phase (Codesa II). When those talks collapsed in the wake of the June 1992 Boipatong massacre, a decision was taken to bolster the DRCs through the addition of international observers—from the United Nations, the European Community, the Commonwealth, and the Organization of African Unity. As "the eyes and ears of the international community," their presence at rallies and marches "caused participants to show greater restraint" (Gastrow 1995, 73). Constitutional talks soon resumed, in a revised format, and quickly achieved governance through a Transitional Executive Committee, a transitional Constitution of 1993, and the April 1994 watershed election of a transitional Government of National Unity, headed by Nelson Mandela.

With the emergence of these bodies, the standing of the Peace Accord structures as the only legitimate bodies in South Africa was superseded. To conduct a free and fair election, however, the Independent Election Commission required thousands of campaign and polling monitors, virtually overnight. The DRCs were drafted for that task, and in less than three months conducted 456 workshops to train 12,577 peace monitors.

Post-election, however, the connotations of the NPA seemed inconsistent with the Rainbow Nation of the New South Africa; many felt that a truly democratic government should not have to rely on a public-private joint venture of this sort. Despite plentiful testimony on continuing need for the NPA structures— acute in some regions and local communities—the Internal Peace Institutions Act was repealed and its structures were sent into "early retirement." On April 6,

1995, the National Peace Accord was honored in Parliament and the document turned over for permanent display in the library of that legislative body.

How the National Peace Accord Fulfilled the Three Identified Needs

It is our contention here that the NPA did essentially fulfill each of the three needs that Laue had identified as prerequisites to achievement of the developmental track, and that CCI in South Africa did achieve that trajectory during the early 1990s.

Preventive Mediation

If community conflict intervention is to mature and be useful in dealing with the longer range issues of justice and social development that spawn disputes, it must focus more on preventive and policy-making functions (Laue 1982, 66).

Beyond settling community disputes and ensuring that public gatherings could be held peacefully—what Laue (1982, 66) would call "case-by-case reactions to conflict or crisis situations"—the DRCs were also charged to undertake genuine peace building, by creating trust and reconciliation among grassroots leaders and security forces and by working with local subcommittees on socioeconomic reconstruction and development. Indeed, perhaps the greatest contribution of the DRCs was their democratizing, community-building role (Nossel and Shear 1992).

Residents were for the very first time witnessing local leaders, sitting around the same table, who in the past would not have spoken to each other. In some areas no communication had existed between the IFP, the ANC, and other rival groups. Police and defense force members had not been able to establish normal communication channels with many black activists in townships. To have community leaders, police, political groups, tribal chiefs, and church representatives jointly addressing community issues had never happened before. It helped to create a measure of trust among members of the peace committees that it is possible to work with "enemies" for the common good. Political tolerance and the notion of political pluralism is therefore being introduced by example into every community in which an [LDRC] is established (Gastrow 1995, 68–69).

Less widely, these DRCs did also take on an actual policy-making function, serving to negotiate a far-reaching agreement on some important community issue—often an issue of community development or reconstruction (despite the national failure to implement the proposed parallel socioeconomic subcommittees). A handful of these agreements (Port Shepstone, Bruntville/Mooi

River, Mpumalanga) received considerable national publicity, and excited wide interest in this potential.

Cross-level Linkages

The field of conflict intervention now has developed to the point where serious questions are being addressed regarding the applicability of techniques across system level: "A thorough exploration of these linkages is among the most important next steps in the development of conflict intervention." (Laue 1982, 66–67).

Cross-level work was in fact a distinctively central feature of the NPA, as is reflected in its multitiered system of national, regional, and local structures. Through the conscious efforts of the National Peace Secretariat and its expanded subcommittees, none of these DRCs operated in isolation. Experiences in one area, or at one level, became known in other areas and at other levels. Learnings about unanticipated problems or novel techniques were explicitly disseminated through national and regional workshops and through incorporation in the constantly revised training programs. Often enough, these learnings detailed how certain techniques and forms that worked satisfactorily at sophisticated national and regional levels proved inappropriate and unworkable in some deeply rural LDRCs.

Laue's own explication of the need for cross-level linkages particularly emphasized "the linking of community and national peacemaking with international peacemaking" (Laue 1982, 67). The South African case is quite interesting in that respect. As already noted, CCI had received a substantial boost in consequence of certain highly visible international mediation efforts in Southern Africa (Crockett 1992; Ohlson and Stedman 1994; Zartman and Deng 1991), particularly the visit of the Commonwealth's Eminent Persons Group to South Africa itself and the U.S. role in the resolution of the Angola and Namibia questions. More concurrently, the direct and substantial involvement of international monitors in the post-Boipatong work of the NPA proved mutually instructive, as elaborated and documented in the United States Institute of Peace seminar examining that role (USIP 1993). Finally, Buthulezi's invocation of international mediation of an IFP/ANC agreement served as an enabling condition for IFP participation in the 1994 election.

(C) Umbrella Organization

"[I]t is . . . time for conscious formation of the critical mass in conflict intervention" (Laue 1982, 67).

Although structured very differently from NIDR (Laue's best bet in the American scenario), the NPA did consciously, deliberately, and successfully create a critical mass for conflict intervention. Many thousands of local and regional leaders received professional training and considerable direct experience in CCI; at least 250 flashpoint communities established highly visible and influential local dispute resolution committees; mediation and conflict resolution became highly fashionable concepts in all sorts of public discourse; the anniversary of the signing of the NPA was celebrated annually through media happenings and street festivities throughout the country.

Moreover, the NPA did effectively perform all the functions Laue attributes to a true umbrella organization. Its remarkable success in promoting the public visibility and acceptance of CCI (just noted) was achieved partly through national promotional campaigns—complete with logos and songs—but mainly through news coverage and its own recruitment and training efforts. The NPS, through its subcommittees, its workshops, its organization of a nationwide hierarchical system of DRCs, forged dense webs of interdependencies among practitioners and scholars, far surpassing NIDR in serving the function of network development. The NPA, during its existence, far outdistanced all others in its project-funding function, supporting around 261 regional and local dispute resolution forums (each quite extensive in size and duration) and thousands of workshops, to a tune of around fifteen million dollars in public and private funds during 1993–94. Finally, the NPA also performed important clearinghouse functions; everyone in the field worked with and through the NPS, resulting in an unprecedented awareness of others' activities and bringing about a significant degree of intellectual synthesis (reflected especially in the nationally coordinated convergence of training materials and procedures).

The Developmental Track

In sum, the National Peace Accord not only broke new ground in cross-system linkages and applied CCI techniques to "longer term issues of justice and social development," but also provided an effective umbrella organization that produced that critical mass and intellectual synthesis which Laue predicted would fuel a genuine "take-off." Documentation of these dramatic changes in South African CCI during the very early 1990s, and of just how the NPA answered the three identified needs, ought to be much fuller—indeed, such was the fervent wish of the research subcommittee of the National Peace Secretariat all along. Its chairman, Peter Gastrow, is responsible for the best single account available (Gastrow 1995) and for encouraging most of the other accounts and analyses (Nossel and Shear 1992; International Alert 1993; Shaw 1993a, 1993b; Sisk 1994; Odendaal and Spies 1996).

Where Has the National Peace Accord Experience Left the Field?

In South Africa

Is CCI still on "the developmental track" in South Africa? Probably not. First of all, its dramatic take-off there has largely leveled off—such explosive acceleration could not possibly be sustained. Second, Laue's analysis suggests that stability of funding is probably the most important determinant, but the overall level of fiscal support for CCI in South Africa has fallen off considerably. NGOs (of every sort) today face a massive crisis of funding (the European and American monies that had fueled their proliferation having now slowed to a mere trickle), and the substantial levels of government funding formerly provided through the NPA and the IEC have disappeared along with those bodies. Third, no successor has arisen to assume the decommissioned NPA's functions as an umbrella organization for CCI.

But through its dramatic take-off during the early 1990s, South African CCI did reach a far higher plateau. Perhaps more than in any other society today, mediation and conflict resolution are terms of ordinary public discourse. Quite a few localities became so committed to their LDRCs or other community forums for CCI, that they have simply maintained them through their own resources. Similarly, the extraordinary levels of political violence in KwaZulu-Natal (right up through the long-delayed municipal elections of June 1996) persuaded the national government to essentially spare the RDRC in that province, still functioning today. The national government also continues to flirt with new applications of CCI—such as police-community forums, family courts, community courts, and local reconstruction and development boards (though without serious levels of funding)—as do the surviving NGOs, now promoting school mediation and environmental dispute resolution.

The continuing development of formal knowledge by South African scholars (Anstey 1991, 1992, 1993; van der Merwe 1993; Pretorius 1993; Nieuwmeijer and du Toit 1994; Malan 1997) strives to remain cumulative and directional, as witnessed by a nationwide effort to take stock of current lines of research and their likely extensions (Nieuwmeijer, du Toit, and Sebulela 1995; Minnar and Hough 1997).

The number, competence, and reputation of experienced South African practitioners has led that country to both recognize and pursue a self-conscious role as prophet and teacher to other nations, particularly on the continent of Africa.

Globally

For the worldwide field of CCI, of course, the significance of the NPA is theoretical rather than political. That theoretical significance lies primarily in its design: multilateral, multipronged, and (especially) multitiered.

The disappointments of 1990–91 had shown South Africans that bilateral peace agreements tend to founder on unilateral withdrawals; some analysts suggested that a multilateral agreement signed by all the parties might make withdrawal far more costly in political terms. And, in fact, no signatory ever renounced the Accord or actually withdrew from any of the DRCs (although in a very few DRCs one or more parties did temporarily withhold their active participation). Many participants in the drafting of the NPA also believed that the fate of their joint exercise in peacemaking would depend upon incorporating provisions for subsequent peacekeeping and peace building measures. Hence, its multipronged design, providing for the functions of factfinding, justice, order, and socioeconomic reconstruction and development.

National leaders of many participating organizations—having sought unilaterally to restrain violent acts by their own followers—had been frustrated and embarrassed by their inability to leverage certain of their regional and local leaders. As its key design feature, therefore, the NPA took a multitiered approach, calling for leaders at each of these three levels to form their own DRCs.

In its design, then, the NPA constituted a bold and innovative national approach to widespread (and interlinked) violent community conflicts.[5] But does a design of this type actually work?

The question of whether the NPA was a success or a failure turns out to be unexpectedly complex and has surely been overemphasized (Shaw 1993b; Gastrow 1995). Because so few provisions of the accord were ever implemented, it is of course impossible to tell whether that promising design actually worked. The question becomes, then, did the multitiered system of dispute resolution committees succeed or fail?

Critics of the NPA emphasized that several key political organizations never did sign the accord, some signatories periodically withheld their participation, the security forces remained problematic players throughout, and the number of political killings actually increased. These critics blame bad faith (on the part of several signatories, especially the government), bureaucratic inertia, or fuzzy-minded utopianism.

Defenders of the NPA discount these blamings and also contend that the elevated body count measures not the failure but rather the success of the NPA. That argument develops as follows. First, because the Peace Accord was undertaken by the political elites as the necessary stepping stone toward constitutional negotiations, the fact that Codesa opened only three months after the signing of the accord signifies that the NPA quickly fulfilled its primary function. Second, as nearly all commentators concede, the changed political circumstances posed by constitutional negotiations greatly raised the stakes for several parties. Third, as political violence then became a far more serious undertaking for some, the very nature of political violence changed drastically; the lethally efficient and anonymous raids of high-powered hit squads (generating far higher body counts) came to displace the highly public street counter-demonstration violence which the NPA had been designed to control. Hence, the elevated body count can be said to reflect the success of the NPA in two senses: as a stepping stone to constitutional negotiations, and as a control on partisan confrontational demonstration and counter-demonstration events.

A less roundabout defense of the NPA cites the many localized successes of its dispute resolution committees—occasions where it does seem clear to close observers that violence was averted through LDRC functioning, by controlling effects of rumors, inflammatory remarks, demonstrations, and street confrontations. The most widely appreciated instance, no doubt, was the funeral day for the assassinated Chris Hani; in the Johannesburg area (where the regional and local committees had quickly developed detailed agreements among the parties) virtually no violence occurred, whereas the Cape Town area (absent comparable agreements) suffered very serious political violence (Sisk 1994).

Indeed, many commentators locate the overall successfulness of the NPA in its having established, within many flashpoint communities, a multiparty communication/problem-solving forum that was the first step toward effective local governance.

Finally, to support that interpretation, many defenders of the NPA point to the alarming rate of attempted and actual assassinations of RDRC and LDRC members, presumably by parties interested in preventing the emergence of such multiparty community forums and their promotion of grassroots democracy. But whatever one concludes regarding the success or failure of the NPA, the field of CCI learned from that experience a great many lessons about how to design and implement peace accords.

Program Design Problems

Numerous critics of the NPA (e.g., Midgley 1995) have attributed many of its tribulations to the fact that it very definitely emerged through a top-down (rather than a bottom-up) process of design. This trenchant criticism has served to prod the field into serious consideration of both the difficulties and the limitations of top-down design of such agreements. Peter Gastrow (1995) presents an unusually detailed and analytical account of the actual design process from which the NPA text emerged. Timothy Sisk (1995) was spurred to a deeply theoretical analysis of the nature and limitations of elite settlements, drawing heavily on the works of Michael Burton and John Higley (Burton and Higley 1987; Higley and Burton 1989). But, in a way, the genius of the NPA lies in its (top-down) creation of the system of regional and local committees to eventually engage the grassroots leaders in bringing the spirit of the NPA codes alive in localized contexts. Not enough has yet been written about how that system managed to do so.

A second criticism is that the NPA's function of socioeconomic reconstruction was poorly thought through. Although properly cognizant that destroyed homes and public buildings often constituted major local issues—redressable through funds for reconstruction—that provision of the NPA essentially ignored previous South African research (Byerley and Hindson 1992) which showed that the availability of reconstruction/development monies enormously elevates the stakes for local political contentiousness. Perhaps it was partly for this reason that the local subcommittees for socioeconomic reconstruction and development were never actually implemented, despite the passionate interest of the NPC chairman and the earmarking of public funds for that purpose.

Another design flaw was vague and inadequate provision for code-enforcement. The primary reason for this weakness was that the adjudicatory and enforcement procedures of the accord required multiparty consensus and cooperation. Even the decision to submit a dispute for adjudication or arbitration required a consensus in practice. In retrospect, an independent body would have had a much better chance of enforcing the agreed code of conduct (Gastrow 1995, 63).

Finally, the NPA has been called a (counter-cultural?) First-World solution to a First World/Third World problem, a solution unresponsive to the harsh realities of that social interface, including:

- the continuing importance of traditional leadership (chiefs, village headmen)
- socioeconomic realities (e.g., although DRC members did receive reimbursement of costs for attending meetings, many grassroots participants could not afford to attend the next meeting until reimbursement had been received for the previous one)
- linguistic realities (the document-heavy process was not friendly to the many DRC members who were illiterate; moreover, the English language—unfamiliar to many—was the medium for all NPA documents and nearly all DRC deliberations)
- spatial segregation (exaggerated by apartheid regulations, spatial segregation of ethnic groups dictated longer travel to DRC meetings, with atten-

dant economic costs and risks to personal safety in travelling through the territories of other groups)
- political intolerance (even within many white communities)
- a culture of violence
- two contrasting police cultures
- lack of organizational discipline (especially between national, regional, and local levels)

Implementation Obstacles and Successes

The NPA experience teaches the field of CCI a good deal about the difficulties of implementing peace accords of this nature.

First, the NPA was, for long, only a social policy. That is to say, it was a social compact rather than a public policy; during the crucial early months of implementation, much of the NPA lacked any basis at law. That it was a social compact, entirely voluntary in nature, lent real gravity to the fact that several important parties never signed the accord and thus were never bound by any of its provisions.

Second, the Accord was essentially a symbolic policy (Nakamura 1990)— the signatories endorsing the concept rather than making real commitments to its particulars, and bypassing the Accord structures for bilateral discussions at critical junctures.

Third, in this climate of a negotiated transition to democracy, political conditions changed rapidly and significantly. The attention of the political elites was deflected from the NPA by their rapid passage to second and third steps in that transition, before most of the Accord ever got started. The centrality of anticipatory jockeying in that constitutional process led to changing stakes in peace for several parties, and this in turn led to that changing face of political violence described above.

Therefore, by reason of these three rather distal factors hindering implementation, two other, more proximal factors arose. First, insufficient resources were committed to the establishment and operation of NPA structures. Cash was particularly scarce; the government contributed only (highly bureaucratic) reimbursement of direct cost of DRC meetings. Infrastructural support for DRC operations—telephone, fax, copying, mailing, and the like—derived almost entirely from in-kind contributions by nongovernment parties (often, a local business or church); clerical staffing was quite rare. Time is ever scarce in modern South Africa, and was either volunteered or an in-kind contribution. Most DRCs could manage only enough time to meet quite occasionally, and committee effectiveness was adversely affected by absences and tardiness.

Second, capability and know-how were often limited. Everywhere, meeting logistics and security were serious problems that restricted frequency of DRC activity. These problems were especially acute in the black townships; where could a sufficiently large and secure space be found, and how could participants get there safely? Further, most DRC participants lacked even rudimentary knowledge of the provisions of the NPA; for the longest time, it was available only in official pamphlet form, only in English, and in scant quantities. Limiting, too, was members' lack of skill or training, particularly in mediation and negotiation.

Fortunately, most DRCs somehow managed to cope with these proximal obstacles of insufficient resources and limited capability/know-how. A key here was the top-down, pyramidal nature of the implementation process. The NPS—national political leaders well-connected with the social elites of business, church, and academy—organized the eleven RDRCs, each of which assisted numerous localities of their respective regions in implementing LDRCs. Those at top levels thus rapidly accumulated much practical experience and ingenuity in dealing with problems of limited resources and know-how, so that even the most challenging of local situations could be helped.

A second key in this process was the role played by CCI professionals, very effectively mobilized by the NPS and most RDRCs to deal with the problem of limited capability and know-how. Their professional skills, experience, and reputation for neutrality were conducive to some serving as chairs (or facilitators) of DRCs; many more served as trainers, providing DRC members with rudimentary knowledge of mediation, negotiation, and the provisions of the NPA.

DRC Organization and Operation

Most of these dispute resolution committees were clumsy and inefficient contraptions, pretty much all wrong from the theoretical perspectives of group problem-solving and process design. That they did function, and often with tangible success, was due in good part to two design features. What lent these structures their almost unprecedented legitimacy was their inclusivity. DRC membership was never confined to NPA-signatory organizations, but instead was meant to include all politically significant organizations in the relevant geographic area. Reinforcing that foundation of legitimacy was the provision that DRC actions would be decided by consensus, not by voting. While these ideals of inclusivity and consensus proved difficult to define and to achieve, DRCs struggled diligently to practice them, drawing deeply on that expansive reservoir of social goodwill so notable among South Africans. Again, despite the continuing efforts of an NPS subcommittee on research, the wide range of DRC interpretations and tactics have been the subject of far too little documentation and analysis.

Conclusions

Our aim in this chapter has been not simply to analyze the distinctive justice views of CCI or to document and analyze the troubles and triumphs of South Africa's NPA but, more importantly, to harness these in probing Laue's sociological analysis of the paths the field of community conflict intervention may take, and of the conditions that influence its actual course in various places and times. Central in this respect is his conceptualization of the best-case scenario, the "developmental track." Our chapter apparently stands as the first historical look back on Laue's forecasting. We conclude that it remains questionable whether CCI took the developmental track in the United States in the 1980s, but that it definitely did so in South Africa during the early 1990s. In the process of reaching that conclusion, we hope that we have helped illuminate the deeper conceptual meaning of the "developmental track."

Suggested Study Questions

1. Why did the field of community conflict intervention follow the "developmental track" in South Africa rather than in the United States?
2. How do the justice ideals of community conflict intervention relate to the values of the liberation movement in South Africa?
3. Does diffusion of the ethos of collaborative conflict resolution throughout civil society eventually dictate its pursuit within a country's legal and international sectors as well, or do successes of mediation in legal, labor, and international arenas pave the way for its applications in political life and civil society?
4. What were some of the principal difficulties associated with the application of community conflict intervention practices in South Africa?

Notes

1. This phenomenon is, actually, quite congruent with the philosophy of the CCI field: adapt; let it bubble from the ground up; spread it around rather than make it exclusive—even though we lose energy, boundaries, and commonality along the way. A strength of the field is thus also a weakness.
2. At that time, the University of Missouri and the University of the Western Cape jointly proposed a path-breaking proposal for faculty exchange. We ourselves worked with Laue to develop a detailed plan for faculty exchange in the specific area of community conflict resolution. The proposal was funded by the United States Infor-

mation Agency, but by the time designated for Laue's visit to UWC he had already moved to George Mason University. Our own visit, scheduled for the second round, was moved up to January 1989. Thanks to Ampie Muller and Jannie Malan at UWC, we were sent to visit nearly all of the CCI programs operating at this tense moment near the end of P. W. Botha's presidency. Those links have brought us back to South Africa nearly every year, and served to involve us directly in the workings of the National Peace Accord, beginning in January 1992.

3. It was during this period that Laue and some of his associates at the Conflict Clinic (transferred from UMSL to GMU) did visit South Africa to provide consultation and training to some of these new programs.

4. The full text of the National Peace Accord is reprinted in Gastrow (1995) and in Anstey (1993).

5. This idea of a three-tiered system seems to have gained some currency in other national settings of community conflict (Lederach 1994), such as the Central American peace accord (Child 1992).

References

Anstey, Mark. 1991. *Negotiating Conflict.* Cape Town: Juta.

———. 1992. "Mediation in the South African Transition: A Critical Review of Developments, Problems and Potentials." *Geneve-Afrique* 30: 141–63.

———. 1993. *Practical Peacemaking: A Mediator's Handbook.* Cape Town: Juta.

Burton, Michael G. and John Higley. 1987. "Elite Settlements." *American Sociological Review* 52: 295–307.

Byerley, Mark and Doug Hindson. 1992. "Peace Pacts and Urban Reconstruction." *Work in Progress* 80: 31–33.

Child, Jack. 1992. *The Central American Peace Process 1983–1991.* Boulder, Colo.: Lynne Rienner Publishers.

Crocker, Chester. 1992. *High Noon in Southern Africa: Making Peace in a Rough Neighborhood.* New York: Norton.

Friedman, Steven, ed. 1993. *The Long Journey: South Africa's Quest for a Negotiated Settlement.* Johannesburg: Ravan Press.

Gastrow, Peter. 1995. *Bargaining for Peace: South Africa and the National Peace Accord.* Washington, D.C.: United States Institute of Peace Press.

Hare, A. Paul, ed. 1983. *The Struggle for Democracy in South Africa: Conflict and Conflict Resolution.* Cape Town: Centre for Intergroup Studies.

Haysom, Nicholas. 1992. "Negotiating a Political Settlement in South Africa." *South African Review* 6, 26–43.

Higley, John and Michael G. Burton. 1989. "The Elite Variable in Democratic Transitions and Breakdowns." *American Sociological Review* 54: 17–32.

Horowitz, Donald L. 1991. *A Democratic South Africa? Constitutional Engineering in a Di-*

vided Society. Berkeley: University of California Press.

International Alert. 1993. *Report of the Mission to South Africa to Evaluate the National Peace Accord and Its Peace Structures*. London: International Alert.

Laue, James H. 1982. "The Future of Community Conflict Intervention." *The Journal of Intergroup Relations* 10(2): 61–69.

———. April 1988. "The Ethics of Power and Justice." *Intergroup: A Newsletter of Conflict and Peace Studies and Activities in South Africa* 1–2.

Laue, James H. and Gerald Cormick. 1978. "The Ethics of Intervention in Community Disputes." In Gordon Bermant, Herbert C. Kelman and Donald P. Warwick, eds. *The Ethics of Social Intervention*. Washington, D.C.: Halstead Press.

Lederach, John Paul. 1994. *Building Peace: Sustainable Reconciliation in Divided Societies*. Tokyo: United Nations University.

Malan, Jannie. 1997. *Conflict Resolution Wisdom from Africa*. Durban: ACCORD.

Mandela, Nelson. 1994. *Long Walk to Freedom: The Autobiography of Nelson Mandela*. Randburg: Macdonald Purnell.

McCall, George J. 1995. "Racial and Ethnic Conflict: Perspectives from Community Intervention." *Research in Human Social Conflict* 1, 219–37.

Midgley, J. R. 1995. "Legislating for Peace: An Overview of Attempts to Promote Peace in South Africa." In Mervyn Bennun and Malyn D.D. Newitt, eds. *Negotiating Justice: A New Constitution for South Africa*. Exeter: University of Exeter Press.

Minnaar, Anthony, and Mike Hough, eds. 1997. *Conflict, Violence and Conflict Resolution: Where is South Africa Heading?* Pretoria: HSRC Publishers.

Nakamura, Robert T. 1990. "The Japanese External Trade Organization and Import Promotion: A Case Study in the Implementation of Symbolic Policy Goals." In Dennis J. Palumbo and Donald J. Calista, eds. *Implementation and the Policy Process*. New York: Greenwood Press.

Nieuwmeijer, Louise, and Renee du Toit, eds. 1994. *Multicultural Conflict Management in Changing Societies*. Pretoria: HSRC Publishers.

Nieuwmeijer, Louise, Renee du Toit and Theledi Ernest Sebulela, eds. 1995. *Conflict Management Research in South Africa*. Pretoria: HSRC Publishers.

Nossel, Suzanne, and Marion Shaer. 1992. "Groundswell at Grassroots: The Challenges Posed by Peace Accord Dispute Resolution Structures." Paper presented at the annual meeting of the South African Association for Conflict Intervention, Port Elizabeth.

Odendaal, Andries, and Chris Spies. 1996. *Local Peace Committees in the Rural Areas of the Western Cape: Their Significance for South Africa's Transition to Democracy*. Cape Town: Centre for Conflict Resolution.

Ohlson, Thomas and Stephen John Stedman with Robert Davies. 1994. *The New is Not Yet Born: Conflict Resolution in Southern Africa*. Washington, D.C.: Brookings Institution.

Pretorius, Paul, ed. 1993. *Dispute Resolution*. Johannesburg: Juta.

Salem, Richard A. Fall. 1994. "Foundations of Mediation in a Culture of Violence." *Dispute Resolution Magazine* 12–14.

Shaw, Mark. 1993a. *At the Cutting Edge of Peace? The Functioning and Future of the Local Peace Committees of the National Peace Accord.* Johannesburg: Centre for Policy Studies.

———. 1993b. "War and Peace: Resolving Local Conflict." *Indicator SA* 10(3): 63–68.

Sisk, Timothy D. 1994. "South Africa's National Peace Accord." *Peace and Change* 19: 50–70.

———. 1995. *Democratization in South Africa: The Elusive Social Contract.* Princeton, N.J.: Princeton University Press.

Sparks, Allister. 1995. *Tomorrow Is Another Country: The Inside Story of South Africa's Road to Change.* New York: Hill and Wang.

United States Institute of Peace. 1993. "South Africa: The National Peace Accord and the International Community: Highlights of an International Seminar." Washington, D.C.: United States Institute of Peace.

van der Merwe, Hendrik W. 1989. *Pursuing Justice and Peace in South Africa.* London: Routledge.

van der Merwe, Hugo. 1993. "Relating Theory to the Practice of Conflict Resolution in South Africa." In Dennis J. Sandole and Hugo van der Merwe, eds. *Conflict Resolution in Theory and Practice: Integration and Application.* Manchester: Manchester University Press.

Zartman, I. William, and Francis Deng, eds. 1991. *Conflict Resolution in Africa.* Washington, D.C.: Brookings Institution.

10

European Integration and Irish Disunity?

Paul Dixon

> "The final solution is union. It is going to happen anyway. The historical train—Europe—determines that. We are committed to Europe. Unionists will have to change. This island will be as one."
> —British government representative to Sinn Fein,
> March 23, 1993, *Setting the Record Straight: A Record*
> *of Communications between Sinn Fein and the British Government,*
> October 1990–November 1993 (Sinn Fein, 1993, 28).

Introduction

AS THE HISTORY OF Northern Ireland was littered with an ever increasing number of failed peace initatives, leading commentators and politicians in the 1980s began to look to the process of European integration to resolve the "outdated" ethnic conflict which continued to plague Northern Ireland and which has more recently embroiled the Balkans. Just as the historic antagonism between France and Germany had become reconciled through membership in the European Union, many involved in seeking a peaceful resolution to the Northern Ireland conflict began to hope that within a European framework Britain and Ireland could, at last, find peace also. European citizenship, it was envisaged, would transcend and transform petty nationalisms and traditional allegiances. In a European super-state it would not matter whether you were an Irish nationalist or a British unionist. Yet, even during Britain's first application to join the European Economic Community (EEC) in July 1961, I suggest that the fault lines of future divisions over Europe within and between Irish nationalism and British/Ulster unionism were emerging.

Contrary to the theory of "modernization" which suggested that the spread of economic integration and interdependence between states would create common interests among different social groups and thus diminish, if not completely erode national and ethnic identities, this chapter argues that the dominance of the theory of "modernization"—that growing economic integration and interdependence between states would diminish ethnic ties and lead to political unity—actually contributed to the division between nationalists and unionists over EEC membership. There was (and to a considerable extent still is) (Bew and Dixon 1994) a widespread expectation among both nationalists and unionists that "modernizing" forces such as the EEC would promote Irish unity. Although this belief has contributed to the support within Irish nationalism for EEC membership, it has evoked a corresponding hostile attitude of unionists towards Europe. The debate over European integration has tended, therefore, to reinforce simultaneously unionist fears and nationalist hopes that the process of modernization and economic integration would inevitably result in the unity of Ireland. The European question, I suggest, rather than transcending sectarianism, was one among a number of issues which, by raising uncertainty over Northern Ireland's constitutional future, exacerbated sectarian tensions during the crucial sixties period.

Modernization and European Integration: The Early Years

The United Kingdom (U.K.) applied to join the EEC in July 1961. This critical decision, it should be noted, was taken at Westminster rather than at the Northern Ireland parliament, Stormont. It underlined both Northern Ireland's continued subservience to London and the province's increasing vulnerability and subordination to modernizing factors beyond the regional parliament's ability to control. In the late 1950s and early 1960s the question of European integration had conspired with a number of other factors to end Northern Ireland's state of "splendid isolation" from the rest of the U.K. and the outside world.[1]

The unionists, wishing to maintain their position within the U.K., feared that the growth of economic integration and international cooperation would have political implications which would undermine the security of their constitutional position within the U.K. by eroding Stormont's economic and political autonomy. In many ways, their fears were justified. Northern Ireland was both becoming integrated into British economic planning policy and, at the same time, more and more dependent on subsidies from Westminster. The region which was also seeking to attract foreign capital became increasingly open to foreign influence. In addition to these external forces, the nascent Northern Ireland civil rights movement was also starting to attract limited British interest.

The 1950s and 1960s also saw the Republic of Ireland beginning to emerge from its diplomatic and economic isolation. The Irish government was using international fora, such as the U.N. and the Council of Europe, to push its case for the removal of partition. Closer trading links with the U.K. would culminate in the signing of an Anglo-Irish Free Trade Agreement in 1965, which was designed to reduce tariffs and increase trade between the U.K. and the Republic of Ireland. The rapprochement of the prime ministers of Northern Ireland and the Irish Republic, Terence O'Neill and Sean Lemass, respectively, was a symptom of this new more interdependent world in which the unionists now found themselves.

European Unity—A Prelude to Irish Unity?

The unspoken assumption of the original six members of the EEC was that economic integration would lead to European political unity. Indeed, the British had opposed membership of the EEC on the grounds that it was a supranationalist body, preferring a model of intergovernmental cooperation. When Britain made its application to the EEC, there was a widespread assumption that joint action between nation-states on economic matters would lead to cooperation on other political matters. The supranational agency, the EEC, would progressively undermine the independence of the nation-state and loyalties would be increasingly transferred from the nation towards a European identity. Some academics believed this process was inevitable (Pinder, 1991, 212).

If the modernizing assumptions of many EEC supporters were correct, then the erosion of state sovereignty and borders would have profound implications for Northern Ireland. Indeed, Irish nationalists have maintained that the corollary of European integration is Irish unity since the attachment of the unionists to the U.K. is "artificial" while the economic unity of Ireland is "natural"—particularly with the opening up of the Irish economy in the 1950s. So, moderate nationalists argue, Irish unity will occur before Europe becomes a super-state. By contrast, militant Irish Republicans as well as some pro-European unionists, have argued that given the dependence on the U.K. of the Irish economy, North and South, the result of growing economic integration is likely to be the unity of the "British Isles" rather than Irish unity.

Irish Nationalism and European Unity

Politicians in the Irish Republic have long viewed moves towards European cooperation as a means to unite Ireland. As far back as 1954, Liam Cosgrave, the Minister for External Relations, argued that Irish participation in the EEC might promote the healing of the division of Ireland. As the Republic emerged from isolation this argument was to achieve more prominence.

Isolation or aggressive policies tend to divide us more and more fundamentally from the majority of our fellow-countrymen in the Six Counties. On the other hand, the more we direct our activities towards playing a part suitable to our means and geographical position in the solution of the great problems that confront Western Europe as a whole, the more it will become apparent to the people of the Six Counties also that their destiny is one with ours, just as ours is one with the peoples of Western Europe (Hederman 1983, 48).

Sean Lemass, the Irish prime minister, argued in 1961 that "in the context of membership of the European Economic Community, any economic argument for partition will disappear; north and south will have exactly the same problems and exactly the same opportunities within the wide European market" (Dail Eireann, Parliamentary Debates, Official Report vol. 91 col. 2577). In 1961, during a debate in the Dail on the Republic's application to the EEC, Lemass said that "in the context of a European economic union, the partition of Ireland will become a patent and obvious absurdity . . . This may be opportunity knocking at our national door and if so we must not allow ourselves to be deterred by excessive caution or pointless fears from opening the door and grasping opportunity with both hands" (Newsletter 16/8/61). Similarly, even the leader of the Irish opposition party, Fine Gael, James Dillon, maintained that membership of the European Community would reduce the economic importance of the border and bring about Irish unity.

According to Miriam Hederman (1983), the appeal of European unity was more "a means of getting out of the straitjacket of British-Irish preoccupations" than a concern with partition (p. 16). The argument that European unity would produce Irish unity protected the republican flank of those politicians in favor of opening up the Southern economy. However, it was also likely to alienate unionists from the promotion of European economic integration on political grounds since they feared nationalist predictions would come true. The "common-sense" argument that economic integration leads to political union has a simple and powerful logic, one which seems to have given it influence in the North as well as the South.

Northern Ireland and Europe: First Attempt

The British Government's application to the EEC in 1961 underlined Northern Ireland's growing subjection to "national" and international influences which were beyond the Stormont parliament's ability to control. The modernizing assumptions of Euro-enthusiasts were accepted and echoed in Northern Ireland by politicians across the ethnic divide, regardless of whether or not the implications of those assumptions were welcome.[2]

In July 1961, the Northern Ireland Parliament debated EEC entry. The fact that the British application had been made by a Conservative Government, which traditionally had close ties with the Ulster Unionist Party, may have constrained Unionist criticism of EEC entry. The low salience of the issue may also have facilitated this. John Andrews, speaking on behalf of the Unionist Government and reportedly in favor of the EEC, said "It is not . . . for us to judge what is the best course for the U.K. to adopt for real and lasting prosperity . . ." (Northern Ireland Parliamentary Debates, vol. 49, col. 142, 6/7/61). This statement expressed the essential powerlessness of Stormont to take fundamental decisions affecting the future of the region.

There was some opposition among Unionist MPs to the EEC. William J. Morgan, for example, spoke up against EEC membership, believing that the British would lose both economic and political sovereignty in the EEC (Newsletter 13/7/61). Later, another Unionist MP, Andrew Hunter, feared that Southern Irish workers would come to take Northern jobs and argued that "economic integration will be followed in a decade or so by political integration" (Newsletter 28/8/61).

In the absence of strong Unionist Party opposition to the EEC application in Stormont, it was left to David Bleakley, MP of the "unionist" Northern Ireland Labour Party (NILP), to raise the political implications of EEC membership for Northern Ireland's constitutional position in the U.K. He said that if the North was ignoring the constitutional implications of the EEC then the South was not.

Our problem viewed from Strasbourg would look very different than the same problem does when viewed from Belfast. But in the future a great deal of our problems may well be viewed from Strasbourg and there may be a very natural tendency to regard our economy and the political situation that derives from it in a light very different from what we would ourselves . . . Eire will have direct representation in this new community and will therefore have great influence in it which will not be matched by either the representation or influence we are likely to have (Northern Ireland Parliamentary Debates, vol. 49, col. 99, 6/7/71).

Bleakley was concerned that the surrender of sovereignty by the U.K. to the Common Market Parliament "would imply . . . surrender of sovereignty *vis-a-vis* ourselves and Mr Lemass" and that this trend might become more marked as time went on. The right questions had to be asked now before such a movement gained momentum "as economic movements are apt to do" (Northern Ireland Parliamentary Debates vol. 49, col. 100, 6/7/71). Another NILP MP, T.

W. Boyd, called for a declaration from the British Government ". . . that no decisions which would be taken in relation to the Common Market will affect the constitutional rights of this House to decide its future" (Northern Ireland Parliamentary Debates vol. 49, col. 138, 6/7/71).

Both nationalists who spoke in the debate, Cahir Healy and Francis Hanna, supported membership of the EEC. Echoing Lemass, Healy argued that "the logical development of a united Europe is surely a united Ireland" (Northern Ireland Parliamentary Debates, vol. 49, col. 111, 6/7/61). Albert McElroy, of the Northern Ireland Liberal Party, also saw a united Ireland emerging from EEC membership, since the border would disappear and there would be a levelling of social services (Purdie 1990, 75).

Irish republicans, on the other hand, saw growing economic integration between Britain and the Republic, through common membership of the EEC and the signing of the Anglo-Irish Free Trade Agreement, as a means by which Britain could ensnare the Republic and maintain its domination (Purdie 1990, 127). C. D. Greaves, of the Connolly Association, argued that if the EEC ended all borders and Europe was one big country "there would be no partition of Ireland" but "would there be an Ireland to partition?" (Greaves 1963).

The prospect of entry into the Common Market was the theme of many of the platform speeches of the Protestant Orange celebrations on July 12. W. F. McCoy, QC and MP, feared the breakup of the Commonwealth if Britain joined the EEC, while the Attorney-General W. B. Maginess said "The world was becoming smaller and no country could live in isolation, nor could any country afford to remain unchanged in a changing world" (Newsletter 26/9/61 quoted in Aughey and Hainsworth 1982, 100).

There may also have been a religious concern amongst Protestants at joining a Catholic-dominated EEC (established by the Treaty of Rome!). Certainly this was a factor raised by unionists in later debates on the EEC. The publication by the Conservative Central Office of a leaflet reassuring its members that there were no religious implications of membership would suggest that misgivings over religion were not just confined to Northern Ireland.

Given the approaching entry of U.K. into the EEC, the Unionist leadership tried to calm unionist anxieties over Common Market membership. Brian Faulkner, Minister of Home Affairs, told a demonstration of the Royal Black Institution[3] that the real border between the North and South of Ireland was political, not economic, and the border was a recognition of the existence of two different ways of life (Newsletter 28/8/61). R. W. B. McConnell, MP, also distinguished between economic integration and political integration: "It is not the land frontier which divides the people of Ulster and Eire; it is only the geographical expression of differences of loyalties and ideologies which are fundamental and permanent" (Newsletter 28/8/61). On a trip to Northern Ireland, Selwyn Lloyd, the Conservative Chancellor of the Exchequer, commented that U.K. entry into the EEC would not mean a weakening of the border between Ulster and Eire, although he did not dispute that an economic treaty would have political repercussions (Newsletter 31/8/61).

Although the first British application to the EEC failed due to French objections in 1963, the prospect of membership had started a debate in Northern Ireland. Even in these early stages, hair-line cracks had appeared—along which future splits between pro-European nationalists and anti-European unionists would emerge.

The Second Try: 1967

In October 1961, Herbert Kirk expressed the Unionist leadership's position on the EEC: "Whatever was finally decided for the good of the United Kingdom it followed, that, on balance, it was good for Ulster" (Aughey and Hainsworth 1982, 96). This integrationist formula may have been acceptable to Unionists while their Conservative allies were in power at Westminster, but would it still hold true with a British Labour Government holding the future of Northern Ireland in its hands? In 1964, the British Labour Party was elected into office. In 1967 Harold Wilson, the British prime minister, applied for membership in the EEC.

Wilson appeared to favor a united Ireland, or at least not oppose it. In response to a question from Sean Dunne TD at the Council of Europe, January 23, 1967, the *Irish Times* reported Wilson as saying "that the Anglo-Irish free trade treaty would result in closer economic unity in Ireland. The question of unity, he added, was a problem for the people of Ireland to solve, and nobody would be happier than the British people if the Irish could find a solution. . . . He said that if the North and South could make up their differences, they would have his blessing upon them, and, indeed, spare him the trouble of answering further questions on this score" (*Irish Times* 24/1/67). The talks between O'Neill and Lemass and the signing of the Anglo-Irish Free Trade Agreement in 1965 fuelled hopes that the political unity of Ireland would follow from economic integration.

A debate on Europe was held at Westminster on May 8–10, 1967. There was a 426 majority for seeking entry to the EEC. Six out of the eleven Ulster Unionist MPs were counted among the twenty-six Conservative MPs opposing entry. One Unionist MP abstained and four voted for the motion. Ulster Unionists were therefore disproportionately represented among the ranks of EEC opponents. This contrasted with 1961 when no Ulster Unionist MPs at Westminster had voted against the Conservative Government's application.

The leader of the Unionist MPs at Westminster, Lawrence Orr, was the only Unionist to speak in the three-day debate. He opposed negotiations with the EEC on industrial, agricultural, and economic grounds. He was also concerned at inroads on British sovereignty (*Belfast Telegraph* 11/5/67). Stanley McMaster MP wanted assurances over the safeguarding of employment and agriculture. He tabled a motion which was signed by all eleven Ulster Unionist MPs calling for 1) an inquiry into the effects of EEC membership on less prosperous regions, 2) the government being free to give economic aid to development areas, 3) an inquiry into the effect on British farmers of an increase in the price of foodstuffs (*Belfast Telegraph* 4/5/67).

The Unionist Party leadership, however, continued to favor EEC entry. In April 1967 the Stormont Premier, Terence O'Neill, said on a visit to Germany: "This is a time of great change and development in Europe. Fateful decisions have to be taken, which may determine the political and economic structure of our Continent for generations. . . . I speak for Northern Ireland, the most westerly Atlantic bastion of the United Kingdom, and I tell you tonight that we are Europeans with a European destiny" (O'Neill, 1969, 190). Brian Faulkner also spoke of the benefits of EEC membership (Newsletter 4/5/67).

The moderate unionist newspaper the *Belfast Telegraph* favored entry into the EEC. Geoffrey Fitzsimons wrote: "It seems inevitable, too, that Stormont will have to abandon some of its autonomy in economic and financial matters. But anxiety that the constitutional identity of Northern Ireland could be in danger have little basis in fact" (*Belfast Telegraph* 3/5/67). Following the overwhelming vote at Westminster in favor of EEC entry the *Belfast Telegraph's* editorial argued: "This is a time for Northern Ireland to remember that its truest interest continues to lie in the larger unity, whether of the United Kingdom, the British Isles or Europe" (*Belfast Telegraph* 11/5/67).

In November 1967, Stormont debated the consequences of EEC membership for the first time since 1961. Austin Currie, the Nationalist MP for East Tyrone, moved the motion and raised civil rights issues. He asked the Unionist Government whether the EEC would find Northern Ireland's draconian Special Powers Act or its restricted franchise acceptable. Currie also pointed to the divisions within Unionist ranks over membership and noted that speeches made outside the House on EEC membership "emphasised the possible political implications rather than the economic implications" (Northern Ireland Parliamentary Debates, vol. 67, col. 1815/6, 14/11/67). The Nationalist Party, he said, were "dedicated pro-marketeers" who "accept fully the possible political implications as well as the economic implications of entry into EEC" (Northern Ireland Parliamentary Debates, vol. 67, col. 1816, 14/11/67). Currie argued that entry into the EEC would mean the end of the border. Citing the example of the German *zollverein* (a nineteenth-century customs union) and the unification of Germany he stated that "economic unity came about and political unity inevitably came after it" (Northern Ireland Parliamentary Debates, vol. 67, col. 1831/2, 14/11/6). Entry into the EEC and the subsequent increase in North-South cooperation would bring Ireland closer together. John Richardson, MP for South Armagh, endorsed Currie's view: "We know that the Common Market will bring our whole country together. A united Ireland is what we all want to see" (Northern Ireland Parliamentary Debates, vol. 67, col. 2038, 14/11/67).

Indeed, it appeared that Northern Ireland prime minister Terence O'Neill had embraced the rhetoric of modernization, even if he did not take it to antipartitionist conclusions. For O'Neill, Northern Ireland's old sectarian ways were to be discarded as an outdated legacy of history, and the region was to share the "modernized" world's preoccupations and divisions over economic and social matters. In his "Ulster at the Crossroads" speech in December 1968, O'Neill asked: "Is a freedom to pursue the un-Christian path of communal strife and sectarian bitterness really more important to you than all the benefits of the British Welfare State?" From this it could be argued similarly: is your attachment to national identity really more important to you than all the benefits of North-South or European cooperation? In the debate on the EEC in November 1967 O'Neill turned the logic of modernization against the Nationalists. He argued:

The same people who urge that North and South will merge into a common European identity in the EEC would resist with equal vehemence any ideas that the Republic and the United Kingdom will merge into a common British identity under reciprocal free trade. Yet they cannot have it both ways. In logic, if the removal of tariff barriers will have these profound political effects in the one case they will have it in the other as well (Northern Ireland Parliamentary Debates, vol. 67, col. 1837, 14/11/67).

O'Neill further ridiculed the notion "that the Border has been kept in being in all these years by the Republic's tariffs on cat food and cardboard boxes" (Northern Ireland Parliamentary Debates, vol. 67, col. 1837, 14/11/67). Ulster would remain British "because that is the freely expressed political will of its people" (Northern Ireland Parliamentary Debates, vol. 67, col. 1838, 14/11/67). However, O'Neill did accept that EEC membership had political as well as economic implications for Northern Ireland, but it was "a long step from anything resembling a unified or federal form of European government" (Northern Ireland Parliamentary Debates, vol. 67, col. 1838, 14/11/67). Nevertheless, even the prospect of a politically united and possibly Catholic-dominated Europe was likely to be unsettling to unionist opinion. There was also a continuing fear of an influx of workers from the South who would vote nationalist.

By 1967 the issue of Europe was coming to be seen increasingly in sectarian terms. There were clear divisions within Unionist ranks over the question of EEC entry. Indeed, a majority of Unionist MPs at Westminster now opposed entry, where in 1961 none had voted against Britain's application to join the EEC. Prominent among Unionist objections to the EEC was the fear that membership would undermine Northern Ireland's constitutional position within the U.K. The Nationalists had come to the same conclusions and therefore supported EEC membership on the grounds that it would lead to Irish unity.

Richard Rose's survey of Northern Ireland public opinion in 1968 testifies to the polarization of the electorate on the European issue along sectarian lines. A majority of Catholics favored membership of the Common Market while a plurality of Protestants were against: Protestants were only narrowly against the EEC by 36 percent to 30 percent while Catholics were in favor by 56 percent to 14 percent. Rose argued that "the reason for this is the belief among Protestants and Catholics that the lowering of national barriers between the United Kingdom and the Common Market countries would inevitably be followed by moves to unify Ireland" (Rose 1971, 285).

Third Time Lucky: 1973

Unionism

The crisis of the late 1960s—the eruption of the civil rights protest into street fighting and the deployment of British troops in August 1969 divided unionism (Byrne 1997). The "moderate" O'Neillites were both more amenable to Westminster's demands for reform and more prepared for compromise with nationalists than unionist "hardliners." This moderate/hardline unionist division also coincided with the pro and anti-European split among unionists. There was a similarity of principle in sharing power at both the regional and European level. As the Alliance Party's leader on the power-sharing Executive, Oliver Napier, put it, "there is nothing sinister in the words 'power sharing.' Power sharing is something which is the rule rather than the exception throughout Europe" (Northern Ireland Assembly Report [1973] vol. 1, October 16, 1973, quoted in Hainsworth 1983, 57).

In the debate on membership in the early 1970s Brian Faulkner, the Northern Ireland premier, took a similar modernizing line to that taken by O'Neill in 1967. Membership of the EEC would bring Northern Ireland and the Republic closer to the U.K. He argued that the harmonization process and the dismantling of tariff barriers inevitably reduces the significance of frontiers. It would clearly bring Northern Ireland and the Republic closer together, but it would also bring the Republic and the U.K. as a whole closer together.

Talk of "natural units" which does not look beyond the Irish Sea is purblind. When frontiers are no longer a barrier to the free movement of trade, or a line of demarcation between different fiscal, social or economic systems they will remain primarily as a mark of people's continuing sense of national identity and loyalty. In such a context it would become even clearer than it is today how foolish as well as immoral it would be for any one to seek to remove frontiers against the will of the majority of the inhabitants. And if it were to be accepted the Border could at last receded from the forefront of many minds. If the United Kingdom enters the EEC our main lines of consultation and communication must be with the British Government (Northern Ireland Debates, vol. 83 8/12/71).

The Government Chief Whip and Minister of State for Finance, Captain John Brooke, argued that the inevitability of economic interdependence and the trend of history was leading Britain to the EEC (Aughey and Hainsworth 1982, 96).

The weakness of this "moderate" pro-European unionist view was its acceptance that European political union was inevitable—only some way off. This "inevitability" threatened to take the future of Northern Ireland out of the hands of both Stormont and Westminster and leave the constitutional future of the region at the mercy of the European Community. Given the international unpopularity of the unionist cause, and the dominance of Catholic countries in the EEC, that prospect was likely to cause great alarm to many unionists.

The Northern Ireland Government, meanwhile, was embarrassed by its powerlessness to influence the decision to apply for EEC membership. Although this was a matter for the British government, Faulkner's government "had to be seen to be influential, to have some say in deciding the destiny of Northern Ireland. . . . At each phase, Unionists were at pains to stress that Stormont ministers and officials had the ear of Government ministers in London and the sympathy of the Commission of officials in Brussels" (Aughey and Hainsworth 1982, 97)

In 1971, with violence escalating in Northern Ireland, the Ulster Unionist MPs at Westminster threatened to withhold their support from the Conservative Government (Norton 1978, 49). They wanted stronger measures taken against terrorism. In October 1971, six of the eight Ulster Unionists and Ian Paisley, leader of the "hardline" Democratic Unionist Party, voted against the principle of entry into the EEC. The decline of pro-European unionism coincided with the failure of a powersharing assembly in Northern Ireland and the demise of the moderates. By 1975, the dominance of anti-European unionists was apparent.[4] A poll of the members of the Constitutional Convention found that out of the forty-seven "hardline" unionists thirty-eight opposed the EEC. The poll showed "the EEC issue was becoming resolved along sectarian lines" (Moxon-Browne 1978, 29). A DUP anti-EEC handbill for the May 1975 European referendum justified opposition to the EEC by quoting Irish prime minister Dr. Garret Fitzgerald's support for it as a means of uniting Ireland. The EEC was also opposed on the grounds that it was dominated by Catholic states. The DUP leader, the Reverend Ian Paisley, claimed the Pope referred to the Virgin Mary as "the Madonna of the Common Market" and his Democratic Unionists were opposed to anything connected with Rome and a "Roman Catholic super-state" (Moxon-Browne 1978, 31).

The Ulster Unionist Party's hostility to the Maastricht Treaty signed in 1992, which accelerated the process of European integration, contrasts starkly with the perhaps half-hearted Europeanism of the early 1960s. Those who had been in favor of the EEC, O'Neill and Faulkner, had become tainted by their association with "un-Ulster values—compromise, cross-border dialogue with the annexationist Irish Republic, and power sharing with Republicans" (Hainsworth 1985, 122). The demise in support among unionists for power-sharing and the European Union are logically connected. Both are *perceived* by unionists as giving up the power to determine their future to outsiders, people who are often hostile to their cause. Given this unionist isolation this reluctance to trust power to others is not so surprising (Dixon 1995).

Nationalism

The three Northern Irish Catholic MPs at Westminster most probably voted against entry into the EEC in 1973 for republican and/or socialist reasons. However, the trajectory of the principal nationalist party, the SDLP, was in a pro-European direction. In 1972, the SDLP published a policy document, *Towards a New Ireland*. This proposed a National Senate of Ireland whose basic function "should be to plan the integration of the whole island by preparing the harmonisation of the structures, laws and services of both parts of Ireland" (SDLP 1972, 6). It would build on the "obvious" common ground and "necessary" common interests between north and south. Europe was "looking to the future with a vision to end the old quarrels. Old and bitter enemies are settling their differences and are working together in a new and wider context of a United Europe" (SDLP 1972, 2). The SDLP's manifesto for the 1973 Assembly, "A New North, A New Ireland," spoke of bringing about Irish unity within the context of the EEC. By the time of the EEC referendum in 1975, the SDLP was in favor of Europe. It was hoped that cross-border cooperation under the ambit of the EEC was more likely to be depoliticized and, therefore, successful. This would diminish the economic significance of the border and bring a united Ireland nearer (Butler and Kitzinger 1976, 156). The SDLP still adheres to this position. In 1992, their submission to talks on the constitutional future of Northern Ireland organized by the Northern Ireland secretary of state, Patrick Mayhew, argued that the European Community offered the "most conspicuously successful and original" model for resolving national conflicts (Submission by the SDLP to the interparty talks, May 11, 1992).

Republic of Ireland and Britain

The weight of opinion in Britain and the Republic of Ireland was more inclined to agree with ultra unionists than republicans that the effect of European integration would be Irish unity.

The success of Britain and Ireland's third application to the EEC boosted theories that Irish unity would result from economic cooperation. Garret FitzGerald, who later became Irish Prime Minister and signed the Anglo-Irish Agreement 1985, in his book *Towards a New Ireland* (1972), was one of the most prominent exponents of Irish unity through EEC cooperation. The effect of Britain and Ireland joining the EEC, he argued, was "likely to be uniformly direct towards easing that path to a united Ireland" (FitzGerald 1972, 104). The economic rationale for partition would become eroded by the EEC. The common interests of the North and South of Ireland on agricultural and regional policy would draw them together and distance them from the interests of highly developed Britain. Furthermore, within the context of EEC membership the transfer of sovereignty over Northern Ireland from Westminster to Dublin would lose some emotional impact if sovereignty was also passing to Brussels (FitzGerald 1972, 108). Northern Ireland might also gain greater representation and influence in Europe through association with the Republic rather than with the U.K.

While the British Labour Party opposed EC membership, it was widely assumed that economic cooperation, accelerated by EEC membership, would lead to Irish unity. James Callaghan (British Prime Minister 1976–79), in his book *A House Divided*, came out in favor of Irish unity and suggested that it could come by North and South developing "the habit of working together on matters of common interest" (Callaghan 1973, 187). On the pro-European wing of the Labour Party, Shirley Williams argued that EC membership, cross-border economic projects, and North-South cooperation would help to bring Northern and Southern Ireland together, and hinted that this might result in political unity (House of Commons Debates, vol. 846, c.149 and c.150, 13/11/72). Since its conversion to Europeanism, in the mid-1980s the British Labour Party has argued that "the partition of the island will be undermined by the process of greater European integration" (McNamara 1990), a view now shared by a large swathe of nationalist opinion in Ireland both North and South (Bew and Dixon 1994). There were reports that, by 1971, the thinking of the Conservative Government was also evolving in the direction of Irish unity. Echoing much nationalist thinking, reunification was seen by Conservatives, not "as a dramatic act of policy" but "as the eventual result of a growing together process. For in the meanwhile—and the meanwhile might be twenty or twenty-five years—Northern Ireland must be made a place worth living in. The development of common interests between the two islands, facilitated by common membership of the European Community, must become the basis of cooperation, if not coalition, between the two communities in Northern Ireland" (*The Guardian* 22/11/71). During the secret "contacts" between the British government and Sinn Fein in 1993, the British representative claimed that European integration made Irish unity inevitable.

Conclusion

During the period under consideration the dominant assumption in Britain and Ireland among unionists, nationalists, socialists, and some conservatives has been that growing economic integration and interdependence through membership of the European Community would bring about Irish unity. This assumption probably laid at the heart of unionist opposition to the EEC. Faulkner and O'Neill's pro-European unionist case that modernization would result in the Republic rejoining the U.K. has achieved much less prominence or credibility—least of all, perhaps, among unionists themselves. When unionists argued this pro-European case it was handicapped by the accompanying acceptance that European economic integration would at some point result in European political union. This raised the prospect of Northern Ireland's constitutional fate being left in the hands of an unsympathetic Catholic-dominated EEC and was, therefore, likely to exacerbate unionist anxieties. As early as 1961 these anxieties were being aired. By 1967, the Euro-scepticism of many unionists was already apparent. The European question heightened unionist constitutional uncertainies at a time when they feared that the processes of modernization and economic integration were shifting power away from Northern Ireland and undermining the region's ability to control its own future. The modernizing assumptions which were widespread in the 1960s have not been born out by the passage of time (Connor 1990). On the contrary, rising ethnic consciousness has gone hand in hand with modernization. The tendency of closer European integration seems to be towards increasing the cultural and political importance of the regions, rather than the creation of new and larger states. Rather than transcending ethnonationalism in Northern Ireland, the European Union has provided a new forum where these can be played out. Nevertheless, the assumption of the inevitability of Irish unity continues to inform nationalist and republican thinking. The assumptions of modernization are reflected in the documents which have underpinned the recent "peace process": the Downing Street Declaration; the Framework Documents; and the Good Friday Agreement. The apparent acceleration of modernizing processes during the recent "troubles," including the growth of European integration and the onset of "globalization," have not resulted in a shift of unionist attitudes towards Irish unity. If anything, unionists are more adamant about remaining part of the Union with Britain as they were thirty years ago (Dixon 1995).

Suggested Study Questions

1. Which processes in industrialization do you think Modernization theorists believe will lead to the erosion of ethnic and national differences? Why?
2. Does European integration make Irish unity inevitable?
3. How could pro-European unionists argue that European integration would lead to Northern Ireland, and perhaps the Republic of Ireland, being more closely tied to the Union with Britain?
4. Which passages, if any, in the Downing Street Declaration 1993, the Framework Documents 1995, and the Good Friday Agreement 1998 echo the assumptions of the nationalist interpretation of modernization theory?
5. Has economic integration eroded ethnic and national divisions or led to greater conflict in the United States? Or between the United States and Canada and Mexico?

Notes

1. For a full explanation of this argument see Paul Dixon, *The Politics of Peace in Northern Ireland*, London: Macmillan (1999 forthcoming).
2. The hope that the EEC would develop into a supranational federal Europe has persisted since the Community's foundation. But progress towards this goal has waxed and waned, and by 1961 the EEC did not appear to be the supranational "threat" feared by some at the Community's foundation.
3. The Royal Black Institution is the senior branch of the Orange Order, committed both to unionism and the defence of Protestantism.
4. The leader of the hardline Ulster Vanguard, William Craig, came out in support of the EEC. It has been suggested that divisions over Europe may have contributed to Craig's split from the main body of unionism in September 1975 (Butler and Kitzinger 1976, 156 and 283).

References

Aughey, A. and P. Hainsworth. 1982. "Northern Ireland and the European Community—The Localisation of Politics." *Moirae* 7.

Bew, Paul and Paul Dixon. 1994. "The Labour Party and Northern Ireland." In *The North-*

ern Ireland Question: Perspectives and Policies. B. Barton and P. J. Roche, eds. Aldershot: Avebury.

Butler, David and U. Kitzinger. 1976. *The 1975 Referendum.* London: Macmillan.

Byrne, Sean. 1997. *Growing up in a Divided Society: The Influence of Conflict on Belfast Schoolchildren.* Cranbury, N.J.: Associated University Presses.

Callaghan, James. 1973. *A House Divided.* London: Collins.

Connor, Walker. 1990. "Ethno-nationalism and Political Instability: An Overview." In *The Elusive Search for Peace.* H. Giliomee and J. Gagiano, eds. Oxford: Oxford University Press.

Dixon, Paul. 1995. "Internationalization and Unionist Isolation: A Response to Feargal Cochrane." *Political Studies* 43(3): 1–19.

Greaves, C. Desmond. 1963. *The Irish Question and the British people—A Plea for a New Approach.* Connolly Association.

Hainsworth, Paul. 1983. "Direct Rule in Northern Ireland: The European Community Dimension 1972–79." *Administration* 31: 12–35.

Hederman, M. 1983. *The Road to Europe: Irish Attitudes 1948–61.* Dublin: Institute of Public Administration.

Kollinsky, M., ed. 1978. *Divided Loyalties: British Regional Assertion and European Integration.* Manchester: Manchester University Press.

Lyne, T. Winter. 1990. "Ireland, Northern Ireland and 1992: The Barriers to Technocratic Anti-partitionism." *Public Administration* 68(3): 1–24.

McNamara, Kevin. 1990. Text of address by Kevin McNamara MP to Irish Labour Party seminar. London: The author.

Moxon-Browne, Edward. 1983. *Nation, Class and Creed in Northern Ireland.* Aldershot: Gower.

New Ulster Movement. January 1972. *Northern Ireland and the Common Market.* Belfast: NUM.

Norton, Peter. 1978. *Conservative Dissidents.* London: Temple Smith.

O'Neill, Terence. 1969. *Ulster at the Crossroads.* London: Faber and Faber.

Pinder, J. 1991. *European Community—The Building of a Union.* Oxford: Oxford University Press.

Purdie, Bob. 1990. *Politics in the Streets.* Belfast: Blackstaff.

Rose, Richard. 1971. *Governing without Consensus.* Boston: Beacon Press.

11

Negotiating End Games: A Comparative Analysis of the IRA and ETA

Cynthia L. Irvin

Introduction

IN OCTOBER 1984, the Irish Republican Army (IRA) captured the attention of the world press when it bombed the Brighton Hotel and very nearly succeeded in assassinating Margaret Thatcher during the Conservative party conference. In May 1985, Sinn Fein, the political party which represents the interests of the Irish republican movement, pushed the IRA off the front page when it secured almost 35 percent of the nationalist vote in its first non-abstentionist campaign for seats on local government councils in Northern Ireland.

In August 1994, almost a decade after the Brighton bombing, the IRA once again struck a surprise blow against British rule in Northern Ireland that seized the headlines of the world press. Only this time, the news was not about bombs or ballots, but rather the IRA's announcement of a cease-fire to begin as of midnight of August 31, 1994. Eighteen months later, however, the IRA would once again rock the center of London with a massive bomb. By August 1997, the IRA had agreed to renew its cease-fire and Sinn Fein prepared to enter into public, political negotiations with the British government for the first time since 1922. Eight months later, on April 10, 1998, Sinn Fein would sign the Good Friday Peace Agreement which provides the framework for the nonviolent resolution of the conflict in Northern Ireland.

In 1986, at the Sinn Fein *ard fheis* (party conference) where the historic decision that had initiated a radical shift in the Republican Movement's political strategy was taken, i.e., the delegates' decision to drop the party's long-standing constitutional prohibition against its candidates taking seats in the Irish Parliament, another historic statement was being made. However, despite the sizeable contingent of international journalists present in Dublin's Mansion Hall, the address of Jose Luis Enparanza (Txillardegi), one of the founders of the radical Basque nationalist organization ETA (Euskadi ta Askatasuna [Basque Homeland and Freedom] which seeks to secure the right of the Basque people, now divided into seven provinces, four of which are located in the Spanish state and three which are located within the French state), went largely unnoticed by the media. Had the media been listening they would have heard Txillardegi, then Senator to the Cortes (Spanish parliament) for the radical Basque nationalist party Herri Batasuna (Popular Unity), announce major changes within his own party regarding its participation in the Basque parliament. Like Sinn Fein, Herri Batasuna, since its founding in 1978, had refused to participate in either the Spanish or Basque parliaments, on the grounds that they were illegitimate political institutions imposed on Basques against their will.

In February 1987, Herri Batasuna, following an intense internal debate, would amend its policy and nominate a candidate for the position of *lehendakari* (president) in the autonomous Basque parliament.[1] The Herri Batasuna candidate, Juan Carlos Yoldi, who was under arrest for suspicion of ETA activities, was deliberately chosen to symbolize the dual strategy of armed struggle and electoral mobilization which the Movimiento Liberación Vasco Nacional (MLVN – Basque Movement for National Liberation) endorsed and Herri Batasuna was prepared to implement. Some months later, Herri Batasuna succeeded in winning a seat to the European parliament[2] and replaced the conservative Basque Nationalist Party (PNV) as the most popular party in the Basque provinces of Spain.

A decade later, however, while peace talks between all the parties to the conflicts have resulted in cessations of violence by both IRA and loyalist paramilitaries[3], an agreed political settlement and the election of a new power-sharing Northern Ireland Assembly, the MLVN (despite the announcement of a cease-fire by ETA on 16 September 1998), has yet to secure the formal commitment of either the Basque regional government or the Spanish government to a negotiated political settlement of the violent conflict which has cost the lives of over eight hundred persons.[4] Further, facing increased repression by the Spanish state which in December 1997 imprisoned all twenty-three members of the Herri Batasuna leadership on the grounds of "collaboration with a terrorist group" and in July 1998 closed the Basque daily newspaper, *Egin*, on similar grounds, the radical Basque left formed a new electoral coalition, Euskal Herritarrok (People of the Basque Country), to contest future elections as the leadership feared that Herri Batasuna would be declared illegal.

The Decision to Halt Violence

"By what conventional or unconventional arithmetic," as Crenshaw[5] has asked, was the IRA convinced in August 1994 to proclaim a unilateral halt to violence, reciprocated in October by loyalist paramilitaries? By what calculus was the decision taken to terminate the cease-fire and to resume the IRA's campaign in Britain with the Docklands bomb in February 1996 and then to reinstate it in August 1997? By what measures has ETA evaluated the relative costs and benefits of continuing its armed actions versus a declaration of a cease-fire? These questions are difficult to answer, not only because of the ongoing and contentious discussions regarding the implementation of the Good Friday Agreement in Northern Ireland and the lack of a formal peace process in the Basque country, but also because both the IRA and ETA are highly secretive and clandestine organizations. Despite these limitations, this chapter attempts to illuminate why the IRA was able to disengage from violence and an agreed political settlement was reached in Northern Ireland and why prospects for a similar Basque peace process in the near future appear uncertain. The following review focuses on key events in the evolution of the Northern Ireland peace process and the search for a negotiated settlement to the conflict between Basque nationalists and the Spanish government country during the period 1987–89.

IRA Cease-fire: Dynamics

Beginning in 1990, a series of secret meetings were held between representatives of Sinn Fein and the British government.[6] These meetings were viewed by the Sinn Fein representatives as indicating a serious interest by the British government in establishing a process to resolve the conflict in Northern Ireland.

In February 1992, Albert Reynolds replaced Charles Haughey as *Taoiseach* (Irish prime minister). Significantly for Sinn Fein, Reynolds, unlike previous prime ministers, was both willing to take risks and clearly determined to participate actively in the nascent peace process. Most importantly for the IRA, he sought to engage rather than exclude republicans.

In the 1993 Northern Ireland local government elections, Sinn Fein recaptured much of the electoral ground it had lost to the SDLP (Social Democratic and Labour Party) in the 1989 election.[7] Although still reeling from Gerry Adams's loss of the West Belfast Westminster seat in 1992 to the SDLP candidate, Joe Hendron, these results reassured Sinn Fein that its grassroots constituency remained solid and committed. With this support, Sinn Fein was in a position to go to the IRA and argue that the party could no longer be excluded from any future negotiations regarding the Northern Ireland conflict, and that, therefore, they could guarantee that the interests of the republican community would be represented in any settlement to emerge from such negotiations.

On September 25, 1993, Gerry Adams, together with John Hume, the SDLP leader, announced they were suspending the talks process they had begun in April 1993. However, the announcement indicated that they had come to a broad agreement on an initiative which "aimed at the creation of a peace process." However, an IRA attack on what was presumed to be the meeting place of the Combined Loyalist Military Command (CLMC) on the Shankhill Road in Belfast and which resulted in the deaths of the bombers and eight Protestant civilians appeared to signal the IRA's disapproval of the initiative. The loyalist response, which involved the shooting deaths of six Catholics, appeared to confirm the death of any moves towards a political settlement. The British government, however, in the hopes of rebuilding a peace process before the violence spiraled out of control, initiated secret talks with Sinn Fein. Following those discussions, and after consultation with the Irish government, the British and Irish prime ministers issued a joint statement from 10 Downing Street on December 16, 1993, which outlined their commitment to seeking a negotiated resolution of the conflict.

In January 1994, Albert Reynolds publicly backed his commitment to working with republicans in creating the conditions for peace by rescinding Section 31 of the Irish Broadcasting Act which had prevented a generation of Irish people from seeing or hearing republican activists on television or radio. Sinn Fein now had tangible proof of Dublin's commitment to the peace process with which it could bargain with its grassroots supporters and the IRA for support of its emerging peace strategy. Sinn Fein's bargaining position was also enhanced by the success of the IRA in importing extremely large shipments of war material into Ireland during the mid-1980s. The stores of military equipment both ensured the IRA's capacity to carry out a long-war strategy if necessary and reassured those suspicious of the intentions of the SF leadership that electoral politics would not mean a running down of the war machine.

Clinton's February 1994 decision to grant Gerry Adams a visa to enter the United States,[8] despite considerable pressure and opposition by both the British government and many U.S. officials not to do so, also improved Sinn Fein's bargaining potential with the IRA which could not ignore the worldwide media attention that discussions between Adams and U.S. government officials had generated. In addition, Clinton's active engagement in the Irish peace process enabled the Sinn Fein leadership to persuade the IRA that the United States could be called upon to act as a guarantor of the peace process in the event the British should prove less than willing to engage actively in the negotiation stage.

On July 24, 1994, Sinn Fein held a special party conference to decide whether to accept or reject the Downing Street Declaration as the basis for future negotiations. Initial comments by Sinn Fein leaders indicated that there was considerable doubt within a section of the party regarding the declaration. To assess prospects for the declaration's acceptance by the IRA, British government officials, Patrick Mayhew, then Secretary of State for Northern Ireland and Michael Ancram, then Political Development Minister at the Northern Ireland office (NO) met with Gerry Adams and Martin McGuinness in mid-August. Assured, as a result of these discussions, that the British government was committed to a meaningful talks process, the IRA issued its historic cease-fire of August 31, 1994.

Given that circumstances appeared to be ripe for a major transformation in Northern Irish politics from a situation of violent conflict and polarized pluralism to one of negotiation and political accommodation, why then we must ask, did the IRA end its cease-fire some eighteen months after it had begun?

IRA Cease-fire Collapse: Dynamics

Between August 1994 and February 1996, Sinn Fein had been transformed from the public voice of republicanism to a political party of both national and international significance. Clinton's March 1995 decision to allow Sinn Fein to raise funds in the United States resulted in the opening of an official Irish republican lobbying organization, Friends of Sinn Fein, in Washington, D.C. Sinn Fein's role as a legitimate, indeed, key participant in the Irish peace process had official U.S. sanction. Also, the financial resources of Irish-America would now legally[9] be available to Sinn Fein, a fact which helped to reassure hardliners within the republican movement that the political struggle would not take resources away from the military campaign should the need arise to continue it. The large and diverse Irish-American lobby, whose divisions had long mirrored the divisions within Irish politics, was now also united and was willing, ready, and able to deliver domestic and international political clout and considerable financial support to Sinn Fein. Peace dividends were real, and peace was tangible if not quite present.

In the Republic of Ireland, prime minister Reynolds acted swiftly on his promises to respond in a real and positive manner to a cessation of violence by the IRA. Within a week of the cease-fire, Reynolds publicly welcomed Adams and Hume to the Irish parliament buildings. Dublin had now confirmed its commitment to an inclusive peace process and America had also responded with resounding support. The question now became would Britain respond in kind; and, could Britain convince the Unionists to engage in the peace process as well?

In hindsight, it is tempting to state that events surrounding the Westminster vote on the Maastricht Treaty in July 1993 accurately foreshadowed the reluctance and hesitancy that would characterize the British response to the cease-fire. At a minimum, Major's dependence on the vote of the nine Unionist MPs to ensure ratification of a portion of the Maastricht treaty illustrates one of the significant domestic constraints on Major's response to the Irish peace initiative. One of the first manifestations of Major's reliance on the Unionists was Britain's withdrawal in November 1993 from the secret contacts it had established with Sinn Fein and the IRA in 1990.[10]

With a majority of only one, and a general election looming in Spring 1997, Major's dependence on the support of the Unionist MPs to sustain his government limited his ability to pressure Unionists to engage in substantive all-party negotiations. Also, increased discussion of Scottish devolution, and potential, though perhaps improbable, moves toward independence by Scottish voters, placed further pressures on the British government's commitment to "self-determination" for the Irish people, particularly as Major had made the Union a primary theme of his 1992 General Election Campaign.

With these constraints in view, the use of delaying tactics[11] by Major to prevent the collapse of his government made excellent domestic politics. However, these delays weakened the very support base that the Sinn Fein leadership had relied upon to convince the IRA that politics could now secure what armed struggle had not—namely, serious negotiations on the future status of Northern Ireland. As month after month passed, and precondition after precondition was set, then met, while a precise date for the beginning of all-party talks was never mentioned, it became increasingly difficult for the Sinn Fein leadership to convince the IRA as well as its own members and constituents that its political strategy was working.

IRA Cease-fire: Reinstatement

The beginning of 1997 did not appear to augur well for a reinstatement of the IRA cease-fire. Indeed, the first quarter of 1997 was marked by a series of IRA attacks.[12] However, the results of the May 1 British General Elections would produce a new set of political opportunity structures that would contribute to the republican leadership's calculation that the benefits of a new IRA cease-fire outweighed its potential costs.

The election of Tony Blair and the Labour Party to government in Westminister with a majority of over 150 effectively ended the veto which the Unionist MPs had held over John Major. Further, unlike Major, Blair had campaigned on a platform of devolving power from London to Scotland, Wales, and Northern Ireland. Coupled with the spectacular results of Sinn Fein[13] which saw not only Gerry Adams re-take the West Belfast seat but also the election of Martin McGuinness[14] for Mid-Ulster, both the British government and Sinn Fein felt they could engage each other without fear of loss of support. On May 16, Blair traveled to Northern Ireland where he expressed his commitment to work for a political settlement to the conflict and re-opened exploratory contacts between British government officials and Sinn Fein which the Major government had broken off.

The results of the May 21 Northern Ireland local government elections, which saw Sinn Fein further increase its share of the total vote to 16.9 percent and capture the position of largest nationalist party on the Belfast City Council, provided the party leadership with a powerful bargaining chip in its internal negotiations with the IRA, as well as with the British and Irish governments. The IRA, however, was not yet convinced of the British government's commitment to a negotiation process and on June 16, 1997, it shot dead two police officers of the Royal Ulster Constabulary (RUC). The British government responded quickly by banning further contacts with Sinn Fein officials. The IRA and Sinn Fein were now faced with the prospect that peace talks might proceed without them. Their bargaining power, however, was restored due to the widespread loyalist violence which surrounded the traditional Orange Order parades in Portadown and Belfast. With the total collapse of the nascent peace process now looming, the British and Irish governments responded on June 25 by issuing proposals on decommissioning which met one of the key demands of the IRA, namely, that there would be no requirement of a weapons handover prior to Sinn Fein's full participation in all-party talks. Approximately one month later, on July 20, 1997, the IRA renewed its cease-fire.

The Basque Case

On June 10, 1987, Herri Batasuna delivered a "ballot bomb" by winning a seat in Spain's first European parliament elections and replacing the PNV as the most voted Basque party. The fact that Herri Batasuna had received over fifty thousand votes from outside the Basque provinces, as well as a high percentage of the immigrant vote within the four Basque provinces,[15] was equally shocking to parties of the Left and Right. Representatives of these parties, who, having attempted to dissuade voters from supporting Herri Batasuna by proclaiming that "a vote for HB is a vote for ETA" began, privately at least, to fear that 250,000 people did, in fact, support ETA.

Despite these displays of popular support for Herri Batasuna, negotiations with ETA, as Clark[16] has noted, "remained a low priority for the Spanish government until June 19." On that day, a bomb, placed by an ETA unit in the parking lot of a busy supermarket (Hipercor) in Barcelona, exploded. The blast wounded thirty-nine persons and ultimately took the lives of twenty-one. Although official inquiries later established that if the police had acted on ETA warnings loss of life could have been avoided, the bombing led the Spanish government to resume the contacts it had opened with ETA representatives the previous year in Algeria.

The Argel Talks: Setting the Stage

On August 28, 1987, the official spokesman of the Spanish government, Javier Solana, told a press conference that "there have been and there will be" contacts with ETA, thus publicly acknowledging for the first time that negotiated settlement was a possibility. On September 5, ETA responded with a communique in which it offered a cease-fire in exchange for negotiations, albeit negotiations which accepted as non-negotiable ETA's minimal political conditions: the incorporation of the province of Navarra into any new Basque political entity; amnesty for Basque political prisoners; and recognition of the Basque peoples' right to self-determination (the KAS Alternative).[17]

While the Spanish government considered its response, French security forces would inflict significant damage to ETA's infrastructure through the arrest of Santiago Arrospide Sarasola, one of ETA's top leaders, and the seizure of a vast amount of documents which would lead to the further arrest of more than one hundred ETA members or supporters by the end of October. However, less than two weeks after the arrest of Arrospide, ETA's authorized negotiator, Antxon Etxebeste, would engage in a series of highly significant meetings in Algeria with the Spanish government delegate to the Basque Autonomous Community, Julen Elgorriaga. The meetings were held in two phases: the first on October 15–16, and the second on November 21. These meetings were particularly meaningful in that the Spanish government was represented not by a police official as previously, but rather by someone who could speak for the country's political leadership. Despite the symbolic significance of this meeting, the principal obstacle to negotiations remained the question of the recognition by the Spanish government of the Basque's right to self-determination. As Elgorriaga explained, not only was such recognition impossible given existing constitutional structures, but also that it would be politically suicidal for the González government.

While ETA and the Spanish representatives considered each other's proposals, the González government sought to increase the political pressure on ETA and Herri Batasuna by passing a non-partisan anti-terrorist pact[18] in the

Spanish parliament. Such a pact, Madrid viewed as serving to illustrate to ETA and HB the strength and coherence of the forces allied against them.

On November 21, a second meeting took place between Etxebeste and Elorriaga. This meeting is particularly significant as, for the first time, the Spanish government explored the possibility of the inclusion of Herri Batasuna representatives in the negotiations. The rest of the month would witness widespread speculation within various media sources regarding the status of the talks. One of the most widely held views was that the PSOE (Spanish Socialist Party), which was confronting elections in 1990, viewed the opportunity to negotiate a settlement with ETA as ensuring the election of the socialists to another term in office.

On December 11, 1987, however, the gains made in these negotiations all but disappeared in the smoke of yet another ETA bombing, this time, of a Guardia Civil barracks. The deaths of eleven residents, including five children, evoked widespread condemnation and the public withdrawal of the Spanish government from any formal contacts with ETA while it continued these sorts of attacks. On the same day, however, that the Spanish government publicly announced it was breaking off contacts with ETA, the Spanish state security director, Rafael Vera, flew to Algeria. Once in Algeria, Vera, using an intermediary, delivered a message to Etxebeste in which the Spanish government requested that ETA initiate a truce for sixty days to give them time to renew contacts as the furor over the barracks bombing subsided. If ETA accepted the proposal, the message implied that the Spanish government would commit itself to renewing meetings to prepare a negotiating commission. As the New Year approached, it appeared to ETA that negotiations were finally at hand.

The Argel Talks: Setting the Table

While ETA viewed the new year with high hopes, the other Basque parties, particularly the PNV, fearful of being excluded from any negotiations, and thereby, of the probable loss of support to Herri Batasuna, began work on the formulation of a Basque anti-terrorist pact on the model of the Madrid act passed the previous November. The ratification of the Basque pact, known officially as the "Accord for the Democratic Normalization and Pacification of Euskadi"[19] on January 19, 1988, by all the parties participating in the Basque parliament,[20] with the exception of Herri Batasuna, not only affirmed the illegitimacy of any negotiations regarding the status of the Basque country which did not include representatives of all political parties, it effectively isolated, at least for a time being, the representatives of Herri Batasuna within Basque political institutions.

As a counter-offensive to this attempt at isolation by the Basque parties, on January 29, 1988, ETA published a communique in the Basque newspaper, *Egin,* which detailed its communications with Madrid. In the communique ETA stated that, "As a sample of their disposition to dialogue, during a mutually agreed upon period no longer than sixty days, ETA would observe an official partial truce that would involve the provisional cessation of executions, except in the case of chance confrontation." In exchange for this truce, ETA proposed that:

The conversations should be renewed in the period immediately following confirmation of the truce, under the premise of a future [negotiating] commission made up of both delegations at the highest level, whose composition should be studies by each of the parties, along with the agenda, and with a political content, to be established by both delegations, and with the expressed willingness to constitute a negotiating frame work leading to a negotiated political solution to the conflict.

As Clark[21] has noted, this communique represented an attempt by ETA to resolve two of the long-standing obstacles to a settlement: the timing of an ETA cease-fire and the negotiation of political issues. To resolve the timing problem, ETA suggested a two-stage meeting. First, before hostilities ceased, a preliminary meeting would be held to confirm the willingness of both sides to continue negotiations. Then, after the cease-fire was in place, further negotiations could be undertaken. Second, to reduce the difficulties involved with having Spanish government representatives negotiate political issues with representatives of a "terrorist" organization, ETA agreed to invest their negotiating authority in the hands of Herri Batasuna representatives. What ETA did not, perhaps, sufficiently anticipate, would be the political pressure placed on the González government by the Spanish right and even by conservative Basque forces. Although the exact reasons may not ever be known, the Spanish government chose not to respond to ETA's communique for nearly a month. Finally, on February 20, 1988, Elgorriaga returned to Algeria for what would be his final meeting with Etxebeste. Instead of the definitive answer to ETA's proposals which Etxebeste had been anticipating, Elgorriaga responded that his only mission was to discuss the conditions for a cease-fire. The mutual misunderstandings of both parties resulted in the immediate collapse of the talks. ETA would illustrate its sense of betrayal with a vengeance, kidnapping a wealthy Spanish businessman, Emiliano Revilla, from his home in Madrid on February 24, 1988.

The Spanish government's response, was, once again, to announce publicly that it was withdrawing from contacts with ETA. In July, however, González appointed two Basques to key positions in the cabinet: minister of the interior and minister of justice. ETA appeared to respond favorably by softening somewhat its attitude towards the implementation of the KAS Alternative and on October 30, 1988, ETA, in a daring illustration of its abilities, released Revilla within a few yards of his home in the center of Madrid. That same day, ETA would release a communique offering a bilateral two-month truce to renew talks with the Spanish government. In December, the Spanish government responded by proposing high-level meetings in exchange for a unilateral two-week truce. ETA accepted the Spanish offer and announced the truce on January 7, 1989. On January 23, ETA made public the meeting in Algeria between Spanish government officials and Etxebeste and announced they had agreed to a roundtable for political talks. ETA also announced that a two-month bilateral truce had been agreed upon and was in place. A few hours after the ETA communique was published, the Spanish government, as had been agreed, issued its own statement confirming the meetings.

Between January 25 and March 22, 1989, five meetings took place in Algeria. The Spanish government was represented by Juan Manual Eguiagaray and Rafael Vera. The ETA delegation included Antxon Etxebeste and two other ETA members. An Algerian mediator was also present. On March 27, 1989, ETA issued a communique reporting on the meetings with the Spanish delegation which detailed the points agreed (known as the "eight points") and announced the renewal of the truce. As before, the Spanish government was to respond with its own communique ratifying the points agreed. This time, however, the Spanish communique not only failed to ratify the agreed points, but also invoked the two juridical issues at the core of the conflict: the inviolability of the Spanish constitution which asserts the territorial integrity of the Spanish state, and the constitutional legitimacy of the Basque autonomy statute. Madrid, in issuing this response had effectively ended the Algerian talks. ETA issued a new communique in which it asked the Spanish government to reconsider its position. No reply, however, would be forthcoming. Eight explosions in the Spanish railways network on April 4, announced ETA's confirmation of the collapse of the talks. The "war," tragically, was back on.

Avenues and Obstacles to Peace

As the review of these two cases has illustrated, the IRA and ETA have, at certain times, appeared more willing to renounce armed struggle, while at others more determined to continue killing. Having examined the political environment in which these historic decisions were made, this chapter suggests that three factors appear to have played a central role in the calculations of both the IRA and ETA regarding the relative costs and benefits of continuing their campaigns: the level of regime responsiveness, the political competitiveness of Sinn Fein and Herri Batasuna, and the level of resources, both human and material, available to the Irish republican movement and the MLVN.

Regime Responsiveness

In both the Irish and Basque case, expressions of interest by the State governments in a search for a negotiated settlement resulted at a minimum, in encouraging debate within the Irish republican movement and the MLVN regarding the pros and cons of continuing the use of violence. In both cases, expressions of commitment to such a process resulted in provisional or tactical cease-fires. In the Irish case, real commitment to such a process by the Irish and British governments was, ultimately, able to convince the IRA and the republican community that the costs of continued violence were far outweighed by the benefits to be gained through a permanent cessation of violence.

In the Basque case, however, the unwillingness or inability of the Spanish government to commit to official negotiations, much less a negotiated settlement, has served to sustain support for the violent operations of ETA, as evidenced by the consistent electoral support for its political voice, Herri Batasuna.[22] Among the factors which appear to have influenced the different responses of the British and Spanish governments to the political demands of the IRA, one appears particularly significant: the foundation for the territorial connection.

In the Northern Irish case, the British government's primary interest in maintaining control of the territory has been its strategic importance to the defense of the "mainland." Thus, a pragmatic rather than an ideological form of nationalism might be said to characterize British-Irish relations, at least from the point of view of Westminister.[23] With advances in defense technology and the demise of the Cold War, the political, social, and economic costs of a continuing conflict in Northern Ireland were seen to outweigh any costs incurred through facilitating an agreed peace settlement reflecting the right of the people in Ireland, both North and South, to self-determination.

Unlike the British government, Spanish monarchs, General Franco, and successive Spanish governments have maintained an ideological commitment to the integrity of the Spanish state. While relatively accepting of regional differences within the Spanish state, there is very little tolerance for the recognition of the Basque nation, and even less for the view that what is seen as a constituent part of the Spanish state should have the right to secede from that state. Thus, for Madrid, the costs of the conflict are far less than the costs of the potential secession of the Basque provinces.

Political Competitiveness

In both the Irish and Basque cases, increased levels of electoral support for the political parties associated with the paramilitary organizations was shown to facilitate cessations of violence. In the Irish case it should be noted, however, that the failure of Sinn Fein to perform well electorally in the Republic of Ireland also contributed to the calculations of the costs and benefits of the armed struggle. Sinn Fein was aware that nationalist voters in the North recognized, if they did not directly experience, the effects of state violence and thus were more likely and willing to tolerate and support the anti-state violence of the IRA. The party also realized, however, that the majority of the voters in the Republic, who were not confronted with the daily reminders of British "occupation," were unable or unwilling to support Sinn Fein while the IRA continued its armed campaign. Thus, the party confronted the dilemma of needing to be seen to support the IRA in the North to sustain its electoral support, and the need to distance themselves from the armed struggle in the South if it was to increase its appeal. Once the republican leadership was assured of the commitment of both the Irish and British governments to a negotiated settlement which did not involve a concession of military defeat by the IRA, the benefits of political struggle clearly outweighed those of military struggle.

Another factor influencing the ability of Sinn Fein to persuade the IRA of the advantages of a cessation of violence was the congruence of the SDLP with republican goals, specifically, the goal of a united Ireland. While the two parties may differ in regard to their positions on socioeconomic issues, and the means by which to achieve a united Ireland, there was agreement between the two parties on the desirability, if not necessarily the inevitability, of a united Ireland.

In the Basque case, the strong performance of Herri Batasuna in the 1987 European and provincial elections did increase the relative weight of political struggle within the MLVN. However, within the MLVN, support for Herri Batasuna was perceived as being an endorsement for the strategy which had, to date, been directed by the leadership of ETA and coordinated by the leadership of the KAS. That ETA carried out the Hipercor bombing after the successful campaign can be viewed either as a response to the failure of the Spanish government to acknowledge Herri Batasuna's success as a sign of the determination and desire by Basque nationalists to secure the right to exercise self-determination, or as a reminder of who, ultimately, would determine the shape of any negotiated settlement.

Another factor which would influence ETA's calculation of the costs and benefits of continuing its armed campaign was the fragmentation of the Basque nationalist electorate. Unlike the Northern Irish case in which the nationalist electorate was divided effectively between two nationalist parties which, while disagreeing on tactics, nonetheless agreed on Irish unity and independence as their ultimate political goal, the Basque nationalist electorate is effectively divided among three parties who not only disagree on tactics, but who also vary in their preferences regarding the relationship of the Basque country to Madrid. While a majority of Herri Batasuna supporters view independence as their preferred goal, the PNV and EA constituency is divided among those who favor the status quo, increased autonomy, revised federalist arrangements, and independence. The coordination of a broad nationalist movement in favor of negotiations for self-determination has, therefore, proved more difficult to secure and sustain among the Basque parties, than among the nationalist parties in Northern Ireland. The success of the Northern Irish parties in reaching an agreed settlement of the conflict, has, however, served to encourage a wide-ranging discussion process among Basque political parties and other social movement organizations. On September 12, 1998, participants in this discussion process signed an accord, the Lizarra Declaration,[24] which represents a tentative declaration of all the signatories to seek a political resolution of the Spanish-Basque conflict.

Movement Resources

In the review of the Irish case, it was noted that the success of the IRA in importing arms and other military equipment during the 1980s served to assure IRA militants that it had sufficient resources to continue the war, if necessary, and that, therefore, the transfer of resources to Sinn Fein would not endanger the army's operational capacity. Also, the traditional willingness of a segment of the large Irish-American community to support the war effort served as a cushion for IRA coffers. Many within Sinn Fein, however, also acknowledged that the Irish American lobby would be even more forthcoming with financial support once the IRA had declared a ceasefire. In addition, the potential power of the Irish American lobby to induce political support for the nascent peace process by the Clinton administration, particularly in a situation of an existing IRA ceasefire, would necessarily weigh heavily in any cost-benefit calculation of the relative value of an IRA cessation of violence. The value of the Republic of Ireland (despite its own campaign against the IRA) as a relatively accessible sanctuary and base of operations for the IRA, versus its value as a political ally in the search for Irish self-determination, was also a key calculation for the republican movement. As events have illustrated, once the Irish government had convinced the IRA of its commitment to facilitating Irish self-determination, its political value was seen as far outweighing its military value in securing movement goals.

In regard to the Basque case, the division of the Basque nation by two imperial states, France[25] and Spain, was seen to impose considerable costs, financially and organizationally, on the MLVN. In particular, French successes in uncovering and arresting members of the ETA leadership and key ETA units created a considerable drain on movement resources. Consequently, the diversion of movement funds to political activities had to be much more strongly justified than did similar transfers in the Irish case. Although the vigorous anti-ETA campaign by French security forces could also be viewed as having increased the costs to ETA of continuing its armed struggle and thus raising the benefits of political struggle, the failure of a positive response by the Spanish government to the political gains of Herri Batasuna effectively negated the level of benefits accruing from nonviolent struggle. Another key difference in the resources available to the two movements is that, unlike their Irish counterparts, the MLVN does not have access to the support of a large and politically influential Basque diaspora which it can rely upon either for political or economic support or even to focus international media attention on their political situation.

Looking at table 11.1, it would appear that the differences in the factors present in the Irish case and absent in the Basque indicate that prospects for the negotiation of an agreed political settlement in the Basque case are, at present, limited, though not implausible.

Summary and Conclusions

The review of the Northern Irish peace process and attempts to initiate a similar process in the Basque country has illustrated the complexity of the decision-making process involved in the calculations by the IRA and ETA as to the relative costs or benefits of disengaging from their use of political violence to secure movement goals. In contrast to the view that the members of such groups as the IRA and ETA are psychologically drawn to violence and irrationally committed to "terrorism,"[26] this chapter has demonstrated that the decision to end violence can be analyzed in instrumental terms, which take into account that organizations seek to survive as well as to achieve ideological objectives. Underground organizations can and do come to perceive that the usefulness of violence is declining and that other alternatives offer more promise. Among the factors found to be of particular significance in the calculations of the relative costs and benefits of disengaging from violence were 1) the degree of regime responsivness; 2) the competitiveness of the political wing of the movement; and 3) the resources, both human and material, available to the movement.

Table 11.1 Factors Facilitating or Limiting Negotiated Resolutions of the Northern Irish and Basque Conflicts

Condition	Northern Ireland		Basque Country		
	British & Irish Govt. Unionist & Loyalist Parties	Sinn Fein & SDLP	Spanish Parties	MLNV	PNV/EA
Recognition of Need for a Political Solution to Conflict	Present	Present	Present	Present	Present
Official contacts between Governments and Opposition to confirm willingness to negotiate and cease violent actions	Present	Present	Present	Present	Present
Unofficial contacts between Government/State parties to discuss negotiations	Present	Present	Present	Present	Present
Agreement among nationalist parties regarding the minimal conditions necessary for an acceptable agreement and entry into negotiations	Present	Present	Absent	Absent	Absent
Agreed cease-fire by paramilitaries or agreed reduction/withdrawal of state security forces	Present (LVF exception)	Present (Not CIRA)	Absent	Present	–
Acceptance of inclusive talks without preconditions and without restrictions on final settlement	Present	Present	Absent	Present	Unstated

Table 11.1 continued

Condition	Northern Ireland		Spanish Parties	Basque Country	
	British & Irish Govt. Unionist & Loyalist Parties	Sinn Fein & SDLP		MLNV	PNV/EA
Agreement to accept outcome of popular referendum on political settlement	Present	Present	Absent	Present	Present
Agreed commission for decommissioning of paramilitary weapons	Present Commission established, timetable still pending, IRA & Loyalist paramilitary agreement in principle		Absent	Absent	Absent
Recognition and involvement of paramilitary prisoners in political discussions/talks process	Present	Present	Absent	Present	Unstated
Agreement on the transfer and policies for early release of paramilitary prisoners	Present	Present	Absent	Absent	Absent
Recognition of need for a political solution to conflict	Present	Present	Absent	Present	Present
Official contacts between Governments and Opposition to confirm willingness to negotiate and cease violent actions	Present	Present	Unknown	Unknown	Unknown
Unofficial contacts between Government/State parties to discuss negotiations	Present	Present	Present	Present	Present
Agreement among nationalist parties regarding the minimal conditions necessary for an acceptable agreement and entry into negotiations	Present	Present	Absent	Absent	Absent

Table 11.1 continued

Condition	Northern Ireland			Basque Country	
	British & Irish Govt. Unionist & Loyalist Parties	Sinn Fein & SDLP	Spanish Parties	MLNV	PNV/EA
Agreed cease-fire by paramilitaries or agreed reduction/withdrawal of state security forces	Present (LVF exception)	Present (Not CIRA)	Absent	Present	NA
Acceptance of inclusive talks without preconditions and without restrictions on final settlement	Present	Present	Absent	Present	Unstated
Agreement to accept outcome of popular referendum on political settlement	Present	Present	Absent	Present	Present
Agreed commission for decommissioning of paramilitary weapons	Present Commission established, timetable still pending, IRA & Loyalist paramilitary agreement in principle		Absent	Absent	Absent
Recognition and involvement of paramilitary prisoners in political discussions/talks process	Present	Present	Absent	Present	Unstated
Agreement on the transfer and policies for early release of paramilitary prisoners	Present	Present	Absent	Absent	Absent

Suggested Study Questions

1. What role(s) have Sinn Fein and Herri Batasuna played in the search for negotiated resolutions of their respective conflicts?
2. What role(s) have countries external to the conflicts played in their search for peace?
3. What factors might account for the Clinton administration's interest in the Northern Ireland peace process?
4. What were some of the main obstacles to an IRA cease-fire?
5. What are some of the similarities and differences in the responses of the PSOE-led Spanish government and that led by the Partido Popular?

Notes

1. The Basque parliament is located in Gasteiz (Vitoria) in the province of Araba (Alava).
2. Elections for the European Parliament were held on June 15, 1987.
3. A splinter group from the IRA, the Continuity IRA (CIRA), which rejects the terms of the current political agreement, continues to engage in acts of violent opposition. So too does the Loyalist Volunteer Force (LVF), a splinter group of the UVF, which also rejects the current peace accord.
4. As of October 1999, the Spanish government of Prime Minister Aznar had agreed only to discuss the transfer and release of ETA prisoners.
5. Martha Crenshaw, "Negotiating the End Game: A Case Study of the IRA." Unpublished paper, 1996, p. 3.
6. The extent to which the British government's decision was affected by the IRA mortar attack on 10 Downing Street on February 7, 1991, which exploded in the garden while Major and several top conservative officials were meeting in the Cabinet room is yet to be determined. However, it is at least plausible to suggest the IRA's act focused the attention of the prime minister on the political situation.
7. Sinn Fein increased its proportion of the vote from 11.3 percent to 12.5 percent thereby increasing its number of seats from forty-three to fifty-nine.
8. Adams had previously been denied visas to enter the United States on the grounds that he was a member of an organization which espoused the use of violence and had been unable to enter the United States since being elected President of Sinn Fein in 1983.
9. While fundraising for the republican movement has a long history in the United States, previous organizations such as NORAID, which were required to register as an agent for a foreign organization, were closely monitored by U.S. government agencies, as funds raised by NORAID events was generally suspected of channeling funds to the IRA.
10. Further proof of Major's desperation was evidenced first in the British government's initial denial that the contacts had ever taken place and then, when denial was no longer possible, in the government's attempt to manipulate the facts to suggest that

the contacts had begun at the request of the IRA.

11. Among the delaying tactics adopted by the British were 1) resisting "clarification" of what republicans viewed as the critical point of the Joint Declaration, 2) demanding evidence that the IRA's term "complete cessation" was sufficient to be interpreted as a "permanent" cessation, 3) introducing decommissioning of weapons as a precondition to official meetings between senior British ministers and Sinn Fein, and finally, 4) establishing an electoral requirement for participation in all-party peace talks, despite the findings of the George Mitchell and his team that inclusive all-party talks should begin as soon as possible and that decommissioning be dealt with during negotiations.

12. On February 12, the IRA shot dead a British solider, Stephen Restorick, at an Army checkpoint. On April 3, there was a widespread disruption of highway traffic in England as the IRA called in warning of bombs planted on major motorways and on April 5, the famous international horse race, the Grand National, had to be postponed due to IRA bomb threats.

13. Sinn Fein secured 16.1 percent of the total vote, its best performance to that date in Northern Ireland elections.

14. As Martin McGuinness is viewed within the republican movement as the public voice of the IRA, his election was particularly seen as an indication of grassroots support for the Adams' leadership and "peace" strategy.

15. Four provinces within the Spanish State, Vizcaya, Guipuzcoa, Alava, and Navarra are viewed by Basque nationalists as forming an integral part of the Basque nation. Only three provinces, Vizcaya, Guipuzcoa, and Alava, however, are included in the Basque Autonomous Community and represented in the Basque parliament.

16. Robert Clark. 1990. *Negotiating with ETA: Obstacles to Peace in the Basque Country 1975–1988*. Reno: University of Nevada Press, 190.

17. KAS, the Patriotic Socialist Coordinating Committee, consists of members of the MLVN who participate in various social organizations including, youth, feminist, cultural, and trade unions, among others and seek to coordinate support in favor of Basque self-determination. The KAS political platform, supported by ETA, is referred to as the KAS Alternative.

18. The Madrid anti-terrorist act was introduced on November 5 and ratified on November 10, 1987.

19. *Euskadi* is the Basque term for the territory comprised on the four historic Basque provinces in the Spanish state.

20. The Basque party, Eusko Alkartasuna (Basque Solidarity), was allowed to sign "with reservations."

21. Robert Clark. 1990. *Negotiating with ETA*, 216.

22. Since its inception in 1978, Herri Batasuna has consistently received between 15 and 20 percent of the popular vote in the Basque country.

23. Among those residents of Northern Ireland identifying themselves as British, however, it is precisely their suspicions of Britain's pragmatic view of the position of

Northern Ireland that has helped to fuel past resistance to any discussions or negotiations regarding changes in the status of Northern Ireland within the United Kingdom.

24. The Lizarra declaration was signed by representatives of the twenty-three political
    parties, labor unions, and grassroots groups that participated in the Ireland Forum
    (discussion of the Accord in Northern ireland) promoted by Herri Batasuna. The
    name of the accord comes from the place, Lizarra, in the province of Navarra where
    the accord was signed.

25. Three Basque provinces, Labourd, Basse Navarre, and Soule, known together as
    Ipparalde (Northern Basque country) are located within the French state.

26. For an overview of various psychological interpretations of terrorism see Walter Reich,
    ed. *The Origins of Terrorism: Psychologies, Ideologies, Theologies, States of Mind.* Cambridge:
    Cambridge University Press, 1990.

References

Adams, Gerry. 1982. *The Politics of Irish Freedom.* Kerry: Brandon Publishers.

Bell, J. Bowyer. 1979. *The Secret Army: A History of the IRA 1916–1979.* Dublin: Academy
Press.

———. 1993. *The Irish Troubles: A Generation of Violence, 1967–1992.* Dublin: Gill and
Macmillan.

Bruce, Steve. 1992. *The Red Hand: Protestant Paramilitaries in Northern Ireland.* Oxford:
Oxford University Press.

———. 1994. *The Edge of the Union: The Ulster Loyalist Political Vision.* Oxford: Oxford
University Press.

Bruni, Luigi. 1987. *E.T.A.: Historia Politica De Una Lucha Armada.* Bilbo: Txalaparta.

Clark, Robert P. 1980. *The Basques: The Franco Years and Beyond.* Reno: University of Nevada Press.

———. 1984. *The Basque Insurgents: ETA, 1952–1980.* Madison: University of Wisconsin
Press.

———. 1990. *Negotiating with ETA: Obstacles to Peace in the Basque Country, 1975–1988.*
Reno: University of Nevada Press.

Clarke, Liam. 1987. *Broadening the Battlefield: The H-Blocks and the Rise of Sinn Fein.* Dublin:
Gill and Macmillan.

Conversi, Daniele. 1996. *The Basques, the Catalans, and Spain: Alternative Routes to Nationalist Mobilization.* Reno: University of Nevada Press.

Coogan, Tim Paul. 1987. *The IRA* (2nd edition). London: The Pall Mall Press.

Crenshaw, Martha. 1985. "An Organizational Approach to the Analysis of Political Terrorism." *Orbis* 29: 465–88.

———. 1990. "The Logic of Terrorism: Terrorist Behavior as a Product of Strategic Choice." In *Origins of Terrorism: Psychologies, Ideologies, Theologies, States of Mind.* Walter Reich, ed. Cambridge: Cambridge University Press.

Hampson, Fen Osler. 1996. *Nurturing Peace: Why Peace Settlements Succeed or Fail.* Washington, D.C.: United States Institute of Peace Press.

Ibarra Güell, Pedro. 1989. *La Evolución Estratégica de ETA.* Donostia: Kriselu.

Irvin, Cynthia L. 1992. "Terrorists' Perspectives: Interviews." In *Terrorism and the Media.* David L. Paletz and Alex P. Schmid, eds. London: Sage Publications.

———. 1999. *Militant Nationalism: Between Movement and Party in Ireland and the Basque Country.* Minneapolis: University of Minnesota Press.

Irvin, Cynthia L., Francisco S. Llera and José M. Mata. 1993. "ETA: From Secret Army to Social Movement – The Post-Franco Schism of the Basque Nationalist Movement." *Terrorism and Political Violence* 5(3): 106–34.

Irvin, Cynthia L. and Edward Moxon-Browne. 1989. "Not Many Floating Voters Here." *Fortnight* 270: 6–8.

Linz, Juan J., Manuel Gómez Reino, Francisco A. Orizo and Darío Vila. 1984. *Conflicto en Euskadi.* Madrid: Espasa-Calpe.

Mallie, Eamonn and David McKittrick. 1996. *The Fight for Peace: The Secret Story behind the Irish Peace Process.* London: Heinemann.

McGarry, John and Brendan O'Leary, eds. 1990. *The Future of Northern Ireland.* Oxford: Oxford University Press.

———. 1995. *Explaining Northern Ireland: Broken Images.* Oxford: Blackwell Publishers.

O'Brien, Brendan. 1995. *The Long War: The IRA & Sinn Fein.* Dublin: The O'Brien Press.

O'Malley, Padraig. 1983. *The Uncivil Wars: Ireland Today.* Belfast: The Blackstaff Press.

———. 1990a. *Northern Ireland: Questions of Nuance.* Belfast: The Blackstaff Press.

White, Robert W. 1993. *Provisional Irish Republicans: An Oral and Interpretive History.* Westport, Conn.: Greenwood Press.

Zirakzadeh, Cyrus Ernesto. 1991. *A Rebellious People: Basques, Protest and Politics.* Reno: University of Nevada Press.

Zulaika, Joseba. 1988. *Basque Violence: Metaphor and Sacrament.* Reno: University of Nevada Press.

Zulaika, Joseba and William Douglass. 1996. *Terror and Taboo: The Follies, Fables, and Faces of Terrorism.* New York: Routledge.

About the Contributors

JOHN A. AGNEW is Professor and Chair of Geography at UCLA. He teaches courses on political and economic geography, European cities, and international political economy. He has co-authored *The Geography of the World Economy* and is the author of *Geopolitics: Re-Visioning World Politics* as well as numerous articles on European regionalist movements, particularly the Scottish Nationalist Party and the Northern League in Italy in *National Identities, International Political Science Review,* and *Transactions of the Institute of British Geographers.*

SEAN BYRNE is Assistant Professor of Dispute Resolution and Director of Doctoral Studies at Nova Southeastern University. He teaches courses on ethnic conflict, international conflict resolution, theories of conflict and conflict resolution, and violence prevention. He is the author of *Growing up in a Divided Society: The Influence of Conflict on Belfast Schoolchildren* and is co-author with Cynthia Irvin of *The Politics and Practice of External Economic Assistance in Resolving Protracted Ethnic Conflicts: Lessons from Northern Ireland.* He is also the author of numerous articles on youth and conflict, third party intervention, and the escalation and de-escalation of ethnic conflict in *Ethnos-Nation, International Peacekeeping, Mind and Human Interaction, Nationalism and Ethnic Politics, Peace and Conflict Studies, Journal of Intergroup Relations, Security Dialogue* and *Terrorism and Political Violence.*

NEAL CARTER is a Lecturer at Saint Bonaventure University and a Ph.D. candidate in political science at Syracuse University. He teaches courses on ethnic conflict, comparative governments, Canadian and European politics, and international relations. He is the author of articles on ethnic and regional conflict appearing in such journals as *Political Psychology, Peace and Conflict Studies,* and *The Maxwell Review.*

KATHLEEN A. CAVANAUGH is Lecturer of Political Science at University College Dublin. She teaches courses on ethnic conflict, political violence, international law, nationalism, Irish and British politics, and international relations. She has published articles on the escalation and de-escalation of conflict in Northern Ireland in *Merip, Fordham International Law Journal, Journal of Palestinian Studies,* and *Terrorism and Political Violence.*

PAUL DIXON is Lecturer of Government at the University of Ulster at Jordanstown. He teaches courses on ethnic conflict, comparative government, Irish and British politics, international relations, and European politics. He is the author of *Northern Ireland: Power,*

Ideology, and Reality and numerous articles on British and Irish politics appearing in such journals as *Democratization, Political Studies, Review of International Studies, Etudes Iralndes, Irish Political Studies,* and *Nationalism and Ethnic Politics.*

MIRANDA DUNCAN is an Adjunct Assistant professor at the University of Missouri-St. Louis who teaches classes specially designed to synthesize theoretical understandings of conflict with practical application for its resolution, and conducts training in team building, community collaboration, negotiation, and mediation. She is also a Practitioner of Dispute Resolution, and Community Development Specialist, University Outreach and Extension at the University of Missouri-St. Louis.

CYNTHIA L. IRVIN is Assistant Professor of Political Science at the University of Kentucky where she teaches courses on ethnic conflict, social movements, political violence, comparative and European politics. A former United States Institute of Peace Jennings-Randolph Peace Scholar, she is the author of *Militant Nationalism: Between Movement and Party in Northern Ireland and the Basque Country* and is co-author, with Sean Byrne, of *The Politics and Practice of International Economic Assistance in Resolving Protracted Ethnic Conflicts: Lessons from Northern Ireland* (forthcoming). She has authored or co- authored a number of articles on political violence, ethnic conflict, the Northern Irish conflict, and the Basque conflict in the *British Journal of Political Science, Ethnos-Nation,* and *Terrorism and Political Violence.*

HO-WON JEONG is Assistant Professor of Conflict Resolution at George Mason University. He teaches courses on ethnic conflict, international conflict resolution, global issues, development in Africa and South East Asia, cross cultural conflict, theories of conflict and conflict resolution, and violence preventions. He has published *The New Agenda for Peace Research, Conflict Resolution: Dynamics, Process and Structure,* and *Peace and Conflict Studies: An Introduction.* He serves as the editor of two journals, *International Journal of Peace Studies* and *Peace and Conflict Studies.* He has authored or co-authored a number of articles on development, global issues and peace, and international relations in *Peace and Change* and *Peace and Conflict Studies.*

GEORGE J. McCALL is Professor of Sociology at the University of Missouri-St.Louis. He teaches courses on conflict resolution, Africa, methodology, and theories of conflict. Among his published works are *Social Research: The Craft of Finding, Social Psychology: A Sociological Approach,* and *Identities and Interactions: An Examination of Human Associations in Everyday Life,* as well as a number of articles on ethnic conflict and policing, third party interventions, and conflict resolution in such journals as *Social issues, Public Opinion Quarterly, The Journal of Psychology, Social Relationships, Journal of Interpersonal Violence,* and *The International Journal of the Sociology of the Law.*

JOHN D. NAGLE is Professor of Political Science and International Relations at Syracuse University. He teaches courses on democratization, comparative political systems, political elite recruitment, and the evolution of the left political thought in the West.

Among his published works are *The National Democrat Party: Right Radicalism in the Federal Republic of Germany, System and Succession: The Social Bases of Political Elite Recruitment, Democracy and Democratization: Post Communist Europe in Comparative Perspective, Confessions from the Left: On the Pain, Necessity and Joys of Political Rethinking,* and *Introduction to Comparative Politics: Challenges of Conflict and Change in a New Era,* as well as numerous journal articles.

FREDERIC S. PEARSON is Professor and Director of the Center for Peace and Conflict Studies at Wayne State University. He teaches courses on ethnic conflict, international conflict resolution, international relations, and peace studies. Among his published works are *The Spread of Arms in the International System, Arms and Warfare: Escalation, De-escalation and Negotiation* as well as numerous articles in such journals as *International Studies Quarterly, Journal of Conflict Resolution, Journal of Peace Research, International Affairs, Orbis, West European Politics,* and *The American Academy of Political and Social Science.*

BRIAN D. POLKINGHORN is Assistant Professor of Dispute Resolution and Director of Practicum Studies at Nova Southeastern University. He teaches courses on environmental conflict resolution, methodology, theories of conflict and conflict resolution, and system design. He is the author or co-author of numerous articles in such journals as *Alternatives, Peace and Conflict Studies,* and *GSA Today.*

JESSICA SENEHI is a doctoral candidate in social science at Syracuse University and an Adjunct faculty member at the Farquhar Center, Nova Southeastern University, and in the College of Liberal Arts at Florida Atlantic University. She teaches courses on cross cultural conflict, gender and power, ethnic conflict and nationalism, violence prevention and conflict resolution. She has published a number of articles on storytelling and conflict resolution, gender and conflict, ethnic conflict, and nationalism and neuropsychology in *Brain and Language, Mind and Human Interaction, Neuropsychology,* and *Encyclopedia of Feminist Theory.*

MARK SUPRUN is a Ph.D. candidate in the Department of Political Science at Columbia University. He has spent a considerable amount of time serving as an election monitor in the Ukraine. He is co-author of *Violence and Disorder: The Future of Our Cities – A Forum on the Issue of Community Violence.*

MITJA ZAGAR is Professor of Political Science and Constitutional Law, and the Director for the Institute of Ethnic Studies at the University of Ljubljana. He teaches courses on ethnic conflict, international and constitutional law, political behavior, and conflict resolution. He was instrumental in helping to draft Slovenia's new Constitution in 1991. He has authored or co-authored a number of articles on international law, ethnic conflict, human rights, and third-party intervention in the *Journal of Ethno-Development* and *Treaties and Documents.*

Index

Index

Democratic Unionist Party, 184–85

Double minorities, 55

EEC *see* European Union

Egin, 191

Elgorriaga, Julen, 197, 199

Embedded liberalism, 13

Enparanza, Jose Luis, 191

Environmental Conflict, 80, 93; environmental equity and justice and, 80, 87; sources of, 81; in Bosnia-Herzegovina, 83–84, 89; in Israel, 83–83, 87; in South Africa, 81–82, 87; in United States, 80–81, 87

Estonia, 36

ETA, *see* Euskadi ta Askatasuna (Basque Homeland and Freedom)

Ethnic conflict, 41–42; cultural factors and, 98, 117; demographic factors and, 53; economic factors and, 48–49, 117, 121; environmental factors and, 87, 90; historical factors and, 45–46; language and, 55; natural resources and, 85; political factors and, 48–49, 117; psychological factors and, 56–57, 70, 85, 98; religious factors and, 51–53, 85; symbolic factors and, 56–57, 85, 91–92, 98; myths and, 56–57, 84, 98;

Ethnic frontiers, 116

Ethnic Germans, 28–29

Ethnic mobilization, 68–69, 115, 121

Ethnic separatism, 17

Ethnoterritorial politics, 41

Etxebeste, Antxon, 199–200

European Union, 16, 28, 160, 175

Euskadi ta Askatasuna (Basque Homeland and Freedom), 196, 200, 202–204; Hipercor bombing and, 197; negotiations with Spanish government, 196–97; Argel Talks and, 197–99; KAS Alternative and, 197, 200

Euskal Herritarrok (People of the Basque Country), 191

Faulkner, Brian, 179, 183

Fedotov, George, 33

Fitzgerald, Garret, 186

FLQ *see* Front de Libération du Québec

Folklore, *see also* Storytelling

Foucault, Michel, 100

France, 8, 26, 29–30, 46

Freire, Paulo, 99–101

French Revolution, 8, 24, 30

Front de Libération du Québec, 50

Galtung, Johan, 105

Gastarbeiter, 29

GATT *see* Global Agreement on Tariffs and Trade

Geopolitical orders, 4

Georgia and Abkhazia, 33

Germany, 7–8, 11, 15; Anglo-German naval rivalry, 9; citizenship of, 28; ethnic Turks in, 29

Global Agreement on Tariffs and Trade, 5, 13–14

Goldstone Commission, 159

González, Felipe, 199

Gorbachev, Mikhail, 33–34

Greece, 8

Gulf War, 27

Gypsies (Roma), 127

Hani, Chris, 166

Hartz, Louis, 23

Haughey, Charles, 192

Hendron, Dr. Joe, 192

Herri Batasuna (Popular Unity), 191, 196–99, 203

Hipercor, *see* ETA

Horowitz, Donald, 75

Hume, John, 193

Index

Books of related interest
from Kumarian Press

Aiding Violence:
The Development Enterprise in
Rwanda
Peter Uvin

This book explores the dramatic contradiction inherent in the existence of massive genocide in a country that was considered by western aid agencies to be a model of development. The processes of inequality, exclusion and humiliation that have characterized social and economic life in Rwanda are considered and questions are raised about how development aid ignored and reinforced these characteristics of structural violence.

US $24.95 / Paper: 1-56549-083-5
US $59.00 / Cloth: 1-56549-084-3

Civil Society at the Millennium
CIVICUS, edited by Kumi Naidoo

This publication documents how far civil society has come and provides insight into what its future role will be. The thematic underpinnings examined include globalization, governance, youth participation, women and leadership, sustainable development, government, religion, poverty, indigenous people, volunteering, and technology. *Civil Society at the Millennium* is key to developing a clearer understanding of the role of civil society as a legitimate actor in public life.

US $18.95 / Paper: 1-56549-101-7

Promises Not Kept:
The Betrayal of Social Change in
the Third World
Fourth Edition
John Isbister

This book develops the argument that social change in the Third World has been blocked by a series of broken promises, made explicitly or implicitly by the industrialized countries and also by Third World leaders themselves. The fourth edition takes into account the success stories in the Third World, particularly in East Asia, asking why those experiences have not been more widespread.

US $18.95 / Paper: 1-56549-045-2

Unarmed Bodyguards:
International Accompaniment for
the Protection of Human Rights
Luis Enrique Eguren and Liam Mahony

For years international accompaniment has been successfully implemented as a way to protect threatened human rights activists throughout the world. Here the authors succeed in telling a truly inspirational story of the modern establishment of this new tool in human rights protection.

US $21.95 / Paper: 1-56549-068-1
US $46.00 / Cloth: 1-56549-069-X

Famine, Conflict and Response: A Basic Guide
Fred Cuny

Written by the well-known visionary and "maverick" Fred Cuny, this book focuses primarily on responses to what are now called traditional famines or natural disaster. Cuny's approach lives on as innovative and challenging in that his focus on counter famine measures centers on people's livelihoods.

US $23.95 / Paper: 1-56549-090-8

Inequity in the Global Village: Recycled Rhetoric and Disposable People
Jan Knippers Black

As globalization rapidly replaces the cold war paradigm, disturbing aspects of this transition are often glossed over. The narrow distribution of benefits from globalization has created a yawning gap in wealth and power both among and within states. Jan Black incisively describes increased nationalism, growing refugee populations, and the politics of exclusion in her impassioned style.

US $24.95 / Paper: 1-56549-099-1
US $55.00 / Cloth: 1-56549-100-9

Breaking Cycles of Violence: Conflict Prevention in Intrastate Crises
Janie Leatherman, William DeMars, Patrick Gaffney and Raimo Väyrynen

A timely and clearly defined study of how the international community, working with local partners, can effectively prioritize and target resources on key breaking points in societies at risk of violent conflict.

US $23.95 / Paper: 1-56549-091-6
US $65.00 / Cloth: 1-56549-092-4

The Cuban Way: Charting Its Own Course to Economic Change
Ana Julia Jatar-Hausmann

Focusing on the experiences of the people who actually reside on the island, this book is an original analysis of the economic policies and trends in socialist Cuba.

US $21.95 / Paper: 1-56549-088-6
US $59.00 / Cloth: 1-56549-089-4

Multi-Track Diplomacy: A Systems Approach to Peace
Third Edition
Louise Diamond and Ambassador John McDonald

Unique in its systemic approach to peacemaking and conflict resolution, this book identifies the players (official and non-state actors) and activities that contribute to the peacemaking and peace building process. Diamond and McDonald show how all nine tracks are interlinked and provide resources for each track along with new ideas and fresh perspectives.

US $19.95 / Paper: 1-56549-057-6

Street-Level Democracy: Political Settings at the Margins of Global Power
Jonathan Barker

How people in distinct regions in the world experience and respond to the pressures of change is the subject of this book. His new focus on political settings is a vital step in understanding how global forces and local actions are changing the shape of world politics.

US $23.95 / Paper: 1-56549-106-8

 Kumarian Press is dedicated to publishing and distributing books and other media that will have a positive social and economic impact on the lives of peoples living in "Third World" conditions no matter where they live.

Kumarian Press publishes books about
Global Issues and International Development,
such as Peace and Conflict Resolution,
Environmental Sustainability, Globalization,
Nongovernmental Organizations,
and Women and Gender.

To receive a complimentary catalog or
to request writer's guidelines call or write:

Kumarian Press, Inc.
14 Oakwood Avenue
West Hartford, CT 06119-2127
U.S.A.

Inquiries: (860) 233-5895
Fax: (860) 233-6072
Order toll free: (800) 289-2664

e-mail: kpbooks@aol.com
Internet: www.kpbooks.com

DATE DUE

APR 10 2005			

Demco, Inc. 38-293